The author, age 3 years

My first sight of Freetown & Lion Mountains

Pete Wallace

Me left, with Derek, four days after having dengue fever

My friend Daramy and 'small boy'.

Melchsee Früt, where I regained my strength

Kissy mess, Pete, David, Alistair and Dick

Ma nky, my Civet kitten. I loved it so…

The neighbours, Port Loko.

'General Jackson' my faithful cook and his grandson, standing outside the bank, Port Loko market on the left.

The view from my balcony above the Bank.

One of the Chief's wives dancing.

Climbing above Loch Marie, Scottish Highlands 1983.

*Corfu 1984, Demetri
teaching me to waterski.*

Windsurfing in Vassiliki, Greece 1987.

The night I was nearly arrested, riding a monocycle at 3 am.

On the bike, Vassiliki, 1988

My dear adopted family, god daughter on the obelisk.

Go Ape, age seventy-one.

Giving god-daughter a spin on the 600 Hornet.

CHAPTER 1.

'So what do you do for sex?'

She took me by surprise. We had knocked about on several occasions now, mostly working, sometimes socially, but I had not fathomed Danielle. To be honest, I wasn't interested in her private life. I knew that I liked her, enjoyed working with her. We treated each other with respect, until now. Here I was, driving in the midst of London traffic and this question lanced through the protective carapace I had built so carefully. It was direct, probably the most impertinent remark ever made to me. Cocooned inside my car, protected as I had thought by my position as the most important customer of Danielle's employer, she was mugging me, wrenching open my inner self. Many would have told her to mind her own business. She would have done. I should have.

Dannie liked to talk about herself. Was this another opening gambit for her own disclosures? Instead of telling her to go forth, I replied as truthfully as I could, with humour, quoting Stephen Fry.

'Nothing. I'm on a higher plain, given up on the damp and hairy bits. What ever makes you ask?'

'Sex means a lot to me. Just wondered. Wouldn't do for me to be without. Doesn't it bother you?'

I was confused by this sudden invasion. I have discouraged enquiries into my private life and I am careful what I volunteer. There are areas of my life, carefully wrapped and deposited in my memory bank, that I decided long ago, are best left there, out of sight, unspoken. Take me at face value, or leave me alone. As ex President Clinton says, 'Everyone has things in their life they would rather not talk about.' Many will not admit even that much.

I didn't want to have this conversation. Taking my time, using the need to concentrate on my driving, I thought of a cop out answer. Here in the car, I was a gold fish on a hook in a bowl.

'So have you a boy friend?' The question sounded lame indeed, a cheap ploy to deflect her thrust.

'I'm gay. Thought you had caught on by now. You said the other day, it wouldn't make any difference to you if I was.' Her voice had become more husky, boyish, her Luton accent coming through the prettier voice she normally used with me.

'No, of course it doesn't make any difference. You are Danielle, nothing's changed with me.' I meant it. I had no fear or horror of lesbianism. Yet I had never encountered an 'out' lesbian before. You may think that extraordinary, but times are changing so fast in the 1990s, that what was taboo last year, seems now the in thing. Who was I anyway, to be prejudiced over sex.

Danielle was like no other woman I had ever met. What the difference in her was, I had never analysed. I knew her to be streetwise, cheeky, full of life. She could be the sweetest, the most thoughtful and gentlest person too. She drank pints. She also drank spirits and wine. So did many young women these days. The age of the 'ladette' had begun here in the early nineties.

I recalled the occasion when she had asked whether it would make a difference. We had been in a pub for lunch. The little waitress appeared out of the smoky gloom a smile on her face and huge firm breasts on her chest. Danielle had said, 'I could do with some of that.' Naively, I took it to be merely a desire to have more bust than she in fact possessed, being quite flat chested. Although there had been several lesbian references and jokes, to which I had politely smiled, I assumed that to be the fashionable common vernacular of these twenty somethings in London. I also wondered if this remark was a mimic of her male colleagues, who had expressed their admiration for the same fine full chest on a previous occasion. Either way, I had been too shy, no not shy, too respectful of others privacy, to take her up on it.

Passively, I had laughed and said, 'I'm seriously worried about you.'

'Would it make any difference?' She asked.

'Of course not.' Naively again, I thought her to be testing my attitudes.

It didn't make a difference now, except, that trap was opening up, curiosity, the human's greatest gift and vice. Shamefully, I wanted to see into a lifestyle I knew nothing of. Voyeurism was stirring into life, something I abhor. Yet she was to me still Danielle, the person I liked.

Now I realised, I had been very naive with her. She had told me ages ago on the phone that she was late in because she'd had to 'go down on her girl friend'. I had been so surprised, that I took it all to be a joke. I challenged her and she had said, 'Just joking.' I accepted her answer. That is indeed naive, seeing only what is unchallenging, yet in my defence, she was then a pretty blonde with a bob, in a dress. On another occasion, I had asked if she had a good weekend. 'Lebanese,' she replied. 'What's that?' 'Oh, a lot of us girls went up the West End.' I let that go too, not understanding the pseudonym and having once been to an excellent Lebanese restaurant on Piccadilly.

There is a history to our friendship. I had first known her as Danielle, a small blonde blue eyed woman of twenty-four, who always greeted me with friendliness and a cup of coffee when I came to London to see her company. I recalled our first meeting, one of those rare occasions, when two strangers had both left an impression upon each other and I had detected a mutual friendly interest. Having arrived at her company's headquarters in Southwark, I had found my way via a labyrinth of Victorian passageways, through the ancient building to the sales room. I was dressed in power mode, navy skirt suit, matching bag and shoes, immaculate legs, a hard leather briefcase in one hand, fine navy kid encasing my hands. As I entered, one or two known faces had looked up with smiled greetings as they spoke to customers by phone. Danielle sat at her desk, just replacing her receiver. She wore a white blouse and grey skirt with sensible flat-heeled shoes. Her blonde bob shone in the light from the window. Her lips were covered in pink lipstick. She beamed a greeting.

'You must be Adrienne. Heard you were coming down today. Can I get you a coffee?'

'Thanks. You are?'

'Danielle. We've spoke on the phone. Cor, I must have made an impression.' Her eyes watched for my reaction, her face crinkling in a smile.

'Nice to meet you at last. Sorry, it's funny, you speak to people on the phone, then when you meet, you can't connect face with voice, because you've already imagined a person.' A cliché but true.

'I'll let you off.' She smiled. 'Milk and sugar?' Blunt home counties speech of the working class, what they now call estuary English.

'Black, one sugar please.'

Charlie, a director and one of my more frequent contacts, wheeled a chair up behind me. He shook my hand firmly, vigorously, as he always did. He looked like a pugilist and sounded like one with his deep cockney voice. We exchanged pleasantries, then he turned away as someone else shouted his name and shook a phone at him. Directors in this company worked on the shop floor.

Danielle returned with the coffee in a plastic cup. 'I've stirred it,' she said. 'It's very hot, that's why it's inside another cup, so you don't burn your little fingers.' She almost giggled. 'So, good journey down? Come down today, or have you stayed overnight?'

'Today. Left at seven. Three hours, not too bad.'

I tried to study her face without seeming to stare. At first glance, here was a pretty young blond, hair highlighted, cut just below her ears, a touch of mascara and lipstick, pale skin, pink cheeks. Her eyes were blue and piercing, restless and wary, her lips small with a highly defined cupids bow. Yet there was a strangeness about her face, a detraction from prettiness, but not a fault, not a blemish that would make one later revise the adjective pretty to plain.

'Is that your car out there?'

'I guess.'

'Is it OK? Does it go well?'

'I call it the ergonomic coffin. Comfortable, but death if it hit something.'

She looked puzzled, then laughed throatily.

'I've heard about your driving.'

'What?'

'Oh, just Cass, was saying, joking around, how you crossed the marshes at warp speed.'

'What was that?' Cass was at my elbow. He gave Danielle a stern avuncular look. 'Not been tittle-tattling has she? Sorry I wasn't here when you arrived. Has she looked after you? You've introduced yourselves? Danielle has been here, how long is it?'

'Ten months. I was just joking with Adrienne.' She was nervous that Cass thought she had stepped out of line.

Months later I had picked her out from the others in the company, asking Cass her manager, that she should have more responsibility for our account because I found her so willing.

Long before that, I had noted that there were no women in the sales room. I had asked why? There was no real answer, only a feeling that their particular custom could be rude, printers had a bad reputation and women would not cope, but I had pointed out that other similar companies employed women successfully. There were now five women employed. I silently took some credit for that, although the probability was that with a changing labour market, it would have come about anyway.

Later, Danielle had been put on outside sales, walking the streets of the city, selling to public and private offices and I was invited to use her to sell my company as well. Cass her sales director, pointed out the benefits of a joint sales strategy, something I was well aware of, but I had been guarded, not wanting too close a relationship.   But there were sound reasons for an alliance. We needed a local supplier to service same day supplies to the various ministries.   They were both a business partner and a potential competitor. Better to have them onside.

Dannie and I had more contact as a result. She invited me to stay with her when in London, from the time she had moved there. She had been desperately lonely, I had realised. It was an invitation I had not taken up until six months ago, only to find the door closed. She now had a flat mate, and there was no room she said.

Today, as we sat in traffic, our relationship was taking a new turn, and I was not even aware of it. In future, I would say things to her that I had locked up and not spoken of for years. Here was someone with a secret too, albeit a fairly open one, which was a key to my own closed life. I would find out that she like me, defended the secret of her sexuality even though everyone was actually aware of it. The outcast syndrome, is the common denominator which makes for all sorts of strange alliances in the fight for existence in 'normal society'. That society which excludes, vilifies, criminalises and derides, those who cannot live by its rules and mores of sexuality. Thankfully, that is disappearing though not as quickly as it appears to some.

'You must know that I am a transsexual.' This was the first time I had uttered those words.

It was her turn to come up with a jolt. My eyes flicked to her by my side as we ground to another stop in the heavy traffic. Victoria Street, eleven in the morning. The traffic was unusually tight, under a grey sky, which suddenly felt heavier than it really was. The end of winter, plants were coming into bud, and I awaited the leaves of the plane trees which to me are so evocative of London. Earlier we had passed down Horseguards. St James' Park was a picture of spring, the crocuses past their best, the daffodils not yet in full bloom, the ducks paired off, or pairing, a few marine squabbles causing ripples on London's most beautiful lake. I had slowed so that I could take in the sight, and Danielle had said, 'Great isn't it, London.' It is. I was enjoying it, the life, the effervescence, the excitement and colour.

As we sat in the halted traffic, there was fifteen seconds' silence. Out of the corner of my eye as I gazed ahead at the traffic lights in Parliament Square, I could see she had twisted in her seat, pulling the seat belt to make it more comfortable. She was now half facing me. There was a slight frown upon her face. Her appearance was much changed from the blonde I had first known. She had adopted the androgynous look, short cropped hair, her natural colour, light brown, and although today she wore a skirt suit, she normally wore trousers in which she looked more comfortable. In truth, looking back from this distance, that change had both shocked and interested me, but I had not realised how much at the time. I had even remarked to Cass that she looked more like a boy than a thirty year old woman. He had smiled without passing comment.

'I suspected,' she said, her voice low, more that of a teenage boy than a female of her age, 'there has been talk, one of the mill reps shouted his mouth off, until I shut him up. But I knew another transsexual too when I lived in Bedford.'

'Then you probably know that transsexuals are usually hetero.' I threw this out deliberately to put a barrier between us. It had been Dr Randall's opinion of the sexuality of transsexuals. Now deceased, he had seemed unable to understand that transsexuals do not necessarily embrace a straight lifestyle in their desired sex, nor always wear skirts.

'Yeah? Oh!'

The conversation stopped. We were both shocked out of our easy relationship. I wanted to know more about her, but didn't like to pry. She wanted to know about me, but my sharpness, that edge that protects and deflects, had stunned her as I had wanted. There would not be the usual discussion of Spurs versus Gunners today.

Inexplicably, I reactivated it as though wanting a more intimate relationship. 'I suppose the mill with the loud mouthed rep was.........?' I mentioned a Scottish paper mill.

'How d'you know?'

'Picked up the vibes. I know who he sees when he comes to our office.' Oh yes, I knew of the whispers and sniggers. The bitching went on about much less interesting people than me too.

Driving in the heavy traffic was not the ideal time to carry on a conversation as personal as this. I turned into Whitehall, then Trafalgar Square making for the next call in the Strand. What a city! So many of my friends hate and fear it, would not consider to drive in its crowded streets, nor ride the Underground by night, but I relish it, revel in the noise and bustle and I am entranced by the vivacity that is so evident. Here is all the world. A French girl I met in a bar told me that Paris is more beautiful, a matter of a little dispute between us, but she readily conceded that London had more excitement and more pizzazz

This next appointment was one I hated. The customer was a bibulous boor with no redeeming features shown to me, yet I had heard that he did much work for charity. I was glad to have Danielle with me, for she was better equipped to manage this reprobate with her jokey boyish ways. I turned into the portals of Somerset House, the guard checking my name and my pass.

In the afternoon, after a lunch in a pub with the disgusting customer, we had a long drive to the next appointment out in the suburbs. It was an opportunity for her to speak again of more intimate matters. Even my sharp retort about being heterosexual did not deter her for long.

'So what do you think of the gay scene?' She asked.

'Don't know much about it. My impression is that there's a lot of promiscuity and I wonder why?' How had I arrived at this opinion? It was a mystery, even to me. She didn't deny it.

'How can I explain? If you are hetero you can walk in any pub, see someone and chat them up. For the gay community there isn't that much choice. We're not accepted even yet, so we meet in certain known safe locations, pubs, clubs, cafés. Pent up emotions overflow. We flirt, but it doesn't mean that we are necessarily unfaithful to our partners. Look, in a straight club on a Saturday night, see how many straight men are trying to pull. Anyway, a man will make a pass if he just holds the door open for you.' She chuckled. She meant me when she said 'you', and has said that I encourage men. 'You tart1' she had said. If I do flirt, it is done unconsciously and without intent. Can a polite smile and thank you be so interpreted, I wondered?

I considered her explanation of the gay scene. I knew so little about it that I couldn't make a valid judgement. I certainly knew what a straight club was like and she was right. For a woman it could be like being in a market. Unwanted advances flying upon one, disdainful remarks too. I had never been to a gay venue. I wanted to be a 'normal' woman in the Dr. Randall mould. I knew that those who took me at face value, a skirt wearing, coiffured, made up and 'straight' woman, had their attitudes and expectations changed once they knew my history. I have to admit too that a lesbian fling had been a fleeting fantasy. I liked women and their company, but that is hardly odd.

I'd had a long-term relationship with a married man and two or three other sexual affairs with men since my operation. I considered myself between the trenches, not really qualified to be the long term partner of man or woman, and emotionally I had not sorted out in my mind whether my ideal partner would be male or female. I am a submissive person, sexually and in that, my character is female rather than male. What I knew was that I adored women. I liked their ways. I admired their bodies. I admired men for their strength and uncomplicated emotions, but I was not really happy in their company. Sex was both unfulfilling and uncomfortable. The fear of their discovery of my true status was a real worry. I also knew, that men might find having an affair with a transsexual woman, a threat to their manhood. It was most certainly a risky undertaking. This self-analysis and I believe, realistic view of most men's psychology was both protective and restricting. It had kept me safe.

'When did you know that you were gay?' I caught a flash of pain flicker across her face.

'Huh!' It was almost a gasp of agony. Her voice deepened, and her small handsome features showed concentration as if working out where to start. 'I don't really know. I was raped when I was five.'

I took my hand from the gear lever and laid it on hers upon her thigh. Her hands were large for a slight woman, but exquisite, long smooth fingers and good skin, tapering to well-kept short nails. 'You don't have to tell me,' I said.

'No, 's OK. Long time ago. My father sent me to learn to box after that. Can you believe that? Couldn't handle it, my parents. Not equipped, hadn't the education or the intelligence. Even later in my life, when my periods started, early, I was only eleven and I had to tell my teacher 'cause it started in school, mother couldn't cope. Seemed it was something to be ashamed of. Didn't even get the right size sanitary towels for me. Can't forgive how she behaved. She just couldn't bring herself to explain what was happening to my body and what it all meant. Anyway, I always wanted to be a boy. Climbed trees, played football, got in fights.' She had lapsed into 'estuary English' again. Her voice accentuated that boyishness which set her apart from any other woman I had known.

'Did they get the bastard who did it to you.'

'Yeah, he was nineteen. Got six months, then did five more rapes.'

I took this in with difficulty. From the heart I said, 'Should have thrown away the key.'

'Yeah, right.'

'Do you blame the rape for making you gay?'

'Don't know. No. Nothing's helped has it? I mean my parents attitude, the rape and being a tomboy anyway.'

'So what age were you when you felt different?'

'Seven, nine, thirteen certainly. Hard to say. Just think it was always there. How does one put a date on it, unless it is a sudden revelation.'

'No, one seldom can. I know in my case it's been with me since my earliest memory. I mean I believe I was born wanting and believing that I was in reality, female, although I had a body unmistakably male. I hated my maleness even before I knew what girls were like. It was instinctive.'

'Tell me what it was like, your wanting.' She was looking closely at me. Her eyes puzzled, I could never determine their colour properly. They seemed to change like those heat sensitive crystals one can buy which are supposed to denote mood change.

'Hmm. Well, I was never pansified, effeminate, or so I believe. I behaved like a boy. Played rugby, did things for a dare, I suppose trying to prove something to myself and to disguise my real self. I didn't like myself, didn't respect myself. I just wanted to be, what I was outwardly supposed to be. Only in my mind I was a girl. I would have fantasies, had this fantasy world, and sometimes the real world, my hateful imprisoning masculine world was so unbearable that I had to do something feminine, just to be true to myself.'

'Like what?'

'Like plucking a hair or two from my eyebrows, or experimenting with make-up stolen or bought with great embarrassment. Or trying a new hairstyle, even that was something other boys didn't seem to do. Sometimes I would walk as I thought, like a woman, or skip. I took great care not to let anyone catch me. Yet I'm sure my female side showed through even my 'normal' behaviour. I was treated differently sometimes, as though I was a girl, even though I thought I looked like a boy and I'm sure I did. There must have been something, mannerisms, attitude, speech or as I suspect some less obvious..., quality, perhaps gentleness, that made people sometimes react as if I were female. Unconscious androgyny. I loved it when my sex was mistaken, wanted it to be there all the time, but of course I also feared it, feared the discovery of my true nature. Discovery would have destroyed me in those days, I felt sure then. Attitudes have changed unbelievably in 40 years. Oscar Wilde was persecuted a hundred years ago. Now not only would he survive but be fêted. Gay jokes are not funny anymore, but gay men can make a fortune by being gay.'

'Still not that easy for us. OK for stars but on the streets it's still dangerous.'

'But perceptions of transsexuals have lagged behind gay rights. Jan Morris wrote 'Conundrum' in the late sixties, on her own transsexual journey, but although it opened up the phenomenon, and gave it a certain respectability in 'society', it has not been accepted by the state.* As Mrs Bottomley when Health Minister said, 'The health service will not pay for unnecessary sex change operations', as though they were as whimsical as breast enlargement. About 1992 that was I think.'

'So you're secretive about it.'

'Aren't you about being gay? Transsexualism is still a joke. Homosexuality is supposed to be present in one in ten. Transsexualism, actually feeling and wanting to be, the opposite sex, one in fifteen thousand. People just don't get it. And I don't wonder at that. It seems so inexplicable because most people, the other 14,999 are quite content in their natal sex, even if they are attracted to the same sex.

'Knowledge does change perceptions. I get by, by pretending people don't know. Some men are just as threatened by me as by a gay man. Anyway, is it anything to boast about? Secrecy has been destructive of me, the love of my feminine side and the fear of its revelation hurts. I tried to destroy it; then I would pander to it; alternate emotions consuming me. On two occasions men tried to sexually assault me, and boys at school had crushes on me, some just friendships, but also some which I now know to have been more homosexual in nature. One tried to rape me. At school and after, until I thought I would burst, I tried to conform. I wanted a normal life. At school in my time, it made life so much easier. No one, I think, could have survived if openly gay let alone admitting being confused over their sex.'

'Sounds like a right knocking shop, your school.'

'No it wasn't. Four hundred boys, ten per cent secretly gay maybe. The stories about homosexuality in boys boarding schools, didn't apply. Anyway nothing really happened, not sex anyway. After some of the episodes of feeling girly in that very male atmosphere, I would self-harm, a sort of punishment.

She frowned. 'Self-harm? How?'

'Mostly needles through the skin. Sometimes a cigarette burn. People make a whole drama of that now. It didn't mean that I wasn't enjoying life. There were just moments of deep hatred of myself. I didn't understand. I was twelve when Roberta Cowell came out as having changed sex. We had newspapers at school and it was all over the front of one of them. I was fascinated. I spoke about it to my mother but did not dare say that was how I felt. It was so abnormal. It made the sense of loss I already felt, all the greater. In that boys boarding school, dressed in the strict boys dress of the time with short hair, it was the last thing I wanted. I desired a dress, long hair, pigtails.

'I was in another very male oriented situation ten years later when April Ashley was outed. I was sitting in my bungalow in Pendembu, way up country in Sierra Leone, a bank manager at twenty-one years old. By this time I was cross-dressing in private, making dresses, hand stitching in the light of a Tilley Lamp, paraffin fuelled. The lamp hissed under pressure and I listened to Radio Liberia, Sam Cooke and the Everly Brothers. Cupid was my favourite song.'

There was a silence after this. Heavy traffic and the nearness to our next call interrupted our exchange. Later that day she said, 'Perhaps you would like to meet my partner? Would you like to have dinner with us sometime?'

'Thank you, I'd like that.' I was flattered. Being allowed into her home I considered an acceptance of my sexuality just as I had accepted hers. I was already fond of Danielle. Her confiding in me and this invitation, was progressing the acquaintance into a friendship. Although I was not a homophobe, it was a world that I had neither had the opportunity nor the inclination to enter. I was not clubable. I rather despised those who wanted to separate themselves into small cohesive herds. I wanted a world where all was acceptable within reason. Yet I could not deny that it intrigued me now that I knew someone personally involved in that alternative world. I admit that there have been crushes on women since my change of sexual orientation, but was that lesbianism? Are all those bosom pal women closet lesbians? How could I tell? Should I even bother to think about it? Probably not.

The visit would be an insight into a life that I thought to be much maligned and unnecessarily feared. Many are fascinated by the gay life, covering their real feelings with hate or humour or derision. I had never been like that, having suffered just as much at the hands of the 'normal'. Life was certainly becoming even more exciting though.

As a result of these conversations, I decided to write my story. Over the next months, in hotel rooms up and down the UK, I hammered away on the laptop, sometimes way into the night with tears in my eyes until exhaustion sent me to sleep.

CHAPTER 2.

My early childhood was a matter of some mystery to me. The world I awoke to when I became a thinking, interacting human, was full of not only the unknown but of fear. My earliest memory of this first period of my life was being bathed in a basin before the sitting room fire in a semiconscious state. I remember both my parents being there and I was afraid, not because I was feverish, but the bath was laid on the ironing table near the fire and, it was high up. I was under two years old, yet I have retained that memory. My mother told me that I had whooping cough in 1941. I know it was distressing. I could not understand why I felt so poorly.

Having come into the world at the outbreak of war, just five days after the declaration, my childhood memories are not unnaturally of that event. The next happening to make an impression was having a Donald Duck gas mask. We had to collect this at the ARP* bunker near the railway station. We, my brother, mother and I, descended into a dank shelter staffed by men wearing their armbands and helmets, their badges of office. I remember fighting with them when they tried to fit the horrifying mask. I held my breath against the stench of rubber and shrieked. I won and never set eyes on the obscene thing again. All our gas masks stayed in their boxes on a hook in the garden shed and were never used. I was two years old.

My next vivid memories were of hiding under the dining room table in our North Downs, Surrey house, as the whining engines of German bombers ploughed towards London. The sound they made was wow, wow, wow unlike our own good, friendly sounding planes, which made a continuous thrum. This was because, my brother four years older told me, the Germans had deliberately desynchronised their engines with the intention of striking even more fear into the population. 'A typical swinish Nazi trick', he said, Captain Mainwaring like. My brother knew this because our father worked for Hawker Aircraft who had built the Hurricane, the splendid little fighter that had been the backbone of the Battle of Britain but which was eclipsed in mythology by the more potently and imaginatively named, 'Spitfire'. Certainly the Spitfire was pretty and perhaps the best fighter plane of WW2, but the Hurricane bore the brunt of the Nazi onslaught of 1940.

---

* Air Raid Protection

Considering my birth at the very outbreak of war, I remember a considerable amount. Sheltering from stray bombs seemed a haphazard affair. We had an outside shelter, an Anderson, half underground and made from stout corrugated iron. Half buried with a rough rockery on top, it was something for small children to scramble over. We seldom used it. It ran with water down the inside as condensation collected on the metal. Even wrapped in blankets, as I was when carried into it at night, it was a cold dank place. Also, my parents considered it little safer than staying in the house. I remember using it, but by the time I was three, it had become redundant.

As well as under the dining table, we used the cupboard under the stairs. The way in which our parents made us safe, yet took little or no precautions themselves, was quite remarkable. I remember our being thrust below the stairs while mother carried on cooking the dinner. As soon as, and often before the wail of the all clear siren was heard, we emerged. I found it disturbing that mother should not be with us in safety, after all, what was the use of surviving if we had no mother? My brother protested at having to take these scant precautions. He would far rather have been out looking up into the sky, trying to spot the make of bomber. Of course, familiarity bred contempt.

The Germans left our village alone, if they even saw it, for there were better targets to the north; the great Port of London, the City, and factories. Further North still there were important manufacturing centres, Coventry, Birmingham, Manchester and Liverpool, perhaps our most important port for the North Atlantic. All were just within range, while to the South were the Channel ports. Only stray bombs came our way at first, but when the flying bombs started, we were in their direct and unpredictable course.

We later acquired a Morrison shelter, a stout metal construction that stood in the front room. It was the size of a double bed, just large enough for two adults and two children. But it is my recollection that this too was seldom used.

In 1944 the flying bombs appeared. As was the way of the resilient and defiant British people then, we treated this new and horrible weapon with scorn. Officially known as the V1 it was humorously nicknamed the 'doodlebug'. They were strange looking contraptions belching flames. Powered by a ram jet engine they made a frightful noise like a pulsing jet engine. We soon learnt that while they made a noise they were no threat to us. Someone would 'cop it', but as long as it kept going it would not be our area. We had one or two close shaves. One came down in the field opposite doing considerable damage to other houses. We arrived home one day to find our doors open, blown in by the blast, but they closed again without trouble, the locks still worked and the woodwork was unmarked. Nor was a pane of glass broken. One Doodlebug flew by my bedroom window awakening me, the red blast from the jet pipe lighting up the bedroom. I was terrorised, the flames in the darkness worse than the picture of hell in the Jehovah's suitcase. It came down half a mile away, killing several people in a large house converted to flats.

Today, there would have been an ocean of flowers to mark the tragedy, but then it was just commonplace, the fall of the dice, the turn of a card, the ten pound lottery win. Tragedy was stifled by a stiff upper lip and fearsome force was treated with contempt. The people had a fatalistic attitude to danger. It was a matter of 'if your number's on it'. In the 1980s sitcom 'Blackadder', Baldrick keeps a bullet in his pocket with his name on it, therefore he cannot be killed he thinks. We were more fatalistic. There was nothing to be done, so why make a fuss. Meanwhile one would carry on life to the best of one's ability. The people were amazingly cheerful, resilient and brave. There was no wailing and gnashing of teeth. No fear, just phlegmatic stoicism and scorn for the enemy.

On another occasion, we had just got off the bus when we were rocked by an explosion. This was the V2, the rocket made by Herr Braun who later became the brains behind the US space program. This rocket had fallen ten miles away, but the blast was such that I shuddered, falling to the ground.

There were soldiers everywhere, camped in the pine woods, running around the roads practising street fighting. A convoy came down our road one day, on their way to the south for the 'D' day landings. They were Canadians marching four abreast presumably to the train station. We children stood cheering and waving, though it was all a bit of a mystery to me. The soldiers were in good heart, laughing, waving, throwing us gum, sweets, cigarettes to the women. I was a little thing of four and a half, a smiling angel-like child with a head of cream curly hair. Suddenly, I was snatched up, perched on a soldier's shoulder and carried down the road a hundred yards. They named me 'Snowball', gave me some sweets and set me down to the relief of my mother who had been alerted by my brother. The soldier said he had a child just like me at home.

I seem to recollect that the opening up of the second front was freely spoken of, a logical next step in the war of attrition against Hitler. A pipeline called Pluto was built across the fields we played in and near to where the V1 came down. It seemed to be known that it was to supply the Allies with petrol after the landings in France.

A flying bomb flew right over the house while we were in the garden. I dived for cover, but my brother raced to the front gate to watch as a Spitfire dived to gain enough speed to catch it and shoot it down before it reached London. I was rather ashamed that I had missed the fun, though I was only doing as my brother had told me. He was full of the experience and taunted me for having missed it. The fighters tried to get them while they were over the North Downs where they would do least harm. They developed a technique of tipping them over with the wing tip. This upset the flying bomb's gyro navigation system and caused them to crash.

Walking my brother to school one day, a flying bomb roared right over our heads. On mother's command we dropped to the ground in the gutter, waiting for the roar of the engine to falter that we knew would prelude the thing falling to earth and exploding. Much to my brother's disgust it kept flying, just a few feet above the trees on its way north to London. He would not lie down, sitting up, watching it excitedly. We had become used to these fearful weapons. They came from two directions, and just like the local buses we decided there was an Epsom and a Sutton route. It was all so ordinary to us, yet was all so extraordinary. It demonstrates the human's ability to adapt, to live under whatever intolerable dangers, but still retain a love of life. It explains too, how some poor souls were subjected to the most inhuman conditions imaginable, those in the German death camps, and yet came out sane enough to build successful and happy lives afterwards.

With my brother at school, I was free to do as I wanted. I would disappear up the stairs while mother was preoccupied with housekeeping and her little job on the side, typing manuscripts for authors. I would delve into the rag-bag and dress up in her old dresses, miles too big but with lovely material. Occasionally I would sneak in and play with the scented powder she kept in a bowl, or her rouge. I would receive a scolding. It was a lonely time. My family did not mix with the neighbours.

Father would complain every Christmas, I think for the next 20 years, that at Christmas his whole office went to the pub. He hated it.

Mother pretended to be social, but found fault with nearly everyone. She was either an inverted snob with those she felt better off or disdaining of those she felt below her 'station'. Her sisters too were utter snobs, all three the daughters of a grocer.

Born in 1904, she told me stories of her own childhood, working in her father's shop, weighing the sugar into blue paper funnels, sponging maggots off the bacon with vinegar. She knew the tricks of the retail trade at that time, when every commodity was weighed to order, of weighting the scales with a magnet or a finger, of stones in the currents and even sand in the demerara sugar. The best time in this lonely period was of being in the kitchen, making pastry which I made better than she could, of peeling Bramley apples, so that the peel came off all in one piece, and shelling peas and broad beans.

She had one great friend, Mrs Postgate, Wyn, who lived up our long road, and on certain days she would childmind me. I remember being quite bored, playing their wind up gramophone with records like the laughing policeman. She read books to me and taught me to read. I would be put in the pushchair and wheeled home, picking flowers on the way from those that hung over people's front garden walls.

It was at this time, that I started to have dreams that Wyn cut off my penis, something I desperately wanted her to do in my dream, yet I had no knowledge at all of human anatomy or an inkling of the difference in the sexes. It seemed intuitive that my body was wrong. I can only assume, that just as a fledgling bird pops out of the nest and knows if it flaps its wings, flight is possible, I knew instinctively, that my body was not as it should be.

I was already confused. Toys given to me were few, but none really pleased me. My only favourite was a small soft toy, a panda. My brother's hand me down peddle car, freshly painted and resplendent, was a disappointment. So was a railway engine I could sit on and propel with my legs. I therefore had no toys I liked. The background to my existence was still the war. We could not escape it. Roaring planes in the air, convoys, walking the North Downs and being surprised by soldiers involved in mock battle.

There were news reports, 'The Allies have opened up the second front.', 'The Red army has crossed the Elbe.', 'The British Army has crossed the Rhine'. We had a map, and with mothers help I watched the progress, measuring the distance covered and the way to go. I understood quite a lot in a limited fashion. We doted on the news, listened hushed for the next victory that would lead to the defeat of the hated Hitler. The German people were nothing to us. The destruction of Dresden then, was no more than they deserved, for they had instigated the bombing of the innocent. We never thought about Frau Schmidt and her children living in a cellar, nor of her husband lying dead in the snows of Russia. We felt no humanity towards the enemy at all.

Something that brought home to me the awfulness of war was a photograph in 'Picture Post', a soldier crouched by the side of a shell hole, tears running down his cheeks. There was the suspicion of a body in sight. Here was a grown man, probably a father, far from his home and in a distressed state from exhaustion and the experiences of a fighting soldier. At five years old, I found it painful and worrying. Fifty years later, it was revealed that the photo had been posed. I feel cheated, but the message is still valid. War is dreadful, and any leader that takes a people into it unnecessarily as in the former Yugoslavia or indeed, Iraq, should be locked away in an asylum. Perhaps if our leaders had to be on the front line into battle, there would be fewer wars. When The Cameron Government pushed by William Hague pressed to be involved in Syria, I campaigned via press and letters to my MP against it. My MP voted for intervention and I wrote and accused him of selling out since he had become Minister. None of our interventions have worked out. I will return to this later.

My brother was something of a character. He was nearly four at the outbreak of war, so that all his thinking life was wrapped up in it. He positively loved the excitement of the planes and the soldiers.

He even developed his own uniform of shorts, lumber jacket similar to what is now known as a bomber, as sported by that cretin George W Bush when he declared from the safety of an aircraft carrier that the Iraq war was over. He treasured and wore an army glengarry complete with the badge of the East Surrey regiment. He was somewhat difficult. He would only eat bread, dripping and Marmite, but managed to survive. The family doctor said that this plain fare had all the nutrients one required. I rather doubt it.

Val was also equipped with a rare temper and let it go fairly frequently. Consequently there was a constant queue of parents complaining that little Fred or Shirley had received a thump and that of course they were innocent angels set upon by a devil. To my knowledge, he never bashed anyone without a reason. He just wouldn't accept any lip. He was somewhat anti-social. He regarded most of the mothers round about with utter contempt. There was a street party, either for VJ day, the end of the Japanese war, or for some other occasion to which we were not invited. I would have been but they thought that it was impossible to invite me without my obnoxious brother. Not that I cared. We didn't want to eat their dirty rock cakes and spam sandwiches. To celebrate this affair, we rode our bikes through the middle of the party, then repeated it, just to show what we thought of it.

On another occasion, he investigated an exploded doodlebug, the remains of which lay in the crater it had made in a field a quarter of a mile away. These days, no one would be allowed anywhere near, but in more sensible times, people were not so frightened of their surroundings. From this pit, he managed at ten years old to salvage the jet pipe, some six feet long and heavy. He brought it home in triumph, then dropped it on me because I refused to move, bringing up an egg shaped bump on my head.

Another triumph was constructing a three wheeled cart, complete with steering wheel. I supplied the horse power on the level, the alternative was a bashing, and he careered down the hills with no brakes. Luckily there was so little traffic, one could hear a motor vehicle coming. He had a few near misses, and I silently rejoiced when sometimes, he was deposited in a hedge or stinging nettle bed. The truck was the envy of our friends who were occasionally awarded a go in return for pushing power.

I had a scooter, a lovely one with a brake. In our hilly neighbourhood such a toy was potentially dangerous. I can remember having grazed knees and hands for what seemed months. It was an active mostly outdoors life. Our bikes would allow us to roam for miles, quite unsupervised, and mother and the other mothers, had little fear for our safety. We did indulge in mischief as proper children should, but not in deliberate malice, cruelty or crime. We had so much freedom, yet survived through our own common sense. My brother and I compensated each other, both of us cooling the other's excesses. We scrumped, fruit from gardens, berries from bushes. We built fires and baked potatoes to a char. We liked fires, but never let them get out of control. My brother's bonfire night edifice was something to behold. Fuelled by four or five old motor tyres and all the old scrap wood for miles around, it was the only fire to be seen at before the advent of the organised affair.

The women around us had had a good war. Their husbands had almost to a man, gone to the war. Consequently, the world that I was raised in was very different. Our father was not only too old, but also in a reserved occupation. The other children were fatherless, but it appeared not to harm them. They neither grew up effeminate, nor out of control. But their mothers had to have comfort of some sort and entertaining the gallant troops provided a good excuse. They flooded off to the village hall hops, fraternised with Yanks, Canadians and others. One close friend was always coming in to our house early in the morning, saying that Uncle Brian, Jim, Gary etc., had stayed the night. Her husband was missing in Malaya, never to return. We nastily conjectured that he had gone to Australia after the war rather than come back to his wife. She sang like a nightingale, especially after an uncle's visit, as she cleaned her spotless home. Others had several children during the war, and they certainly could not have been conceived by the respective husbands. Yet when peace came and the men mostly returned, life just picked up where it had left off. Possibly the men were too traumatised to create a fuss.

Even at this young age, preschool, I was fundamentally unhappy. While still in the pushchair, I had demanded while at the hairdressers, a ribbon in my hair, but pulled it out as soon as I realised that I had committed some kind of dreadful sin. The dreams that Wyn delivered me from my horrible body with a pair of scissors persisted. Secretly, I adored the feel of mother's dresses.

While Val was at school, I was alone all the day, or so it seemed. One memory that has stayed with me all my life was hearing Dvorak's symphony no.9, 'From the New World'. That first experience of classical music made a deep incision into my very soul. I retained the memory of that work from the age of four or five and in times of severe stress it has come to my aid.

My brother also had a multifaceted role in my life. He was both guardian and bully. Leader and slave owner. He teased me mercilessly. He must have found me a somewhat fey child, a charge that was also made against me later in life. The dictionary definition of fey is silly or impractical in an artistic sensitive sort of way. No one who has used the word about me has actually been able to explain the meaning. In later life, a friend in Africa thought its meaning 'sensitive with powers of insight like the fairies'! He was a Scot and meant it affectionately.

I was perhaps the least practical in the family, but then I was the youngest. Val liked to make me his slave. For instance, if there were household chores to do, he would get me to do them while he tinkered with his bike. It was the same with any distasteful task, whilst I, thinking as usual of the family unit or rather my mother, would make up for his deficiency. He also liked to lean on me, on the way to school, calling me his leaning post. At the bus stop, he would leave me on guard while he went off to look at shops or cars, or to throw stones into the coal yard.

He liked dogs and still does. One morning the large black Labrador that always barked at us was loose in the lane. I was frightened but not Val. He said, 'good dog,' and patted its head. I watched and said nothing while the dog peed on his foot. It was splendid.

Eventually he was sent to boarding school and I was free. In holiday time, our pleasures were cheap. We didn't go far afield. If we had drawn a circle of six miles radius around our house, it would have been roughly the limit of our world. Within the circle we roamed freely and largely fearlessly. Sometimes, we would wander into the territory of a neighbouring tribe and we would either take to our heels or bluff it out.

We had few treats. A loaf of fresh bread was gorgeous. We ate the inside first, rolling the soft flesh into little balls with our probably dirty fingers. The hollowed crust we considered the best part and we ate that with relish, quarrelling over the choicest, crustiest parts. We still cannot understand why children now shun bread and discard the crusts. Pop, fizzy drinks, were a rarity. R. Whites was our local brand. Ginger beer (Stones), was our favourite, but lemonade was next. We shared a large bottle, quarrelling over the size of the gulps, accusing each other of allowing tongues to be sucked into the bottle. As the bottle passed, we wiped the top hygienically, with a dirty hand. We could buy one Oxo cube for an old penny, 240 to a £1. Sweets were on ration. Mars bars were our favourite, then Cadbury's milk chocolate or Crunchie.

Our mother cooked one meal, tasty, salted and spiced. We ate it or starved. Stews, rissoles, roast on Sundays, cold on Mondays, liver and bacon, steak and kidney pie or pudding, shepherds pie. Potatoes new, boiled, mashed or roast. One green vegetable except when we had two in the garden. That was a rare occurrence, for father had no love of gardening at all. It was plain fare, before the explosion of international cuisine which began in the sixties. It was lovely food, flavoursome and nourishing, and although today I will eat anything and I am passionate about curry, I will defend traditional English food always, as long as it is well cooked. We always had a pudding, milk, steamed, plum duff, or 'dead fly', pies, stewed apple, pancakes. In summer there would be others, cold stewed fruits as well as blancmanges and jelly. How she managed to produce such wholesome food in times of rationing is beyond understanding. There was no black-market for us. We had what was available including whale meat and rabbit, neither of which I liked.

Father liked to make models, trains and then boats. His tool kit was elemental, a few files, a small vice, a hacksaw and a hammer and pliers. He would spend hours of his little spare time, making these models. None were quite right, a near miss in respect of finish would mar them. They were a constant source of irritation to mother, who once put them in the dustbin in the sheer frustration of wanting the garden and house put in order. Father left home at 6.00am, returning at 7.00pm or later. He also worked Saturday morning and in the war sometimes extra hours on top when Hawker had a warplane order to develop. I believe, he just did not have the energy to give to household matters, and that the models were his relaxation. He worked on the dining room table, in time drilling it full of holes until I refurbished it at the age of sixteen and forbade further work indoors.

Until about 1950, when I was 10 and my brother 14, we hardly knew our father. He was a remote figure who sat around for a short weekend. My brother and I both had the toy of the moment, potato pistols. These air weapons had a crude pump action and expelled a potato pellet made by screwing the barrel into a potato. One day, my brother dared himself to shoot father as he nodded off after Saturday lunch. The pellet hit right between the eyes. As father awoke and realisation dawned, a deep growl erupted. It was like a lion being stung by a bee. Val turned tail and fled, while I watched what was unfolding. Surprisingly, father gave up the chase quite quickly, and, believed my brother when he said it had gone off by mistake.

Val liked dangerous pastimes. A favourite was putting calcium carbide in a bottle with a little water. The gas produced would blow a tightly stoppered bottle to pieces. If it failed to explode, we would either pick it up and throw it, or chuck a stone at it. This usually took place in the chalk pit, an old but small working across the road from us. This was also the playground of the Home Guard. They erected a crude tin shelter, its purpose unknown to us. It was about two feet from ground to roof, four feet wide and eight long. It made a fine noise when we jumped on it, but in so doing, we, and the gang reduced it to some broken sticks and a flattened piece of corrugated iron. We awaited results. After several days, we thought we had got away with it. Then of course, the local commander caught up with us and explained to mother on our doorstep that we had destroyed a vital training tool. He made it sound as though we had set the war back by months, except that already, the war was over.

We hit upon a good scam to make money. Most drinks bottles had a return fee. We knocked on doors asking whether they had any bottles to return. The bottles cluttering up a pantry were a nuisance, and mostly people were only to pleased to have them taken away. Some naively thought we would return with the money. Others thought we were working for the shop. Some, especially silly people, thought we were doing it for charity. You can only get away with a scam for a short time, so we quit as soon as the first rumbles of trouble appeared. However, we had lived like royalty for a couple of weeks.

Mother had a hatred of the state system. Consequently, at age five I joined my brother at a private school and one that was in vogue at the time. Progressive education largely left the children to set their own agenda. It was a sort of poor man's Summerhill. One learnt when one felt like it, a choice between the sandpit and reading, hide and seek and arithmetic, was always available. The place was a shambles, but somehow I managed to learn to read and write. After two years, we were both taken away by our disillusioned mother.

My next school was a private high school. At nearly eight years I was backward and started off sitting in the front where the dear teacher could keep an eye on me. By the end of that year, mainly through her encouragement, I was sitting on the back row where the bright children sat. It was a good system and one that should be followed in every school. It meant that the most needy received the best attention.

In the following year I advanced to a higher class. I missed my former teacher. I was now taught by a rather testy man and although I had made up ground in the previous year, there were fundamental gaps in my educational grounding that soon showed up under pressure. I also had to deal with new subjects, Latin, geometry, algebra. The boys were rough in their play too. I became unhappy.

I was saved from this by pneumonia. The whole of January through March 1949 was spent in bed. Initially I was given M & B, one of the new miracle drugs, but it made me violently sick. Keep taking it said the doctor, but within an hour of swallowing the dreaded pill, I would spend half an hour spewing and retching. The doctor then turned to another new drug, penicillin, delivered by injection in the back side. I lay, limp and lifeless, gasping for breath for days, the bedroom heated by a radiant copper fire that was warm, friendly and beautiful. It was that fire that cured me as much as anything, I just loved the warmth and colour of it. Waking from feverish sleep, I would move over towards it in the bed, feel the warmth upon my face, see the bright red and coppery hue of it, hang a limp arm out towards it. I was nine and a half.

Recovered at last, I recuperated with my Aunt Edith the other side of the Hogs Back. Mother put me on a bus alone to Guildford where I changed to another bus and arrived at Runfold near Farnham. Few mothers today would let their children make such a journey. Edith was my mother's elder sister. She had married a Major who had been gassed in the First World War and, having a small private income, Uncle George did nothing. He got up, breakfasted, sat in the drawing room reading the paper and listened to the Home Service of the BBC. He lunched with us in the dining room, then returned to the drawing room, had high tea or dinner and went to bed. He liked a beer with lunch, a whisky in the evening and smoked cigarettes, only a quarter way down ever, the butt then cast into the ashtray. This provided me with a supply of cigarettes which I consumed while swinging on the swing, which was thoughtfully hidden from the view of adults, by a nice box hedge.

Edith was a meagre provider. Uncle George ate his pudding with a tablespoon so that he could finish first and get seconds. She treated me to sweets. With great excitement Aunt Edith and I walked down to the little sweet shop where she bought me a tube of Smarties, still rationed at that time. However, the catch to this generosity was that I was allowed two after lunch. Naturally, I raided the larder where they were kept. My room was usually used by my cousin B, the eldest child of my other Aunt, Ciceley, who lived abroad. B was at boarding school. In the cupboard were all her dresses. I tried them all on and studied myself in the mirror. I was exhilarated by what I saw. I looked and felt a different person, the person I had always wanted to be. I took them off with great reluctance and sadness. This was a reinforcement of the feelings of self dissatisfaction I had felt from my earliest memory. I knew not where it would lead.

I loved my time there, for from seven or eight in the evening till getting up at nine the next day, I could be the person I wanted to be. I loved the house, the large garden with the swing, the woods beyond which reached down to the slow flowing and boggy river Mole. I roved them alone, unafraid, in my own muse. My aunt was mean but kindly. I learnt to construct the wooden puzzle animals they had and, nightly we played Halma before bed.

However, without doubt I was a sensitive child. I felt the vibrations and tensions of my family life very deeply. It is a great failure of character that one is not so full of oneself that other's moods pass by unnoticed. This preoccupation with others thoughts, actual or imagined, and their opinions and actions, has been a source of distress and anxiety all my life, though over the last few years this pain has receded. In amongst all this introspective and speculative angst though, there has been a certain amount of insight that others miss. Years later, at work, I was aware of who was seeing whom, who was unhappy at home. On two occasions, meeting people on the Continent they took one look at me and said 'sympathetique' or 'sympatico', a quality not recognised in this country in the same way and certainly not valued.

It had been easy to learn to hate the Germans, without knowing anything about their barbarism, National Socialism, the holocaust or the fearful destruction they had caused. Not only were their planes nasty, but their uniforms black and grey, breeches rather than trousers, jackboots, high peaked hats, the black Swastika, the black Prussian Cross, the Hitler salute and the fact that they had started a war against innocent and unprotected countries, confirmed all we wanted to believe. Had Hitler succeeded in ruling all western Europe, I would sooner or later have joined the queue for the gas chamber, for I grew up to be a sexual deviant. Along with those with Jewish blood, Moslems, Seventh Day Adventists, Quakers, gypsies, gays, lesbians, Poles, Slaves, Russians, militant priests, conscientious objectors, political opponents, any opponents, mentally ill or damaged, even those physically disadvantaged; all would eventually have been exterminated. That would have been a great many people.

CHAPTER 3.

By the time I had recovered from pneumonia, it was April. Instead of returning to the High School, I went to a cramming school for some intensive education. It was a strange institution. It appeared perfectly respectable. The owner and headmaster, always dressed his portly frame in a smart suit. He used the title Captain, which he had presumably acquired in the war. The premises were an old Victorian House on a corner site in the better Cheam end of Sutton, Surrey. As well as the house there was a large garden and a hard tennis court. The front room and an upstairs bedroom were class rooms.

I was supposed to have extra maths tuition and this took place in the Head's sitting room. I was therefore able to observe the Captain and his wife at close quarters. I found them slightly creepy. Their close encounters and whispered words close to the ear, were disturbing to a young child. They had a glass of whiskey mid morning and a sherry before lunch, a practise completely foreign to my family. What's more, my extra tuition was just working on my own. One teacher a middle aged man, wore a brown tweed suit. He was a pipe smoker, and like my father, tended to drop burning ash around. He had burnt a hole in his trousers, two or three inches below the groin. There were occasional flashes of white flesh which were not conducive to good concentration. It was rather disgusting. I stayed to do my homework and all through the next winter walked home three quarters of a mile in pitch darkness. When a car with its lights blazing appeared, I would run to make as many yards as possible in the light.

I had time to read, and there were a number of books in a little library. One that fascinated was 'Poor dear Esme', a story of a teenage boy pretending to be a girl, I can't remember for what reason. It was a well-known book.

The only game we played was a kind of hockey on the hard tennis court, using a tennis ball and walking sticks. The pupils all seemed nice children. I was happy enough there but my education was only marking time.

In the holidays my brother and I and a few others would roam our North Downs world on our bikes. We often did wrong, scrumping apples, pears and plums, trespassing, lighting fires, but never letting them get out of control We cycled through passageways and in one particular place, in someone's drive and through their garden to another road which ran behind their plot. There is no doubt that we were every bit as naughty as children today, but we were less truculent, more aware that we were pushing our luck and, quite prepared to be hangdog if caught, promising not to do 'it' again. We would take potatoes to cook in the embers of a small fire. Beech twigs were our favourite fuel. We raised the turf, dug a small shallow pit, lit our fire let it blaze and when only the hot embers were left, put in our potatoes, put the turf over the top and returned in an hour. The potatoes would be done. We were more skilled at fire lighting than any boy scout. We also took precautions to ensure that fires never became out of control.

We had fights with other children over bird nesting. They would take eggs and blow them, a pure waste of wildlife. We also hated attacks on trees, barking and breaking off branches. My brother was a feared opponent, so we usually met little opposition. He had the thugs knack of hitting so it hurt, pulling no punches, single-mindedly going for the quick victory with knuckles to the head or fist into the abdomen. My only duty was to follow.

After a year, I left the crammer's, my education little improved. I attended a prep school, where children bound for public school were educated for their common entrance to public school at thirteen. I would be there for only one term, but it was the happiest period in my childhood. If only I could have spent all my early years there. The school was run by a Scot and it attracted as pupils, the sons of Scots living in Surrey. They were encouraged to wear the kilt, something that was quite new to me. I found it most alluring and wished that my own heritage included Scottish ancestors.

The grounds were extensive and sport was important. The school was a large gothic mansion built about the turn of the century. There were several classrooms, a music room, a library and an outside games room and hall for assemblies. Sport was as important as academia. We started each day with prayers attended by all the staff .The hymns were popular and rousing The teaching was intensive, business-like and fun. When learning is fun, it is easy and I cycled to and from school three miles each way, joyfully.

It was here that for the first time, I came into contact with sex. As a prepubescent boy, I was completely innocent. Suddenly I was exposed to nice and amusing companions whose knowledge far exceeded mine. One boy, a dark haired sallow skinned imp of a fellow, was particularly witty in a vulgar way, with a wealth of dirty jokes and innuendo. It was a great revelation. As a somewhat shy child I took little part in this but managed to keep on terms with everyone.

There was one teacher, who appeared to be a single parent, whose child was in my set. Latham was his name and he was a poor boy, unattractive and he appeared terrified of his father who seemed quite disturbed. Poor Latham had something of Smike about him. His father would quickly fly into a temper, and his poor son bore the brunt of it. One day, he picked on his son for an answer, and when there was none, flew into a rage. There were several murmurings from some of the boys, me amongst them, and calls to leave him alone. These days one would recognise child abuse more easily.

The next day it was my turn. He made me stand, then announced to the class that they should look at a cheat. I denied that I had cheated and demanded the reasons for the accusation. It was an essay I had written on the English subjugation of Wales and Scotland that had caused offence. He said that I had included facts that I had not been taught, some of it wrong. I said that I had written it from memory of reading my history book at home. It was not accepted. He sent me to the Head who questioned me closely and later spoke to my mother. The Head was a kind man and I told him my view of poor Latham and the constant bullying from his father. The next day, I stood again, this time for an apology. The teacher never seemed as terrifying again, and much of his status had gone. The next time his son offended, there was a chorus of disapproval as his father started his bullying tactics. I wonder what became of them.

Apart from that incident, I was happy at Aberdour. The one period that I disliked was the recorder. This 'instrument' may be excellent for teaching the fundamentals of music, but I thought then, and still now, that it is an apology of an instrument with its thin breathy sound. All the pupils made their own instruments from bamboo, some strategically placed holes and a piece of cork. As I had not been there long enough to make an instrument, I was given one from stock. Soon after blowing this whistle, I developed a form of diphtheria in the mouth. The cure was rubbing the inside of my mouth with some foul tasting salts. The upside was that I was excused playing the dratted recorder. This instrument appeared six years later in my education.

Sweets were almost non-existent then, so I improvised. It was a little game of mine to fill with orange juice one of the old penicillin bottles from my treatment for pneumonia. This little treat, kept in my pocket, would come out when I felt I needed it. I had developed a way of taking the rubber top off with my teeth, storing the top in my cheek and drinking the mouthful of sweet juice. While singing 'All things bright and beautiful' in prayers, I felt the need for a swig. Unfortunately, I had never practised singing and storing the top. The top shot down my throat and lodged so that I couldn't breathe. I tried to blow it out in vain, so using lateral thinking, sucked with all the power my lungs could manage. With an audible thud, the top disappeared, never to be seen again. I had given myself a good fright, and gave up the junior hip flask. Years later this too reappeared to frighten me.

I took and passed the entrance exam to Whitgift, a well known grammar school. It would have meant a half hour rail journey each way every day, but I was keen to go there. Mother had other ideas. Instead of Whitgift in Croydon, I found myself shipped off to boarding school in Cambridge.

The Perse was a good school, but right from the start, I hated it. I told my mother that I hadn't cried at all, a truth but although my companions were mostly great, I really didn't want to be there. Shyness made making friends difficult, though I was not unpopular. Even then, they recognised that I was not as other mortals. My terrible secret made me shy as if actually displaying my real self would unveil someone they would hate.

Every child is different, but there was something else about me that I failed to realise but my fellows realised subconsciously. I was a rather zany child, slightly eccentric, and they treated me with amused tolerance. Moore called me mad Nash while begging me for sex. He later became a C of E priest. I hated the regimentation and missed my family. The world was full of rushing about, a mile from school to boarding house, morning, lunch and afternoon, four miles each day. We hurried from classroom to classroom and with new subjects to learn, Latin, French, Sciences.

On the playing field, we were introduced to rugger. Being small for my age, I was useless. When I tackled, my fellows just stood still and passed the ball, sometimes dragging me along. It wasn't that I was fearful or unwilling to play, I was just puny. From that first sports experience, one is judged. Consequently, I was thought no use at any other sport. Soon one gives up and lives down to the expectations. However, I did get my all rounder's badge at athletics and later was an excellent hooker for the third fifteen.

Teachers are indeed a strange race. Why they stay in the profession when they appear to not only hate the job, but also their pupils, is beyond me. In the junior boarding house the assistant housemaster was Mr Croft, of around thirty years of age. He was tall, gaunt, ginger, with sunken cheeks and a bony face and long nose, down which he eyed most boys with cold disdain. He sang hymns in the bath, expected continued silent obedience like some damnable Abbott and we his monks. He liked to give us books to read in our spare time, I liked to choose my own. The first he gave me was Lord Peter Whimsy, even then out of date, and in my opinion stilted. I didn't like it, nor did I like my meagre free time to be organised in that way. I wrote my parents and it stopped. He was also a pervert.

Croft liked to slipper, to use his own vernacular, 'boy's bare bums' in his room just before their bedtime. This would be the punishment awarded for running in the passageways, not sweeping the common room floor well enough, or not washing behind the ears even. He was a real sadist. I was slippered twice by him, I can't even remember what for. The ceremony would go like this. Knock on his door, he would ask you in. In his bedroom, he might be in a suit or even in his dressing gown. He would harangue you on your crime, pronounce sentence in number of blows, then order your pyjama bottoms dropped. Six was the norm. The sound could be plainly heard by all those in the dormitories. Having had the blows you were then expected to shake hands. The man was a psycho; there is no doubt. I would not shake his hand. The housemaster must have heard, but he took no action.

Croft gathered around him a small group of boys whom he convinced to join the Crusaders. He took these fellows punting or for picnics. There was a protective bubble around them. They were never in trouble. I wondered then, whether he had another agenda besides religion, but one of the group of whom I was particularly fond, assured me that there was no 'funny business'.

He became progressively worse, as if getting away with it encouraged his excessive discipline. One boy, the younger of two brothers MacDonald, was always in trouble over a period of months. Mac 2 was a lovely boy, good looking, fair headed, full of life and the joy of it. He was finally slippered three times in a week, all for petty boyish high spirits, nothing malicious or deliberately disobedient, running in a corridor or not sweeping in the corner. He reported it to his parents and Mr Croft was junior housemaster no more. That meant that the eight to thirteen year olds could at last move, talk and generally behave like children.

After another term, Croft left, as did the MacDonald boys. I heard that he only survived a year at the next school too, a well known minor public school in Essex where as it happened Mr MacDonald was a farmer. I wondered if he put the boot in, or whether they found Croft out for themselves. Croft then went off up north, probably to Dotheboys Hall. I heard recently that a friend had also experienced him as a master and bore a grudge even after fifty years. If I met him today, I would still like to smack his unbearable sanctimonious bony face. Of this I am sure, he was sexually depraved. The spanking was only the tip of a sadistic sexuality, most of which he managed to control.

With puberty came certain realisations. I would have body hair. I knew enough about girls to know that they did not or were not supposed to have hair as dictated by fashion, in some of the places where it would grow on me. It was a distressing thought. Most of my peers welcomed it. I should have just accepted it as others did, or taken pride in it, counting the hairs upon the chest, as often happened in the changing rooms, not that I had any, but in my mind it illuminated the future, showed me what I would become and be for the rest of my life. It was a horrible time. Life had little meaning set in the context of a life sentence as a man. I knew that I was destined to be something I was not.

There had been a contra indication in the preceding year, when one breast had started to swell. The pain of this was of nothing to the joy I had felt and I awaited the development of the other tit. It too swelled, and I hoped that some miracle was taking place and my life as a girl was beginning. Alas it was a false dawn. The swelling of the first faltered and subsided after a couple of months, and the other too. It was a terrible disappointment! My breasts had given comfort and for a while helped me to believe that I really was female. I was even more disturbed by their disappearance.

There were boys too, some attracted to me sexually, some just wanting to be pals. I avoided the former. The latter posed a problem, for thinking of myself as a girl, it was easy to have feelings that were more than mate ship, yet I knew that to disclose these feelings would mean the end of valued friendships. It wasn't that I wanted sex with them. I just had feelings of extreme fondness. It meant that my world was full of doubts about myself and how others saw me. My place in the world was uncertain. I was over sensitive, feeling what was not there, hiding what could not be seen. If insulted I merely ignored the insult. I tended to over compensate, camouflaging my female nature by becoming more daring, more fool hardy, better at bike mechanics than my friends, prepared to collapse on a loose rugby ball under the feet of giant forwards from the opposition. It was all extremely frustrating and confusing.

One of the Crusaders, a boy I absolutely doted on. grabbed me and put his tongue in my ear. I was very fond of him so just asked what he thought he was doing. It was so confusing. If I responded positively, then it would be construed as homosexual. Yet as I believed myself to be female, I should have felt able to accept such affection. I was however, just on the side of reality enough to know that this should not happen, especially with this boy who was otherwise pure as the whitest angels wings, clever and an excellent sportsman.

Another boy, Stuart, tried to hypnotise me. Stuart was a country boy from Lincolnshire, and compared to my family, well off. I stayed with him one half term. His father picked us up from Sleaford railway station and somehow seemed to think I was a girl, saying, 'You sit in the front darling'. How I loved that. Well it was half light. He of course realised his error, especially as Stuart said 'Eh? It's not Claire dad,' referring to his younger sister. It was difficult to decide whether he was more confused than I. My hair was conventional, with a Tommy Steele quiff and yet there must have been an aura that misled him. We flew across the dark fens at high speed, laughing and giggling, as the car leaped across the raised camber where minor roads joined ours running along the dyke.

The house was an old farmhouse, red brick and ivy clad. The kitchen was large and warm. Stuart's mother was very good looking and had been a model. She had exquisite clothes, many of which resided in my bedroom. I tried on a ball gown and liked what I saw. This second, serious cross-dressing experience confirmed what I already knew about myself. I hated my male persona, my male body and genitalia. I undressed and went to bed. I cried into my pillow until I slept.

Stuart had a number of old Austin Seven cars, and I was soon driving them around the yard. Then unaccountably Stuart deserted me to see a friend also home from boarding school. I was left to my own devises.

It was suggested that I should ride his sister's pony. She was away at school and had not ridden the animal for sometime due to a strained groin. Saddled up, I was encouraged to ride the pony through the village, Stuart's father following in the car. Outside the village at a cross road, I was told to turn back. As we turned, the pony shied at the road sign, then reared twice, the second time throwing me out of the back end, one foot in and one foot out of the stirrup. It then started to drag me by one leg before anyone could come to the rescue. Luckily it trod on my thigh and pulling at the same time, something had to give. It was the stirrup that snapped leaving me on the ground, my leg numb from being stamped on.

With difficulty, I clambered into the car and was carried home for attention. I made for the bathroom to examine the damage, then had to show the family the large bruise. I had been extremely lucky, but it might have been better had the crown jewels been crushed. The pony was caught two miles away. The accident did not stop me from enjoying the treasures in the wardrobe over the next three days.

Back at school, Ranjit attached himself to me. He liked to sing romantic ballads from current shows. 'Take my hand I'm a Stranger in Paradise' was one and he would reach for my hand which I soon retracted. Being wealthy, he would take me to tea. He was a Malaysian of Indian descent. In holiday time he lived with his elder brother in London. Ranjit never tried anything other than hand-holding. He was very sweet. His favourite songs were 'No other love' and 'Love is a many splendoured thing' from Kismet.

In spite of all these crushes on me, nothing really happened. I did not want sex but love. I don't believe I was considered homosexual, or even, effeminate at that time.

Earlier, I had two bad experiences of molestation. The first was down at the railway sidings adjacent to Cambridge Station where our little gang had said they were going to collect numbers. When I arrived there was no one there. An engine cleaner invited me into the cab of a Sandringham class loco, a real treat for those who had caught the engine spotting craze. I was not that interested, but was tempted by the thought that I could later boast of it. Once hauled up into the cab, the cleaner tried to take down my trousers. When I resisted he made me watch as he masturbated. I told the others about it, and they all went down and gave him some verbal harassment. I was too shy to take the matter further.

The other occasion was summer half term. I had been to the cinema in Epsom by myself and waited at the bus stop to go home. A smart looking man in a new Morris Oxford pulled to a stop asking the way to the Downs Hotel. He was Australian by his accent. He suggested he could take me home if I showed him the way to the hotel. I agreed. There was little spoken then of the dangers of getting into a strange car. When we reached the downs, he suggested a drink at the pub, parking away from the hotel. I said I didn't want one but he insisted, as a thank you. I was starting to feel suspicious and said that I would rather get home. He said it would only take a few minutes. While he was in the pub, I tried the door, making sure I could escape. He returned with a beer and a ginger ale. As I sipped the drink he slid his hand onto my thigh. I threw the drink at him, opening the door with my left hand at the same time, and I was away, under the racecourse fence, across the darkening course and round the other side of the large empty grandstand. I watched for car lights. Some were coming up the road, so I hid behind a heap of road gravel. I peeped out, making sure that it was the enemy. As he came level, I showered the car with a handful of gravel. He didn't slow. I had scared him off. I waited for the bus and reached home safely. Over the next few days I debated whether to report it to the police, but fearful of finding myself in trouble, remained silent, just as many other children do.

Before we took our 'O' levels, Peter Reid and I decided to have a cycling holiday in France. We convinced our parents and the headmaster that it would improve our French, which it did, but neither of us was to know quite how.

The plan was to train to Dover, ferry to Calais, then ride to some friends of Tom's in central France. Our route, would have been Calais, Montrueil-sur-Mer, Abbeville, Beauvais, Paris, Orleans, Bourge, but our adviser, the headmasters wife, said that we must see Chartres, or not see France at all, and especially the cathedral and the statue to the resistance. I did protest that of course we were on cycles, so extra miles could mean a lot of extra time.

'Oh, Northern France is flat. Have you not been?'

We confessed that neither of us had.

'You'll find it very easy going I'm sure and the roads are shaded, because Napolean had poplar trees line the roads to shield his marching soldiers from the sun.'

I fantasised about wearing a kilt for this trip, but with knickers and a slip. Of course I knew that was out of the question, but it was in my mind.

On good advice, we added an extra hundred miles to the route. It would be spring, not too hot, the traffic was sparse, the roads straight and flat, lined with poplars to shield from the wind and give shade just as Napoleon had devised. Poppies would glint and flutter. I imagined a never ending Impressionist landscape. All would be well.

You will of course have guessed that the actualité was different. Leaving Calais at about two thirty, we had forty miles to do on heavy touring bikes with a considerable amount of luggage weighing them down, before we would reach our first nights halt. The roads were open and the cars few. Some roads were straight. The poplars featured prominently. Our first stop was to be at the French youth hostel in the castle of Montreuil-sur-Mer. By the time we had reached Boulogne, having rid ourselves, of eighteen of those miles, we had already learned that from the mouths of the learned often fall crumbs of absolute crap. What might seem flat in a car, is certainly a mountain when peddling up it. Forty-three years later, I drove the same road with friends. Most of it was still recognisable. I even remembered the spot of Tom's accident. But even in the car, it did not seem easy cycling for a novice.

Before Boulogne, there was a little hut by the roadside, presided over by an old peasant woman, black garbed, selling among other things, crusty rolls and bottles of wine. The old lady who presided over this forerunner of today's massive cross Channel trade, was pleased to sell anything to anybody. We purchased a bottle of Burgundy with a nice label and a roll each. We took a short breather to take on the refreshment. Having already had lunch with wine on the boat, what we didn't need was more wine, especially in a state of semi-exhaustion. People drank less of anything in those days and wandering around, can of coke or plastic bottle of spa water in hand was unknown. What we really needed was, spa water. As a result of our snack, almost incapable, we pushed our loaded bikes through Boulogne, reading the next road sign with difficulty.

By the time dusk was approaching, we still had some ten miles to do. We had no lights, had not contemplated cycling in the dark, though my father, always a cautious soul, had mentioned 'you never know'. Just then a friendly and very smelly fish lorry roared down the hill passing us and absolutely crawled up the next incline. By superhuman effort, assisted by alcoholic fumes, we whizzed down the hill, peddled hard and caught it up, both catching hold of the tailgate for a free ride to the top of the hill. We ignored the icy fishy water, which sloshed back at us, letting go at the top. We raced down hill after it, catching it as it slogged up the next rise. Weren't we clever? The miles were simply whizzing away. It was worth putting up with the smell of fish.

So obsessed had we become with the lorry, that safety was forgotten. As we pounded down the next hill in pursuit of the fresh fish, we zoomed round a bend to find a level crossing. Tom, panicking somewhat, put the breaks on hard, and came off on his rump, removing valuable skin. Our semi-captive lorry escaped as we checked the damage. Bravely, Tom continued, well what else was there to do? We finally arrived at Montreuil-sur-Mer, in the semi-dark.

The old town is situated on the side of a steep hill. By the time we had pushed our bikes to the top of the town, the darkness was pitch. We asked our way and were pointed into further darkness, of a quality often sought by undertaker's outfitters, but seldom found. Eventually we made out the castle gates, twin towers guarding them. They were in the usual form of such gates, enormous, but with a smaller one set within. To the side, was a bell pull of the old sort, a rope on a pulley and high up in the tower, one solitary light shone yellowly. We pulled the rope and a bell, as if in heaven, gave resonance somewhat below a tinkle and above a chime. Eventually the gate opened to reveal an old lady, clothed in black, bent of back and crooked of claw. Yes, we had arrived.

She led us to our quarters. We were, apart from her and her invisible son, the only inmates. Having shown us blankets and beds she was off, we thought to stir a large black pot somewhere, while we washed and decided what to do about poor Tom's flank. We were the only inhabitants of that old castle which had seen service as barracks and headquarters in wars from medieval times. Looking in the medicine cabinet, there was nothing that looked really promising, but what had the most antiseptic smell was undoubtedly some cream. I coated it on liberally, with tenderness. It was embrocation. Tom gave a yelp and said, 'That's enough.' We slept, warm, Tom warmer almost certainly than I, locked in, we made sure of that. We awakened still fatigued to a dawn of rural French charm, fallow fields and woods stretching away below the ancient battlements, mist laying ten feet from the ground, and the sun rising over the heights of the town to the east. All the fear and apprehension of the previous evening was gone. Cocks crowed, birds chirruped. It was difficult to even imagine how we had felt the previous evening as we savoured the morning in this tranquil rural French setting. Revisiting it with my friends, I was disappointed to find a tourist attraction, the old gateway drastically amputated because it had been unsafe, the gatehouse room now a tourist shop, the whole place sanitised and deprived of its character. The moat had become a tennis court, a lovely asset for this picturesque French town, but the final destruction of an image I had carried for years.

The drastic and unskilled treatment of Tom's wound proved beneficial. Much of the soreness had disappeared and it had begun to heal. He refused further treatment although I offered my services. We were still fatigued but on course for another hard day.

In two days, long gradients to the top of an escarpment, followed by a welcome but all too short steep descent, with night stops at Abbeville and Beauvais, we cycled uneventfully into Paris. The last few kilometres through St. Denis were so flat and uninteresting that it was rather an anticlimax. Suddenly we had arrived. We wondered how the Germans had felt as they entered the city fifteen years before. It had been a hot two days ride from Montreuil.

So much for the Flat France theory of the dear headmaster's wife. There is a song about 'behind every good man is a good woman'. I have often found that behind every man of import is an extremely silly woman with ideas far beyond her own intelligence. Marriage and childbearing, seem to sound the death knell for intellectual development in some women, particularly in the past, when fewer women returned to work and the stimulation of colleagues.

So at least we had reached Paris. There we stayed at a youth hostel, which appeared to be a large disused public loo, converted to having bunk beds. There was certainly not much room. It was situated on a wide pavement at the city end of the Avenue de la Porte de la Chapelle. During our first night I awoke to the sound of a lorry pulling to a stop outside, then the noise of a chain being pulled through spokes. Our bikes chained together outside, there being no other place to leave them, were gone. By my watch I saw that it was three am. Waking Tom, we ran to the door to find it locked; we could not get out to apprehend the thieves. It was probably lucky for us. Because we had taken all our belongings inside, only our bikes were taken, so although a great blow, we could still be in business if we hitched. A very short discussion arrived at that decision.

Next day, we found our way to the Préfecture and fairly quickly into the office of an Inspecteur, a nice fatherly man, whose English was perhaps a little worse than our French. Although kind and concerned, he told us that we would never see the bikes again, a conclusion which we had already assumed. Les mécs, les voleurs, he said, were very many, and his men, very few. It was he said the very worst district in all Paris, full of, well he didn't like to say, we were too young, but there were les Algeriens. He did take a full description, gave us a note for our insurances and wished us bon chance.

Merde! Shit. We used the word a lot. We saw Paris. Now we had no bikes to slave away on in the heat of good spring weather, it turned cold. The song 'April in Paris', had recently been a hit, but the Paris we saw was a disappointment, not that spectacular, and cold and grey, though we agreed they had made much better use of the river than has London even now. We were too poor and cold to enjoy it. Tom had a thing about Eartha Kitt and kept singing a bit of 'Under the Bridges of Paris'; her recent hit, which could get on one's nerves if one let it. We went into a bar on the Champs Elysée to escape the cold, and ordered a Byrrh. We had seen it advertised everywhere, in every village, and on nearly every wall of those villages. It appeared almost as often as the mystic words, 'défense de pissoir', but when we asked for it, the barkeeper, either couldn't understand us or had never heard of it. In the end he twigged. It was he said, très fort apéritif, pas bon pour les jeunes. He gave it to us anyway.

On a budget of about three pounds, and that over three days, there was not a lot one could do, even thirty years ago. We did the Arc de Triomphe, Notre Dame, not the Sacre Coeur, because Tom said, we've had enough bloody churches, and why slog our guts over there? I should explain that he was bent on farming, and had a farmer's vocabulary. We climbed part of the Tour Eiffel, what a lot of rivets said Tom, more impressed than usual, and we walked along the markets of the Seine bank. That was enough. Paris had had us and we were pleased to look at the calendar and see that according to the grand plan, tomorrow we should be in Chartres.

After taking the Metro to Versailles on the last ticket of our book, we soon picked up the main road. In no time we secured a lift in a new car with a very chatty handsome Frenchman and his elegant and beautiful female companion, who we believed to be his wife. They were as charming as they were an attractive couple, as only the French can be. They were also very concerned, that we had been so badly treated in Paris. They seemed to take it as a personal insult, that two young Englishmen had been so badly used by their compatriots, suggesting that we go on the radio to appeal for the return of our bicycles. He drove like the wind for those times, at a steady eighty miles an hour, which I liked, though Tom seemed to sit rather low in his seat. They advised us to go straight on with them to Orleans, for they said, there was little traffic on the Chartres to Orleans road, and we would have trouble getting a lift. A quick consultation in the back and we decided to stick to the plan. How could we return to school to face the headmaster's wife without seeing Chartres? They therefore deposited us on the outskirts of this gem of Northern France. We said au revoir to a very nice couple. Nowadays, they would not look so benignly on young Englishmen.

In Chartres we found the youth hostel, eventually, having learned a little more French, for the house number was 3 bis 4, which we found meant between 3 and 4. We explored the Cathedral. Yes it was large, imposing too, as I now know, an absolute jewel of ecclesiastical architecture, but to us then, neither students of architecture nor religious, it was another pile of stone blocks with stained glass. The city had possibilities. It was old and compact. The statue to the Resistance was dutifully seen too, but Tom was unmoved also, and next day we were on to Orleans, probably the best Youth Hostel of the lot. It was like an ordinary house, each room having two single beds, and the cleanest crispest sheets. We were the only occupants. It's funny, but I can hardly remember eating in that entire journey, so food must have been a low priority. It was before the onset of convenience foods, there were no hot-dogs, fried chicken, pizzas or jacket potatoes. Two meals only are in my mind now; ravioli somewhere around Abbeville in a roadside cafe, and some chicken with sauté potatoes in Chartres. How I regret the onset of the universal convenience food, America's gift to the world and their contribution to civilization.

We picked up the road to Bourge on a scorching morning. We were carrying our entire luggage in very inconvenient containers made for bikes not humans. Before we had gone a mile, we were sweating. After two, we were ready to quit, but decided to split, giving us twice the chance of picking up a lift we thought. I went on ahead as I walked more quickly. In theory this gave Tom the best chance, for any car would reach him first. He then might or might not persuade them to pick me up too. I of course would try to get them to wait for him, should they pass him by, but stop for me. I soon put a half-mile between us, walking briskly, while Tom adopted his farmer's gait, the heavy-footed scuffing walk one seems to use in wellingtons. A new car with two men in the front seats stopped for me, but they refused to wait for him, and off we went, me in the back of the Panhard, a car no longer made. I turned to watch as Tom ran desperately to catch us up. It was cruel to see and I felt guilty and apprehensive..

By the time we had gone three miles, the cross draught from the opened windows had reduced me from a state of extreme body heat when they had picked me up, to feeling distinctly chilly. I asked if they could close the windows a little, which they did, partially and reluctantly. On reaching Bourge, the town incidentally where the 'Tale of Two Cities' film with Dirk Bogarde was made, I had developed a full-blown sore throat. I downed a bottle of milk to quench it. Tom turned up about half an hour later and we met on the steps of the Cathedral as arranged.

We stayed with his friends, good solid middle class, a wine merchant. After two days I had developed a fever. They called a doctor. Bronchitis was diagnosed. The diagnosis involved taking my temperature, which in France means anally. I would not allow any such assault on a British bottom, nor accept a thermometer into my mouth that had been used in other areas. They had to go out and purchase another one. However, they had their revenge for refusing the anal thermometer. In true Napoleonic fashion, they continued to press their attack in the same area but with more strength, and ordered me to use garlic flavoured suppositories. My whole body reeked. I was as Gallic by odour, as a Parisian taxi drivers breath, but the treatment certainly seemed to do good.

In three days I was well enough to travel. We took the train home, over-nighting in a comfortable hotel in Paris, where we had to share a very large double bed. We slept apart and I slept very well. I could have done with a hug.

So much for La France. I have since learned to love France and the French and have longed to live there.

I wanted to leave school at sixteen, after my 'O' Levels. I hated my life there. The thought of another two years in the oppressive, restrictive prison of that school, was not an enviable thought to me. However my exam results were bad enough that I would have to resit one or two subjects, so without making my feelings known, I dutifully returned to the place I hated, to retake two 'O' levels and study for 'A's. The inner turmoil of sexuality remained my biggest problem. As far as I knew, I was the only person with these feelings. I felt totally isolated. I lived a lie so that I could coexist with my fellows. These factors made work, the assimilation of facts and the use of one's intelligence, doubly difficult. Depression made the assimilation and retention of knowledge an almost impossible chore. I would read a page and drift off into yearning to be female. Not only was I imprisoned in a boarding school, I felt my real self, was imprisoned in a body I hated.

As sixth formers, we did have slightly more freedom, but not enough. We went to bed at ten. We had free periods, not many, but time in the day when we could study as we liked. We also had a great deal of work, and most of it, for one reason or another, I hated. I took English, History and Geography. Our English teacher was a Jew. I am not an anti-Semite, indeed I have a great regard for the race. I only mention his religion or race, I'm never quite sure which Judaism is, because I sought a reason for his treatment of me.

Wally looked like a Jew facially, but in every other way he was an ordinary Englishman. I was a fair-haired, sixteen-year-old. The year was 1957. Was it some subconscious connection of my physical attributes that made him bear down on me so hardly, memories of Hitler's master race perhaps? I had done German and my notebook had my German name upon it. He mentioned this name with a hiss, as though I had placed it there to affront him. Certainly I had never given him cause to hate me, which he appeared to do. Nor was I any admirer of Germany and certainly not one of Hitler. The bullying seemed to increase after a faux pas when pounced upon to read, and having not followed the preceding minutes of the lesson closely, I referred to Samuel Pepys as 'Pepis'. Who knows, in the tongue of the time, I may have been right. Anyway, thereafter I was always greeted by Wally with a sneer. With a mind as troubled as mine, it was a situation that became unbearable. My low personal esteem could not withstand the public denigration he subjected me to. At half term, I lay in the bath at home and would not come out. My distress and lonely tears at the thought of returning to more of the same treatment was a private hell. In the end, it had to be divulged to my worried parents.

When I returned to school, I had no means of knowing what lay in store for me. I was surprised when in Wally's first class, he asked me to stand. What now I thought? Had my confidence in my parents all back fired on me?

'I have to make an apology to,' and said my name, 'why, I am not sure, but everyone must expect criticism at sometime. However, if I have offended, then I do apologise. Now open your books....'

There were some grunts of support for me from around the class too, that was good to hear, and I believe he had a record of this bullying, otherwise my word, uncorroborated, would not have been accepted. It must have hurt him to make even that weak apology. He died a few years later, in his early sixties. In truth he was the pinnacle of my distress, the final body blow to my already frail ego. I did not respect myself and it felt as though no one else respected me either.

I was of slight build, five feet and five and a bit inches, eight and a half stone. The only game that I liked was, oddly enough, rugby. On the rugby field, one could display bravery and dissipate aggression. I ended up as hooker in the third fifteen. In the heart of the pack, foul schoolboys pressed about me, I was almost invincible. We had three excellent hookers in the school, the other two being friends also, Tom of our French trip and Richard who became a C of E priest. We swopped notes and learned from each other the secrets of successful hooking. I was the most weedy. Nevertheless, in the scrum I was a ruthless, but skilful cheat. We hardly lost a scrum, even against the head. Consequently, that year we won our league in all teams, first second and third fifteens. Never before had the third fifteen had such success winning all 12 matches.

On another occasion, I was asked to fill in for the Old Boys first team. I was picked up by car, sandwiched between two of them in the back and whisked away to cloudy Wisbech. It was an uncomfortable journey, squeezed between these hairy old boys who seemed very manly to me. There were mumbles about me as we changed, my size was mentioned adversely. We ran out onto a pitch full of cow pats. Nice, I thought, how did I get into this? The first scrum we won against the head. We only lost one in the first half. Swinging between the giants in the front rows I could reach through and drag almost any ball back. By half time, I was almost a hero. At the end, they bought me a pint and said any time they were short, they would ask for me! No thanks I thought, playing amongst cow pats with hairy great men was not for me. I had proved myself, and that meant everything.

I left school at eighteen, thankfully, and fearfully. With no idea what to do, six 'O' levels and an 'A', not at all outstanding, I felt hopeless. I feel I would have done far better at the day school I had liked in Croydon. But at this distance I have a high regard for the school and for most of my fellows.

CHAPTER 4.

I now had to find work. Summer was drawing to a close before pressure from my parents made me think about finding work. I was aimless. The trauma of school and exams and my madness as I thought of my problem, all conspired to deny any real focus on where I wanted to go or what I wanted to be, other than female. I was living in a never never-land, a sort of prolonged catatonia, outwardly functioning but inwardly bereft of any significant thought.

My mother, clearly worried by my lack of enthusiasm for a future, tried to fathom my wishes and then scanned the employment section of the Daily telegraph. I had expressed interest in going abroad; we still had an Empire in 1958. It was three years before Macmillan's wind of change speech. I had thought to see wildlife in Africa. One means of doing this was to become a colonial police officer, but height and a lack of experience made that goal unattainable. My mother spotted an advert for the Bank of West Africa. Without any research into the organisation, I applied and to my surprise and horror was given an interview

The position was as a trainee for overseas service. I would be eligible for West Africa, when I reached twenty-one. The interview was most friendly, the Secretary who doubled as personnel manager, was a beautiful gentle man, full of the value of the better things in life, like sport, reading, the arts, and emphasised how marvellous it was to work in London, the centre of such things. The way he spoke to me, I envisaged nights at the theatre, dining in Soho and the odd party at the Savoy. He obviously saw something in me which made him offer me a post there and then. What a difference to today's interviews. I felt as if I was meeting a benevolent uncle.

I started the third week in September, five pounds a week paid monthly. I paid something like six pounds a quarter for my season ticket. Firms now pay that for you. After paying my keep, there wasn't much left.

However, even on that meagre sum, young people then could have a life and if we wanted, we could attend practically anything, but it meant watching the pennies. We drew our cash in ten-shilling notes, because they always seemed to be new, you got more of them and they filled your wallet. We did not have money for endless pints of beer, not that that appealed to me and lager was almost unknown. That was not a bad thing. Drink seems to be a god, a prop, an escape or a pastime these days. Drunkenness is accepted as funny in men and latterly in women, when I believe it should be seen as demeaning to the human spirit. The latest rating on drugs puts it as the fifth most dangerous, while cannabis comes a lowly eleventh. I drank then and I drink now, but not to excess and it means nothing to me. If all the pubs closed tomorrow and all the supermarkets stopped selling liquor, I would not mind in the least. We could always open up coffee bars as were popular in the fifties as social meeting places.

The work was varied. As a trainee for overseas service, you moved around from department to department, learning bookkeeping, foreign exchange, debt control. I was not very good at it. It was all extremely boring; the departmental managers were mostly boring little men with no ambition and little vision, I thought then as a callow youth, probably misjudging them. But it was a meal ticket and there was the incentive of foreign service to help one's application.

There was a girl there I was fond of, though we shall never know how much I liked her. Her name was Patricia, and she came from the East End, Dalston, hardly a good area then. Her father was an invalid, I think poisoned by some work prpcess. We never had a date, partly because it took me so long to pluck up the courage to ask her out, she found someone else. We teased each other as we worked. One day, when she had been ribbing me about my 'posh' accent, all day long, I filled her umbrella with the contents of the four-hole punch. I carefully refurled and secured it. When she was waiting for her bus in Gracechurch Street, it began to rain. In times of beehive hairstyles, you didn't let rain spoil the back-combing. She raised her umbrella, pushed it open and was showered with pink and white confetti. She thought it a good joke as did the other bus passengers. She was a sweet petite and clever girl, very family oriented and proud of her East End. Patricia was my first real contact with a girl and made a great impression on me. I watched what she wore and how she wore it. She wanted a gondola basket, the fashion object for a young woman then, and found one and gave it to her, to make up for the umbrella stunt. I bought her a set of Coty perfumes for Christmas. I moved to the next department.

There was a girl there, Kathy, who had a steady boy friend. He was a hard looking Italian type, not a coast trainee, and stopped me on the stairs one day.

'We don't like the way you smile at the girls,' he said.

'Just being friendly. That's the way I am.' I replied. Well, I was a sort of girl and girls smile a lot.

'We're watching you.' He looked at me from under his black eyebrows.

'Keep watching,' I said, 'are you engaged or something.'

'Be careful.'

I walked away, somewhat surprised. I didn't think I had done anything to offend, and didn't take the threat seriously.

Two weeks later they became engaged, but she fancied me and asked me out. Determined to see what would happen, and not wanting to hurt her, I agreed to go. We went to the West End. I had no more idea of how to entertain and amuse her, than I could charm snakes. We started off with a meal at a place on the edge of Soho, followed by a beer in a pub. Then we walked down to the river. It was a beautiful, still and sunny evening. She declared her love for me, poor darling, but by the end of the date she knew and told me that it was not going to work. She could tell that sexually, I was just not interested. I told her honestly, that I liked her a lot, but that would not be enough for her. I said that her boy friend, seemed very keen. He was, she agreed, but she was not sure she loved him. We kissed on the Charing Cross footbridge, she with a mouth wet with desire, and my lips dry with the shock of it. She went back to the boy friend and they were married within a year. It was my first experience of love and how difficult and painful it could be. I hope she has had a happy life.

There was one sport in which we joined. From our office in Fish Hill Street, an annexe to the main building, we could see the top of the Monument erected to commemorate the great fire of London. At teatime in the afternoon, we would have time trials up the two hundred or so steps and down again. It was amazing how quickly we could do it. I went up again a few months ago and suffered vertigo, which I controlled with difficulty. My companion had no idea until I told him later that I had been suffering.

The 'in things', the fashion statement of the time were Italian suits and winkle picker shoes. The latter became ever more exaggerated in form. The toe came to a point, and all the chain shoe shops sold them. As time went on, young things about the city had them made. A place in Battersea would knock out a pair for a fiver, to your own design. That was a considerable amount, twice what one would pay for good shoes off the shelf. I remember Patricia had some really long ones and some of the boys, even longer. It was a tricky business walking in them, for every step meant a lot of toe being left on the ground as the heel rose. The result was that after a time, toes would just crack off. I never indulged in these far out models. I did sport an Italian style suit, single breasted, short collar, years before the Beatles wore the same garb. It was made for me in Cheapside, the shop smelled of crushed spices, sandalwood and cinnamon. We all wore shirts with detachable starched collars, white only. A badly starched and pressed collar would saw into your neck and was extremely painful. Softer shirts, drip dry, and in colours were just gaining popularity. The girls wore, stiletto heals with sharp toes, usually in a colour to match their outfit. Trousers for women were hardly seen, and never at work. The hair was done in a beehive, lots of hairspray and backcombing. Then we thought it was great, now it seems just naff. It could come back in this crazy world. Men had short hair mostly, but there were still Teds about with DA's. Greased down hair was common.

I saw my family GP and told him of my sexual difficulties. He referred me to St. Bartholomew's, where they offered me group therapy. It appeared to me to be a very inappropriate treatment for a very personal problem and having made an initial contact with the psychiatrist running the sessions, my opinion was confirmed. He outlined the treatment as patients sitting round discussing their different problems and inviting comment from each other. Into the bargain, there would be students sitting in. I asked if it worked and he said it was very beneficial, a cop out reply if I ever heard one. It was my view that the case histories disclosed would have a considerable value to a school of psychiatry, but that the treatment would be of no value at all to the patients. I was not ready either, to confess my shame to all and sundry, it had taken all my courage to even raise it with the GP. I did not go back.

There was a fledgling rugby team in the bank and I had made the mistake of saying that I had played for the school and was a hooker. I was pressed to play, and did so. There was a training evening in the banks rest room, using weights. There were no gyms then. We had several matches against other banks mostly and usually got a good beating. We were a weak side, some of the players having next to no skill and compared to our school teams, they were very poor indeed. The skill and aptitude levels of some of them were so low, that I wondered they played at all. My success as hooker was therefore a surprise and a delight to the rest. I remember particularly a match played in that same park where thirty-four years later I would sit with a thirty year old woman and feel love for her, a woman who considered me very feminine, in need of protection and, desirable. I would never have imagined that could happen back then, as we made our way there on the bus, changing into our kit.

The team we played was the École Francais de Londres, a tough outfit, and very quick. I had looked up Lim Meng Lai, my old school friend, for whom I had held a secret passion, and prevailed upon him to play as scrum half, the position he had played at school for the first fifteen. It seemed as if it were just the two of us versus those hard Frenchmen. Both of us succeeded, to be let down by the rest. We had some six footers but with the guts of chickens. I won nearly every ball in the scrum, using all the dubious tactics learned in public school rugby, grinding forty-eight hours growth of stubble into the opponents face, screwing my chin into him and treading on his hooking boot. The idea was to make being in the scrum so uncomfortable that your opponent gave up. I angled my foot so that the ball shot to the rear on entry. All good stuff and enjoyable, effort and pain, bravery in the face of charging Frenchmen, going to ground with the ball and flying into a tackle, trying to keep studded boots out of one's face. The ball went to Meng Lai and was then lost by our so called centres. At the inquest afterwards I called them chocolates soft centres.

Meng Lai said he would never play for us again, the team being so frail, and I quit soon after. I had proved myself braver than any of them and as hard as most.

We saw little of London entertainment because money was so short. In the lunch hour we would go to the West End and back, running all the way to Bank Station, down and up the escalators. Occasionally we went to a show.

There was also study for the Institute of Bankers exams, which meant going to the City College up by the Barbican, where preliminary work was just beginning on the present development. Most of these lectures were very boring and I retired to the library to read American Classics, William Faulkner, Scott Fitzgerald, Hemingway, Bellow, Salinger and Steinbeck. Even so, I managed to pass some of my exams, but failed that which would prove most important, bookkeeping. Debits and credits, profit and loss. were all so boring.

There were still considerable tracts of bomb damage, 15 years after peace had been declared. Most of these had not even been touched, unless to turn them into rough car parks. Some have only been developed in the 1990s. It was yet another sign of our slow recovery from the war. It had sucked us dry of money and of inspiration.

Another lunchtime occupation was going up to Tower Hill. There was always entertainment to be had, the Red Dean giving forth and being heckled, escapologists, getting out of bonds with extremely shaky knots, fire eaters, and religious cranks venting fire and brimstone and dire warnings of the end of the world.

The Thames, over which I walked morning and night across London Bridge, was still a busy place. The Pool of London, that section of the river between London and Tower Bridges, was still a port. The icebreakers from the South Atlantic tied up there. Fyffes banana boats came in from the West Indies. Tugs pulled barges up and down the river and coal lighters came into the Bankside Power Station, now Tate Modern. Billingsgate fish was landed straight off ships and into the market.

Billingsgate fish market was still going strong. You could walk in and buy your fish direct from the wholesaler. The porters amazed by their skill in carrying enormous loads on their specially made leather hats which had a flat top. They also had cafes where you could get fresh crab sandwiches, absolutely delicious, and a glass of sweet tasting milk or a cup of tea. All the character of lower Thames Street has now gone. It has become one of the busiest highways in London, choked all day long with nose to tail traffic. Thirty years later, I would be using it regularly, driving into Westminster from Norfolk or from the Isle of Dogs.

I would soon be off to Africa, and earlier than expected.

CHAPTER 5.

I was in the last birth month for National Service, September 1939. Towards the end of National Service, intakes had been more and more delayed. Whereas my brother went in shortly after his eighteenth birthday, I was six months off my twenty-first before the fateful brown envelope hit the doormat. By this time the Government and Parliament had recognised that taking two years of a young man's life was not only unpopular but unnecessary. The feeling in the military was that these conscripts were now a damned nuisance. No sooner were they trained, they were getting ready to go back to Civvy Street. The services were over manned and there was little for these short-term soldiers to do. The delay on entry meant that I would be twenty-three by the time I had done my two year stint, not what one needs when one wants to get on with life and my bank training would have to start again from scratch..

I had been in the cadet corps at school, so I had some knowledge of the services. There had been drills every week, with parades, punishments, camps and exercises. I knew what a waste of time it all was therefore and my brother's experience as a National Serviceman had done nothing to change that opinion. He had been a driver and spent his time waiting in a cold Humber staff car outside various officers' homes while they fed and roistered. One incident at school that brought home to me the utter stupidity of playing soldiers occurred when I was fifteen. We were on 'exercises', playing battles. The pupil NCO, a fellow called Stone, directed me to crawl through a bramble thicket. I believe he knew I would disobey before he ever gave the order and of course, I did not disappoint him. It was a case of petty and malicious bullying.

I knew Stone well; he liked to inflict pain, liked to bully. He had given me two or three dead legs for no reason other than I was in his presence. As a result of my 'mutiny', I was put on a charge and he was the judge and jury. I would therefore have to run round the school with full packs carrying a .303 rifle, 1914 vintage. Had I the bullets for it, they might all have mended their ways. I refused this punishment too after the first circuit. I was told that I would be reported to the 'Head', to which I replied, 'Go ahead and I will leave the force!'

That's where it ended, his bluff called, he backed down. If he ever reported me, no action was taken. This was I knew, the same sort of treatment which the bullyboy NCOs meted out in the real forces and I wanted none of it. Stone later entered the RAF and became a jet fighter pilot. I believe he was later put on a charge for dangerous flying, 'buzzing' his home, and was dismissed the service.

There were of course more fundamental reasons why I did not want to spend two years in the highly artificial and restrictive confines of the military. Number one was that shortly I would be off to Africa, if allowed to complete my training. Number two was that my mental state would not make me a very good service man. Had there been a war, a matter of threat to the existence of the country and the British way of life, then I would have been in the vanguard I hope. I would have struggled to do my bit, just as faced with a real enemy and machine gun fire, I might crawl through a thicket. I was and am in spite of all sorts of reservations and criticisms of my country, very patriotic. National Service I considered to be a waste of time. The government had obviously come to the same point of view, otherwise why were they ending it? It did not seem reasonable that I should have to suffer a two-year sentence, when others born three weeks later would get away with it. In any case, my inner self reasoned, women are not called up.

Consequently, I ignored the first call egged on by my brother, who had nothing but loathing for the army, non-coms and particularly the officer corps. The second invitation came soon after and fearing the military police turning up on the doorstep, I went. The result was that they found me fit. On a technicality, their failure to do a blood pressure test, I had a re-examination. This time I had a letter from my doctor, reference my sexuality. For good luck, I suddenly had great difficulty seeing with my left eye.

I had an interview with a doctor, who I presume was the chief medical examiner for the Air Force, somewhere in High Holborn. Having asked me to strip and cough so that he could observe and feel that the genitalia were all in working order, he asked a few questions.

'This letter from your doctor, regarding these .... feelings you have, are you just swinging the lead?'

'No. I'm afraid it's true.'

'So what do you feel?'

'I feel that I want to be a woman, that I should have been female, I always have and I am not always able to control that. I believe that I would be subject to considerable bullying, should it become known to my fellows.'

'Your doctor says he considers you might have a breakdown. Do you consider that a possibility?'

That was news to me. He had imparted something that I should have thought was a confidential opinion of my doctor. I was surprised.

'How can I say?'

'Lots of people have these feelings you know. Can't you just put it behind you?' I wondered whether he sat there in lacy underwear beneath his white coat longing for womanhood. Who were all these people who had the same feelings as me?

'Easily said.' I replied, too shy and embarrassed to do myself justice.

He dismissed me. I was free to go, but I would have to await his decision. The illogicality is that homosexual men and women have been fighting to get into the services, while I fought to stay out. What's more, had I just rolled up, affected a camp manner and declared myself to be homosexual, they would have turned me down. Of course, latterly, and years after other more enlightened societies, we have at last allowed gays of both sexes into the forces where they have always existed, serving as honourably as heterosexuals but living in fear of discovery.

I arranged an appointment with Mr Kewley, the avuncular Bank Secretary. I told him that I was being called up. He thought the same as I, that it was all a waste of time, especially as I was in the last intake. He set about arranging my future immediately. Within a week, I received notice of a posting to Sierra Leone, where I would be an accounting assistant in Freetown, the capital. I received an allowance for clothing and equipment, sixty pounds sterling, the equivalent of six weeks money. I went off to Simpsons and had a tropical suit made, one jacket two trousers, (how I longed for a little skirted number), in a subtle shade of moss green. The list of tropical equipment the bank gave me included all sorts of strange paraphernalia, kidney pads and mosquito boots for example and even a pith helmet. I queried some of this stuff and was told that much of it was no longer considered necessary equipment, including the pith helmet and the kidney pads. Why then leave them on the list, I asked? It was the same attitude I would later find in the civil service, 'change nothing, challenge nothing, then you haven't made a mistake'.

There were injections to have, Typhoid A and B, yellow fever, revaccination for smallpox. This meant trips up to the London Hospital for Tropical Diseases situated north of King's Cross. Now one would just go down to the local surgery. I also had to have a medical by the Bank's doctor in Harley Street, who agreed that I was very fit.

The only thing that worried me about my service medical was that should there really be a war, I might have disqualified myself for good. That was a matter of real concern, for I had and have a pride in myself. I have never then nor since wanted to be a misfit, an outcast unable to play a full part in society. This pride has made life the more difficult, in that I would not give in to the pressures within me. However, taking my part in a future war was all hypothetical. Life was moving too fast to worry about what might be. I was on a conveyor belt and there was no way of stopping it other than giving in to my inner self, which prospect was even more daunting.

Within six weeks and two weeks after my birthday on September the eighth, I went to Heathrow, my family coming to see me off. It was a strange goodbye, my parents being particularly undemonstrative, while I felt like hugging and kissing them all. As that sort of sloppiness did not take place in our family, I said a cold goodbye promising to write, shook hands and walked away. My ability to separate my real self from the one that managed to operate in a normal world, took me ever deeper into a life that was a lie.

This was my first civil flight and it was to be on a Comet. Departure was delayed by four hours due to an engine change, so we were held in Departure for two hours. It was not full of shops and restaurants as it is now. My flight was going to Buenos Aires, with stops at Oporto, Portugal and Dakar. I would transfer at Dakar the capital of Senegal, a former French territory, to an Air Liban flight down the coast to Freetown.

The descent into Oporto gave me severe earache. I was tired already, it now being 23.00hrs and there was still a long way to go. We reached Dakar at sometime around six in the morning. The heat as the plane door opened was like walking into a sauna. Having never been further south than central France, I was completely unprepared for the tropics. The air was thick with moisture and the temperature was already 85F. My suitcase arrived by my side as the Comet taxied away, leaving me alone on the airfield sitting on my suitcase, to await Air Liban.

About seven it duly arrived and I was allowed to board. The sight within was far from pleasant. The passengers were a mixture of Africans and Lebanese. Small children seemed to be gambolling about everywhere. In addition to the noise, there was a pervading odour of vomit and I had to pick my way to a seat around suspicious stains on the carpet and bundles, calabashes, rolls of material, and all sorts of other personal paraphernalia. It was a far cry from the sanitary environs of the BOAC Comet that had been full of fashionable Europeans. I had truly arrived in Africa. The one nice thing about that flight was the provision of about a dozen bottles of perfume, French and expensive, in the loo. I helped myself.

When airborne, the smell seemed to decrease. I sniffed my scented handkerchief and occupied myself by looking out of the window. Not much was to be seen as the DC6, a sort of stretched version of the old Dakota with four engines hammered down the coast, propellers humming and beating, some rivets seeming to rattle in their holes, flying over almost unending mangrove swamp. Occasionally, there would be a patch of yellow sand and a few palm trees, perhaps a fishing boat pulled up on the beach, and a few huts in a clearing. Numerous river estuaries were crossed, but no great areas of habitation. It was a fairly depressing sight.

We landed at Bathurst in the Gambia, to let people on and of and to refuel. It was hotter than Dakar. All I can remember about the place was that it seemed to be a wartime field, the runway and most of the walking areas being made of perforated metal. The refreshments were served in an old Nissan hut over which branches from encroaching trees stretched. At least there was shade. I was starting to feel that the real Africa was opening up before me.

At last we touched down at Freetown. The airport was separated from the town by a river, which here at the estuary was some mile or so across. First though we had to queue up for customs. As the place was still a colony, that was not too bad. Four years later, it had deteriorated to a state where the officials were becoming more like pirates or highwaymen. Now, it is even worse and the officials as in many parts of Africa, prey on tourists, trying to extract as many items and chattels as they can, all part of the African method of survival.

The airport was concrete, mostly open air, covered by a high roof. All was painted creamy yellow. At that time, the country was still working its ticket to independence, which would follow almost six months later, so as long as you were within the law, nothing much bad could befall you. My work permit was in order, though the immigration officer let it be known what he thought of expatriate workers. The natives were not friendly.

As I waited to board the coach to the ferry, I watched the lizards dashing about, green and black, bright little eyes, tongues shooting out. They were anything from six to thirty-six inches long. Some were in the process of casting their skins, like careless Brits on holiday, which gave these unattractive animals an even more repulsive appearance. In some palms a few metres away, a family of monkeys swung about. This was it, Africa, the Dark Continent that I had long dreamed of. There was a smell, a heat smell and a smell of decay, musty, dead vegetable, decaying flesh, the smell of the tropics. It was powerful but like other African sensations would disappear from the senses as one became used to them. It was September; the rains ended in July or August, as I would find out later. Everything was starting to burn up again.

At the ferry, we had to transfer ourselves and our baggage to a boat. It seemed to be little more than a converted patrol boat. We had to cling to the side as it tossed across the swirling waters, watching anxiously for our cases to tip off. I struck up a conversation with a returning civil servant, who pointed out that we had a Government minister aboard. I followed his gaze, seeing a small black man in a dark suit and a homburg hat. He also told me that he had never been up country, had no need to and no desire to see it. I thought him rather lacking in curiosity or pioneering spirit and lost interest rapidly. I was taking photos of the bullom boats, a sort of sailing barge, but was soon aware that the occupants were not always pleased to pose. My companion informed me that it was best to ask if you could photograph, as some believed I was capturing their soul in the camera. Whether he was right or not I have no idea, for I experienced no problem after that. Most Africans queue up shyly to have a photo taken, giggling and laughing. As he had never ventured further than the Freetown beach, I wondered what he knew about anything.I hoped there would be someone to meet me on the other side.

The town of Freetown nestles beneath the mountains from which the country gets its name, Sierra Leone, 'Lion Mountains', as the Portuguese had named them. They are not particularly high, just two thousand feet, but compared with the rest of the coastal terrain, they are spectacular. My impression from the approach by sea was of a mouldering, rusting town of mostly two storey buildings, many roofed and even clad in rust-stained corrugated iron, crouched sullenly beneath the thickly verdant mountain. Even in the town, dark green leaves shrouded decaying tin and timber and I would find later that bananas grew wherever a couple of square yards of earth were available.

Clouds hung over the mountain, dark bluish grey, I could see rain falling near the summit, misting, obscuring the detail of houses and forest. Everywhere at sea level looked old, dilapidated and dirty. Even white painted walls were streaked with rusty stains, the colour of the red laterite soil. The stench of decay grew stronger as we approached and the heat was considerable, even on the water. I was quite pleased that I had a hat, to keep the sun off my head, a sort of lightweight trilby, getting towards the white hunter style. I thought it quite the thing when I purchased it in London.

The ferry docked and everyone flooded ashore and seemed to disappear. A young fellow in white shirt and tie and very short shorts leaned against a large black Humber car.

'You must be Nash,' he said.

I nodded and put out a hand. We shook and he nearly took my arm off.

'Where did you get that fucking hat,' he asked, and I never wore it again, I don't even remember what happened to it. Probably, some African is wearing it to this day.

Pete was the manager's assistant. What that meant, I had no idea. In time I would find out. He was amazed by my companions off the plane, used to meeting people off the usual route that was via the Canary Islands. Pete considered my travelling companions to be a bit grim. He asked where I had overnighted, and I told him that I had been travelling all night long.

'My instructions are to take you to the manager now and then you can start work this afternoon. How do you feel?'

'Distinctly jaded,' I admitted.

'I'll take you to the bungalow, then explain to the manager later.'

We entered a great old car, black, huge wings. The engine throbbed powerfully. It was extremely hot inside, with a smell of leather and petrol. The leather seats burnt through my trousers. He tooled the car through the traffic, carefully avoiding dilapidated lorries, some seeming to limp along, either severely overloaded or with a broken spring, mostly Bedfords with wooden bodies that consisted of a flat back with sides, surmounted by an awning. The interiors could be filled with goods, animals, people, or a combination of all three. The fronts were adorned with paintings, what one would call naive, and slogans like 'Zorro the Great', 'Rush Rush Express', 'Speed to God'. The other road users seemed to be mostly taxis, the windows having little stick on vases, with plastic flowers in them, or a woman's headscarf like a knight's favour, flying from the mirror. All the drivers seemed to ride with their backs to the driving door, right hand outside, left steering and changing gear, so that they looked through the windscreen over their right shoulders. This side saddle attitude allowed the driver to catch most of the breeze from the open window. Most wore battered versions of my infamous hat, coerced into mini versions of a cowboy's Stetson. The impression of cowboys was very strong, and in all the time I was there, that never altered. As I would find out, cowboy was a very apt title, for most of them were long on show and short on ability. They were a murderous and crazy lot.

The Humber was so hot. The leather seats remained too warm to sit comfortably, even though all the windows were open. Shimmering heat seemed to bounce off the uneven black tarmac straight up through the floor of the car. It was almost unbearable. Suddenly I felt wan and weak. I had been awake thirty-six hours and changed climates dramatically. At last we arrived at the bachelor accommodation at Kissy, the old naval dockyard, which the commercial world and some ministries used to house their expatriates. Freetown had been a very important base in the Second World War, where practically every convoy to the Far East and Egypt put in to refuel and to avoid the U-boat packs.

Our building was the classic military tropical hut, a veranda all around, protected from the elements by mosquito screens. Within, there were several bedrooms, and a large lounge/diner, with a kitchen off. I was shown my room, north facing as all the bedrooms were, overlooking the bay and dirty rocks of the estuary. This northern aspect was a great asset. The bedrooms were always the coolest rooms and any breeze off the water penetrated the steel insect netting. To move the air around on still nights, each room had a ceiling fan with three speeds. On fast it created a gale, swayed crazily and shook. At night, I would in future lie upon my bed that was in the bedroom's veranda, and watch spectacular lightning across the water.

I was offered a beer or a squash, but no food. It was reasonably cool in the living room, the light subdued and with the ceiling fans whirring rhythmically, I soon fell asleep in one of the Parker Knolls, my feet on the table.

I awoke to find that I had company. There were two of them, another Pete and a Dick. It was soon obvious that they could not stand each other. Pete Morgan wanted to play classical music, while Dick was in love with the music from the film 'Around the world in Eighty days.' Pete accused Dick of liking tasteless rubbish. It was a feud that lasted all the time I was there. They positively hated each other, making no effort to disguise it. Pete would be going up country to take over a small branch in and I had come out to take his place in Freetown.

I looked at my watch to find that it was after five. They ordered tea, and the boys, a most frightening cook who they told me was trying to poison them and a boy, beaming filed teeth, a relic of his cannibal ancestors, presented themselves. The youngster's name was Muli, the homicidal cook, Ali. They carried in cups, a huge teapot and a plate full of mixed biscuits.

We all had tea out of the pot, followed by another cup. When we came to pour a third, it had turned to chocolate. I had difficulty understanding the trick. Was this the first instance of witchcraft? It turned out that they had ordered tea, meaning light refreshments and chocolate to drink. In the African mind this was converted to a pot of tea with chocolate in it. The chocolate being heavier than the tea, sank to the bottom of the pot, and only emerged from the spout after the tea had all gone. It worked quite nicely. It was also an insight into the African mind.

We ate something that night, but I could not remember what. Then the four of us, the other Pete having appeared too, sat around talking and drinking Allsopps beers out of large cans. There was an unholy racket going on, the frogs giving full vent, and the crickets knitting away for all they were worth. I was the only one who could hear it, my colleagues, so used to it that their ears had lost sensitivity, only managing to hear it after concentration. I would learn to ignore it too. Geckos crossed the ceiling, little translucent lizards about three inches long, which were left alone to eat the numerous insects that somehow managed to penetrate the mosquito netting.

Tomorrow I would start work at seven, so we had to leave at six-forty. The dawn would come all too soon.

CHAPTER 6.

That first morning was a nightmare. From the moment we rose, we were in a rush. As European staff, we had standards of behaviour to set to the indigenous staff. Therefore we were never visibly late, never drunk, and never sick. We were clean, smart, correct, knowledgeable, hard working, and polite. There was a dress code; white or khaki drill shorts, white knee length socks and black lace up shoes. We Kissy bachelors, the married expatriate staff had quarters the other side of the mountain overlooking the bay, entered the bank at seven am. I was suddenly surrounded by African staff, some openly hostile, some barely tolerant of the whites in their midst, and many thoroughly incompetent. Added to that, the building was a typical Lebanese built store. Occupying a corner site, it was some thirty metres, by thirty metres. There were no windows, only shutters that were raised all the time the bank was open. Consequently, all the dust and all the noise had free access from the street.

There was of course no air conditioning. The temperature was a nice ninety Fahrenheit minimum. I was informed that this was our temporary abode, a new office then being under construction on the old bank site.

Taking over from Peter, the classical music fan who was off to manage Port Loko branch, my desk was in the farthest corner of the open plan building, and though the quietest point, it was also the hottest, most airless and the dingiest. I disliked the whole situation intensely. The noise from the street was tremendous. Motor horns, the roaring engines of overloaded lorries rumbling by up the hill towards the Cotton Tree and the shouts of the Africans entered this unenclosed space and reverberated off the stark concrete.

I was introduced to the other Brits. Often it was their frailties that were whispered as their distinguishing features, thus Alastair was an eighty a day man, getting through a tin and a half of Senior Service untipped cigarettes a day. James had difficulties with his drink, not a drunkard, just that he could not hold it. His first task in the morning after a night out would be a visit to the loo to be sick, before beginning work. Someone else had a black girl friend, frowned on then, but commonplace two years later, after Independence.

I was as innocent then as I would later be when entering other worlds in my strange life. This whole set up was a world in which I was a blob of oil to their water. It terrified me. I maintained a shy aloof air, as I had at school, giving little of myself, trying to fit, pretending a liking for the riotous bachelor life. I was though, fearful of discovery, feeling different, liking the company of these ebullient young men, but unable to relate to them. Above all I hankered for some tenderness. I wondered why I had come to this stinking country, but what else would I have done? I was terrified of failing and drifting towards the dregs of society, I possessed so little self-respect.

Pete, who had collected me from the dock on arrival, became my guide and protector. Although only four years older, he assumed the role of older brother, even more, sought me out and involved me with his Lebanese contacts and his other European friends. He christened me 'Choochy', I never knew why. When later Dick's fiancée, the famous Eunice came out, Pete teased me about the fluff I possessed where sideboards are supposed to be. 'You want to shave off that Eumig,' he said. 'Eunice,' I would reply, rising to the bait, and we would play out a sort of Simon versus Pete Morgan scene.

This relationship became a problem, for I found myself again in that strange shadow world. He was strong and male, the protector. I felt weak and feminine in his presence. I do not mean that I was girlish, effeminate, but more like a tomboy, playing the male role, trying to prove myself. It was a strange situation. Very confusing, wonderful, a glimpse of a world I longed for, but it was frustrating.

The job was not that onerous, looking after standing orders and periodical payments; decoding the numerous telex transfers of money and other mysterious messages that were sent to us. However, there are pitfalls to be found anywhere, and Murphy's law decrees that slip-ups occur with the most important items.

I made a bad one a few months later. Having had fever, I became run down and anaemic. One morning my nose began to bleed. It would not stop. I tried sitting with my head in various positions, then when that failed, I reclined as far as I could without actually lying on the floor. It still bled. The telexes still appeared. Murphy's had really kicked in on a particularly busy day. Eventually, I just worked on, a handkerchief in one hand to staunch the bleeding held constantly to my nose, while attempting to turn the pages of the heavy code books and calculating passwords, coding and decoding. Still it bled.

Because the Bank never had enough expatriate staff, restricted as they were by the Sierra Leone Government, one was never ill. It was not allowed. You could be dead, or in a coma, but otherwise one did one's duty, worked a good eight hours minimum. We were essential at that time to the efficient running of the Bank, due to the low standards of local education and the temptations which handling money offered African staff whose work we checked each and every day.

Amongst the blood smeared papers was a telex from a large manufacturer and retailer, who had outlets all over West Africa. They were transferring £2,000,000, a lot of money then, simply to play the exchange market and I overlooked it. When the manager found out next day, I was on the carpet. I explained the circumstances that drew no sympathy at all, other than the order to get myself 'bloody well sorted out'. I was ordered to the doctor who diagnosed anaemia and produced an iron tonic. I also managed to find some vitamin tablets, a rarity then, especially in West Africa.

We played hard. No matter what time we went to bed, we had to be in the bank at 7 am. This meant that sometimes, being bachelors and easily bored with life, we were out all night sitting in the beach clubs having worked all day to at least four and often five or six. We lived on a diet of Heineken and peppered chicken. At balance times we worked much later when necessary, in those most unpleasant surroundings and conditions, but no matter the time spent working, it was a matter of pride that we could still go out and play.

I had a particular problem with alcohol. Like James, it just did not agree with me and would soon make me groggy but not drunk. I had discovered this the first weekend. It was my first Saturday; we worked in the morning, then about one, made for the beach. After a cigarette and four Heinekens, I was very ill indeed. Pete allowed me to lie on the floor of his car, the doors open to catch the breeze, after I had promised not to be sick inside it. I was never to be able to drink much more, and later could not tolerate any alcohol at all.

It was our practice to go down the coast on a Sunday, four up in my car, taking a picnic with us. There we found a tourist's dream beach, golden sand, palm trees down to the water's edge and an island, a quarter of a mile offshore. This was where later the Bounty chocolate bar adverts would be filmed. The village was back from the coast, so we were never plagued by beggars. More often than not, we were the only ones there, Africans having little use for beach and sand, and most Europeans staying on the Freetown beaches.

I was not a strong swimmer, so when the boys decided to swim to the island, I agreed reluctantly. Half way across, Pete Wallace said, 'I hope there aren't barracudas, about. They'd take a chunk straight out of your stomach.' It was of course a windup. Nevertheless, I quickened my stroke. Having arrived on the island, we found it was less attractive than our beach, so we turned round and headed back.

Actually, I found these days quite boring, and was glad to pack up around four to head back home. The beach was a hard place to enjoy with sand flies, over a hundred degrees in the sun and over ninety in the shade.

'It'll soon be Christmas, ' Pete said, 'why don't we go up country to see Nigel?'

'How far?' I asked.

'Take your car, not that far if we both drive.'

Later Dick asked if he could come too. Dick was a bit of a dampener, not our sort of person, did not join in and later became a bank inspector. He was prissy, a good banker but a bit stupid. He had been driving up country, and had a bad rattle on the dirt road. He took no notice until the car scrunched to a halt and one front wheel proceeded down the road on its own.

So the three of us set off for Pendembu. It is a road journey of some 300 miles, 250 of them on laterite (dirt) roads. Christmas is the middle of the dry season, not as humid as Freetown during the rains, but up country in the bush, stupefyingly hot. Nigel had informed Pete that he had it all prepared and assured us of a good time.

We arrived hot and dusty. Pendembu seemed as welcoming as a dry well in an oasis, except that the one thing there was plenty of, was beer. Nigel believed in a Spartan existence, saving every penny to take home and open up his own garage workshop. In his backyard resided an old Borgward saloon, a Swedish car that was considered to rival Mercedes. Unfortunately Borgward had become defunct and not even Nigel's ingenuity could make it run. There were signs of other motor carcasses too, as well as welding gear. When Nigel wasn't in the bank, he was out welding things, including one of the road bridges. Technicians of any sort were rare out in the bush.

Christmas day dawned. No decorations, no celebrations, no Queen's speech. No radio broadcasts from hospitals nor promises of snow on the weather forecast. No weather forecast, for everyone knew it would be sun again, all day, everyday until the rains began in May. Our breakfast was a delight, pawpaw or as it is known also, papaya fresh from Nigel's own tree, lime juice and fresh pineapple too from the garden. Bacon followed, but there were no eggs.

"What's for dinner?" asked Pete, provocatively, a sardonic smile upon his swarthy face.

"I've got a goat," mumbled Nigel.

"Goat?" We all chorused. It took me back to my school days, when we performed excerpts from Greek plays. Then one of the chorus had always endeavoured to be last with the line, just as at church, the sexton had always been the last to say amen, cementing his position of importance. On this day, the three of us were in unison.

"Uh, is that it then?" Pete persisted.

"Should be all right," Nigel said, peering at us through his round NHS specs, "have a wander around, I've just got to weld a chassis."

With that he disappeared, bacon butty in hand. After breakfast served by the indomitable General Jackson, later to become my cook, we ambled along the town, kicking dust, avoiding the captive chimpanzee that liked to throw excreta at one, until we came to the railway station. There were a dozen Lebanese stores, a French trading company and two English ones. Apart from the African dwellings, that was it. It was not a bit like Christmas. What was I doing here? The question revolved inside my head yet again.

"Not one of my better ideas," said Pete, "not really worth the journey. Still we've been to the end of the line," he nodded at the railway terminus, "eh Choochy?" He nudged me.

"End of the line, beginning of the road to somewhere," I said sagely.

Dick, Pete Morgan's enemy had said nothing since appearing for breakfast. "Goat," he said now, "spectacular."

Next day we drove the 55 miles to the border with Liberia and Senegal. It could have been almost anywhere in the African interior. Red laterite, which is a gravelly soil, it was hot, dusty, an open market, a sort of exotic car boot sale, a few low buildings and distant palms In the evening we had Christmas dinner, no paper hats, champagne or mince pies and pudding. The goat was edible, a bit stringy but not at all different to lamb. The next day we drove back to Freetown.

Independence came three months later. It coincided with another illness. We had gone to the army cinema and were watching a film of a Neville Shute book, 'On the Beach' a post-apocalyptic novel and extremely depressing. I suddenly felt freezing cold, although the temperature must have been in the upper seventies. By the time we reached Kissy, I was a shivering wreck. They put me to bed covered in blankets. The next day I would not wake, so as it seemed I was in a coma, I was allowed to stay in bed. When the lads returned in the evening, I was out being sick in the loo. I drank water, but was sick immediately. They decided that I needed a doctor and called in the Bank's appointed physician, a nice African Creole lady. She diagnosed malaria in spite of the fact that I had taken the prophylactics religiously. It was our custom in the bachelor house to take our malarial tablet at breakfast time. We all reminded each other. I was given some disgusting medicine that made me sick at once, but I was commanded to take it just the same. In two days, I was starting to keep drinks down. On the evening of Independence Day, I roused myself from my bed and made my way to the lounge to get a drink from the fridge. There were guests sitting drinking with the lads, American officers off one of the US warships that had arrived on a courtesy visit. One turned and looked at me, and I heard him say, 'Good God, who was that, looks like someone from Belsen.'

Back in my room, I looked in the mirror. I could not believe how thin I was, every rib showing and my stomach seeming to cling to my backbone. I was down to seven and a half stone from a usual weight of nine stone. I would eventually get back to eight and a half, but never to nine stone until I left that damned continent forever. According to the manager I was in the wrong for not taking the anti malarial tablets. All my protests to the contrary were ignored and after five days I was in the office again, feeling weak and extremely depressed.

At the weekend, Derek and I drove to the top of the mountains up the steep slope to the University and looked down on the uncomely sprawl of Freetown. It was a rare day, when the place was shrouded in thick grey air, the sun almost expunged by high cloud with smoke haze obscuring the far horizons. Everything looked grey or rusty, dirty and depressing. Even the white painted MV Accra as it lay down at the docks, the ship that transported so many between West Africa and Liverpool, seemed less pristine than usual. Had I not been in company, I would have allowed myself to weep. I was bereft of any happiness. I hated the place, the life, the native people and the work. I hated myself, could not bear to think about my future, and could not believe that there would be a future. Derek my companion, must have sensed my despair, for he rested a hand on my shoulder and said, 'looks like shit, smells like shit and it is shit. Let's go for the curry.'

He hurtled his huge Chevrolet down the twisting mountain roads. We always drove toe to the ground anyway, but today it seemed even faster. The adrenaline pulsed through my veins as the lumbering creaking open top sedan lurched round hairpins on its soft springs and that must have revived me. I recovered enough to survive the next few months. When I at last returned to the UK, the doctors believed that I had in fact had Dengue, aka sandfly fever, similar in nature to malaria, damaging to the kidneys and sometimes fatal. I had been bitten by a sandfly a few days before becoming ill, so I would believe the Bank's London doctor.

The manager decided that I needed toughening up. Like all misfits, and many of the men who had built the Empire, I was being shipped out of civilisation if that was what Freetown was. Summoned by the manager, I was informed that I would be taking over a branch up country, Port Loko where Pete Morgan had gone upon my arrival. As my bookkeeping was extremely shaky, this was a matter of some concern, but there was only one thing to do, accept what fate held for me and somehow get to grips with it. I knew that the clerk was well thought of, therefore I would have a dependable member of staff to help me through the initial trauma.

In the midst of the rains, I was off up country to run this small branch.

The hand over from Pete went well. I confessed my ignorance about the books and he explained it all in a few simple sentences. I made half a page of simple notes. All those boring sessions I had endured at City College were put behind me thanks to Pete. The branch had a turnover of between £50 and £100 thousand a week, so it was all quite simple. The scales fell from my eyes, a eureka moment and the whole thing made sense. Just as well for the clerk wasn't as good as I had been led to believe. Having been assured by the chief accountant in Freetown that the clerk was reliable, Freetown then decided their need was greater than mine.

Later they complained that he wasn't as good as he was reputed to be. Many hours would be spent by me alone, working in the relative cool of the evening, checking and balancing the ledgers that the clerk had written up.

I must describe Port Loko. If the place had been dropped into Europe, it would be one of the foremost tourist attractions. It was a small town of just about three thousand people. It is situated at the end of a thirty-mile creek and a trading centre because of that, the river being the only thoroughfare before the roads were built. Sitting upon a bluff overlooking the river and small wharf, it consisted of a mixture of Lebanese concrete buildings with balconies and flat roofs, contrasting with bungalow style, mud brick and tin roofed African homes. Green everywhere, the mangroves in the creek stretching for miles; coconut palms leaning, their wavering fronds like fancy umbrellas; banana plants, their obscene phallic flowers and elephant ear leaves. In front of the bank was a small square, an African bar blared perpetual 'high life' music on one side, the covered market where the mammies sold their produce took up the opposite side. The fourth side was open, sloping away down to the stream that gurgled through the town in the rains and barely splashed along at the end of the dry season. Here the women did their washing, whirling twisted wet clothes around their heads and smashing them on the rocks, clad in just a sarong. Mostly it was the young women, the junior wives of this mainly Islamic society, who did this chore, their pert breasts jigging and shining with every movement. How I wished to chatter with them and have similar pert breasts.

It was a noisy place, lorries stopping and starting, people shouting, the weaverbirds in the tree above the bar, twittering all day long. The mammies cackled in the market, Arabic music floated down from adjacent Lebanese homes. Here was all the life one would expect of an African and Arab bazaar and all the smells, sewage, decay, cooking meat, wood smoke, cheap scent, dried fish, fresh bread, citrus, sweaty rank bodies, palm oil, petrol and burning engine oil from the abused and toiling lorries.

Vultures floated like V bombers across the sky, to land in the coconut palms. They sometimes came in so close to my first floor living quarters, that I could hear the wind in their feathers, their long bare necks stretched out revealing orange and purple skin and their bright orange eyes searching greedily for food. Their ugliness and coarse feathers contrasted with the skill they displayed in flight, effortlessly soaring and gliding about the rising land.

It was very green. Although the surrounding country was savannah scrub, this little town had an abundance of large trees. It had what could have been a village green, that separated the old town from the new and was traversed by the main road into the place from the south and the capital. This open grassland was one's first sight of the town. Sheep grazed the grass of this green and slept on the road at night, soaking up the residual heat left in the tarmac. It would have been a fine site for a cricket ground.

The old town, built on high ground that sloped steeply towards the river, benefited from a view over the river estuary that stretched for miles all the way down to Freetown, fifty miles away as the crow flies but ninety miles by road. Furthest from the centre, but in actual distance only half a mile, was the airfield, seldom used, and upon which Tim and I would later race our VW Beetles another year. Adjacent to this was the government compound, where mostly expatriate officials lived in bungalows well spaced about another bluff where they would catch the air. The gardens were full of blossoms, but the undergrowth was slowly enveloping the place, native species driving out the cultivated, a kind of simile to the situation in the country at large, as British rule came to an end.

Like most beautiful places, it had an aura about it, ever changing vistas, winding streets. It was a lively place, yet had a tranquillity that would invade the soul. Here Maugham would have been at home, writing his tales of tropical love and tragedy. It was like a Greek village I will mention later, which possesses these same qualities. Away to the north was another compound, older, the seat of government in the form of the District Commissioner's residence and Offices. The compound here was a shady place, umbrella trees providing almost wall-to-wall shade across the close cropped coarse grass.

The town was also the capital of the district, having the prison, the District Commissioner's office, the police station, the district court, public works department, agriculture department, missions and a hospital, as well as a boarding school for boys. It had a town chief, who had his own police and to some extent, his own justice. The British had ruled through these local chiefs, cunningly using these quislings to keep the country peaceful. It was therefore an important little place. Practically all the trade was carried on by Lebanese traders, who in that town were mostly Moslem. There were two African traders, even bigger crooks than the Lebanese.

Up country, I was to find life much different. I was my own master and all the responsibility for the efficient and proper conduct of the branch lay in my hands. This meant that life could be rather sweet provided I worked hard during opening hours that were eight till one. Usually I would be closed up by one-thirty, the place all locked up and the staff gone home. I was then free to do whatever I liked. Some of that time was spent in customer visits, either social or official, but it still left considerable potential to explore and to amuse. At balance times I would work alone far into the night, adding everything in my head, checking each entry until the books balanced to the very penny. At other times there were reports to write, allowing my more creative side to run riot. It caused me trouble later.

Shopping was a thing that needed some thought. It was before the advent of frozen food cabinets even appearing in the furthermost corners of the globe, though my fridge had a small freezer compartment. In Port Loko and later in Pendembu, the only foodstuffs obtainable were tinned or fresh local produce. All exotica had to be purchased from larger towns where European based multinationals had stores.

In Port Loko I made the eighty-six mile dash to Freetown for shopping. Half the distance was on tarmac, a strip wide enough for one lorry only but with dirt strips on either side to run on when passing. This led to frequent accidents as lorries collided head on when neither driver had the sense to give way. Wreckage, and bodies could be strewn for 100 metres when two of these vehicles collided in passing, a sight I saw on three occasions. The other forty miles were on laterite, earth roads which gave off a thick red dust in the dry and turned to mud in the wet season. It took skill to drive safely and at speed on these roads and the driving method was more akin to the Safari Rally than shopping in Kensington.

Port Loko offered different pastimes to Freetown. There was tennis, most afternoons in the dry season. We played on the District Commissioners court, surrounded by a hedge, no one to disturb the serenity other than the Americans from the Peace Corps abusing their rackets. There were other Europeans to see, often a few miles away. There was shooting, exploring the bush with Bob Rattray or Daramy the Bank's messenger. There was target shooting with John Oliphant, or hanging out with the Peace Corps. There was reading, the town having a little library largely of English classics. Books were also available from a library the Peace Corps had been supplied with and many an hour could be passed pleasantly reading undisturbed. What was surprising was that these Peace Corps boys hardly read a book, although serving as teachers at the boarding school. One of their number, George, had brought a large music library though and this broadened my love of classical music. I attempted to paint, rather Gaugin like nudes and sketched bare bosomed market women. I took photos of nearly everything. There were trips to the iron mine club at Marampa 30 miles away, to see films.

When balances did not work out, there was only me to put them right, and the night oil would burn late when it was slightly cooler, the heat, being more oppressive when concentrating hard. My first clerk had been poached by Freetown branch, to be replaced by one who was absolutely useless, a drunk who ended up in prison. He would appear at any time of the morning, his shirt dirty, his body encased in nylon unwashed and rancid. When he punched a policeman in a drunken brawl, he expected me to bail him out, but he had exhausted my patience and good will.

His successor was a timid fellow who hated the bush, longed to be back in Freetown and feared for his life in the land of the Temne. The Freetown Creoles thought themselves a superior race to their inland brothers. He knew nothing about figures and had difficulty adding a column of them. In some ways that was safer than having a flyboy who would fiddle the books, but it meant that I was really a one-person band. My bookkeeping was learned without their help, but I managed. In truth, they did little except enter in the ledgers, and then not accurately

Whereas Catholics sin first and then receive forgiveness in return for an act of contrition, the advantage of being Moslem, I found out, was that Allah could be blamed for everything. The Lebanese spoke a dreadful patois that they learnt from the Africans, a Pidgin English supplemented by some Portuguese words imported when that nation had traded out of Freetown. It was called Creole but is not to be confused with the Creole of New Orleans. They spoke it with the guttural accent of the Arab. Every time they failed to repay a loan, they blamed not themselves nor the weather, nor even bad trading conditions. It was they said Allah. 'Insh Allah,' please god, they would say as they promised faithfully to repay their overdrafts. The trouble was that God did not please, I believe having deserted Port Loko soon after his completion of the world.

'Allah no dey!' they would say as they came to tell me they could not repay the overdraft, 'God is not there,' as if God had shut up his bank and gone on vacation, thus making them break their promise. It was all a trial of wits. They just hoped I would get tired of asking them for the money. It meant that once a week, when I felt they would least expect it, I would descend on them in their stores, assess the stock, look in the till and extract a chunk of the takings, fill in the paying in book, stamp it with the cashiers stamp I carried with me, and return to the bank with the proceeds.

It was tiresome making small talk to these ignorant people whose whole existence seemed to be this small patch of the African bush. Sitting in their shops drinking Turkish coffee, thick black and sweet, soon lost its appeal. Luckily, there were a few Europeans and wherever I went, there were always one or two I could relate to.

In Port Loko it was Bob Rattray. He came from Scotland, 'the kingdom of Fife' and was the regional agricultural engineer. He lived quite alone at the depot twenty miles away, by a wide river across which the sun would set beyond distant palms. We were soon firm friends. I would spend most weekends out there and often afternoons when the bank had closed. Bob was a quiet man, the easiest person I have ever known. We never disagreed, never wanted to do different things. He was inventive, turned a harvester on a pontoon into a sort of riverboat. He had toys; a small speedboat, a large launch and we spent hours on the river.

We hunted crocodile by night, drifting down the silent river in the speedboat; a car headlamp searched for eyes and twelve bores loaded with large shot at the ready. It was exciting, frightening, but I had complete faith in him. In those unenlightened times, the croc was still deemed a killer, a danger to the people and every year there were deaths as the great and vicious amphibians took women doing the washing, children splashing in the shallows, and cattle. The largest I ever saw would have been some fifteen to twenty feet, with a girth of perhaps sixty inches. I killed one, one night, just aiming at the eyes, shot it cleanly through the soft flesh behind the eyes. We fished it out, still thrashing, but it was only the death throws. A woman from the adjacent small village had been taken while washing in the river. I saw the scars upon her leg, the black skin torn and replaced by ugly white and pink skin. She had been lucky, her screams of terror having roused the village blacksmith who had waded in, gripped the jaws of the creature in his large hands and had managed to wrench them apart enough to release her. They laughed about it.

We hunted by day, launching into the bush in Bob's Land Rover, trees whipping across the screen, termite mounds bumping beneath the floor. We waded through flood lands sometimes up to our necks in water, after the wild geese. Once I fell into a hole and disappeared below the surface and he pulled me out. He laughed and so did I. We burned the leaches off our ankles with my cigarettes kept in a waterproof plastic case. I was afraid, there were snakes swimming past, and once a crocodile crossed about twenty feet in front of us, my most terrifying moment, but somehow I knew that Bob could cope with it all. He taught me how to shoot with the twelve bore. We didn't kill a lot, a few bush fowl, and some guinea fowl, some tough old geese, all of which we ate.

He had been a drummer in the Scots Guards, and would make all the drum noises as we marched through the bush, laughing at himself as he did it. He cooked a great brunch, and I cooked dinner. His favourite music was honky tonk classics which I hated, but to see him laugh as it played on his little gramophone, was an amusement in itself.

I was fond of Bob. He had come out to make enough to buy his house back in lowland Scotland, Cupar, in Fife, where his family, wife and two children happily awaited him. He hated the country, was frustrated by the workings of the Agriculture Department and by the tribal and village chiefs he had as customers. He spent not a penny more than he needed to, making his contract pay and sending every spare penny home, the canny Scot. He was not mean, we enjoyed ourselves inextravagantly. He was like an older brother and looked after me. I had a warble fly's egg in my back, and when the grub hatched and began to eat its way to the surface, he told me what it was, coated the skin with Vaseline and starved the thing of oxygen, thus making it race for the surface. He removed and burnt the unwelcome visitor on the end of a pin.

Alas, after three months I had to leave Port Loko and the laughing Temne people, to move to Pendembu, where we had spent Christmas, three hundred miles away among the Mende, the other great tribe of the country. They were very different, not so pretty, coarser featured and more sullen. Pendembu was at the end of the railway line. There was a frontier feel to the place, although it was another fifty miles to the frontier proper. As much as there was a view and perspective in Port Loko, in Pendembu there was only the bush, thick jungle as opposed to Port Loko's savannah, which surrounded the town and spread for twenty miles in every direction. The town ended where it ran up against the almost impenetrable jungle.

As I surveyed the Bank on reaching Pendembu, the whole memory of that ridiculous Christmas ran through my mind. Now I was back in this benighted place, for how long I knew not.

Nigel had met me at the station. As this was the midst of the rains and the roads were impassable, I had sent my car by rail. It would arrive filled with water to the top of the sills, somehow. It would never be quite the same again. I had flown, Freetown to Kenema, then to Segbwema, in some sort of Fokker with canvas seats. We bounced onto the field at Segbwema where we had a branch, and there I sat and waited three hours for the train. There were no other passengers. No food or drink, just sunshine and the lazy drone of insects. Far off there were African voices, some monkey's crashed in the trees.

Finally the train chugged around the bend, steam puffing out of leaky valves. I clambered aboard, first class. Again there were no other passengers.

Nigel showed me the ropes. There was no telephone, only the telegraph at the station, and that was often out as Africans pinched a length of wire, or a tree fell breaking the line. Here was isolation.

The Borgward still sat in the back yard, though the rest of the car detritus had been cleared. I asked Nigel what he proposed to do with the hulking great saloon. "Bury it," he said, "almost ready. Got the labourer and watchman digging. You won't see a thing."

Next day, we rolled the car less its wheels and engine, upside down into the pit. Unfortunately the break drums protruded from the surface. Little hillocks covered them, and Nigel departed.

He had had an accident before my arrival. A customer had asked him to weld a petrol tank. Thinking that he had better get all the petrol out first, he had rinsed it out with water. However, enough residue remained to cause an explosion. Nigel's specs took the full blast and one sturdy lens left the frame and inserted itself, intact, within his eye socket, like a permanent monocle. Blind, he wailed for help and Assaf next door, took him to hospital at Kailahun, twenty miles away. The doctor prised it out and Nigel's sight returned over the next few days. It had been a close shave.

In Pendembu the Lebanese were both Christian and Moslem. They lined opposite sides of the street, not speaking to each other, but speaking ill of each other. They would occasionally have rows as news from home provoked new hatred in this steaming dusty little town in the middle of the bush, more than three thousand miles from their real home. No wonder the Middle East is so beset with warring factions. This town at the back of nowhere had the feel of a spaghetti western settlement.

From Pendembu the nearest centre for shopping was Kenema some seventy miles, all on dirt roads and included a ferry crossing, not always passable when the river was in flood. The other problem associated with the rains was the state of the roads that would turn to a rutted mass of mud, in which lorries would slide and slip, often blocking the highway altogether, sometimes for days.

For important shopping I had to make the one hundred and ten-mile trip to the second town of the country, Bo. To reach Bo with any time to shop meant an eleven o'clock start from Pendembu. I would give notice that the Bank would close early, then leave the clerk in charge with no money, the safes locked and make a dash for the river about twenty miles away. The ferry operated on the current, the angle of attack to the river's flow moving it across the stream. If there was a queue, one could be there some time, as it carried at most three cars, or one lorry and a car.

One morning I arrived at the river to find nothing moving. The car in front of me bore a Liberian number and a CD plate. The driver, a sandy haired, ruddy faced fellow, accompanied by his wife, proved to be our man in Liberia, the British Consul. They were distressed, tired and hungry, and wanting to get down to Freetown. I offered lunch, and we all returned to my bungalow, where General Jackson, my cook soon put a meal together and we shared a few cold beers. After that it was too late for me to go to Bo, but the news was that the ferry had reopened and they set off with an invitation to return if necessary.

Three weeks later when the General Manager was out from London, making visits to see how it was in the bush, he commended me for looking after the consul. There had been a state dinner in Freetown at which the Sierra Leone General Manager, who also doubled as Danish Consul, met Brown of the FO. Nothing passed of my truancy from official opening hours, but I received credit for being a good host! Apparently he and his wife had sung my praises loudly. It was nice to be appreciated for a change after my previous problems with management.

I received a telegram, informing me that the General Manager was to visit. He was in essence managing director, a daunting character for a twenty-one year old to entertain. He would arrive on Saturday, and I had to pick him up from the ferry. The telegram demanded an answer that I would be there. When I tried to send a reply, I found that the line was down. My messenger went to the telegraph office at the station every two hours to see whether it had been repaired. I sensed trouble.

Saturday came and I had still not managed to reply. I drove to the ferry and waited. The great man turned up, bearing a small overnight bag and sporting a trilby hat. As he stepped off the ferry I introduced myself to a red-faced, redhaired and bad tempered Mr Redmayne. There was no response other than to say, 'Why didn't you respond to my telegram?'

'I tried,' I said, 'but the line was down.'

As we reached Pendembu, he spoke for the second time. 'Take me to the telegraph office.'

I sat in the car, hoping that the telegraph manager would not change his story, as sometimes Africans were prone to do. Redmayne was back in a trice.

'Line was down,' he said, with no added apology.

We entered the flat and he threw his bag onto a chair. 'Like to get the business over first. Show me the books.'

We entered the gloom of the closed bank. I produced a Tilly lamp, then the books.

'Don't need your help. Make a cup of tea.'

I left him to it, hoping that I had not dropped a clanger anywhere, and that the books balanced as I thought they had. I took him a cup of tea. The books were all out along the counter. On a balance reconciliation form, he was writing down the various balances, sweat in beads on his florid forehead. I hoped he was not going to have an apoplectic fit. I produced the keys, dialled the combination and opened the safe. Quickly he counted the bundles of notes, then the coin and added that to his figures. He totted it up. I waited, my stomach knotted, chest tight.

At length, he turned. 'Put it away. All correct, I'm pleased to say. Just one thing, one of your pencilled totals was wrong, led me up the garden path. Still you must have found that yourself as you had balanced.'

I cleared away, then joined him in the lounge. Light fell across the room from the front door and from the rear windows. He had collapsed in a chair. He looked deadbeat. I had arranged that the two Irish Catholic fathers would come to dinner to help entertain him. The General would cook two scrawny chickens with all the trimmings. I had even driven to Kenema to get prawns for a starter and tried to get Drambuie which I had been told was his favourite after dinner drink. Two bottles of mediocre wine and beers were stacked in the fridge. I had failed to find Drambuie, probably every bottle had been bought up for this one man. I did have plenty of whisky, Scotch and Irish.

'I hope you haven't arranged anything for tonight. I need a rest.'

'Actually, I have the Catholic fathers coming.'

'Damn.'

'They are good chaps. I'm sure we can get rid of them if you wish.'

'I suppose it will have to be. Now, where am I sleeping?'

'I've put you in my room. It's near the bathroom and quieter.'

'Can I get a bath?'

'As soon as the watchman comes to heat the water, at six. We eat at 7.30, so the evening doesn't have to be that long if you are tired.'

'Think I'll have a siesta, now. Don't want to be a wet blanket tonight. Which way?

I showed him the room. Dimly lit, on the shaded north side of the bungalow, it looked quite restful.

I went to the Assaf's to get out of the way and recover from the tension. I was now looking ahead to the evening with dread. The General had prepared everything for the meal. He would arrive about four to start cooking. I had no worries there.

The watchman turned up early, and I put him to heating up the water. At 6.15 I heard Redmayne stirring. I asked if he wanted his bath now?

'You have yours. I'll follow.'

I bathed quickly in half my normal level of water. I dressed and went to check on the kitchen. All was in order. The fathers arrived early, no doubt looking forward to a free meal and whisky. Redmayne was still splashing in the bath. Eventually he appeared, and I did the introductions. After a couple of beers, the General entered. As usual when I had company, he had dressed in his white ducks. His dark face was polished ebony. He wore his campaign medals and his red fez. He saluted vigorously and announced dinner was ready.

The meal was adequate. The birds were edible, the wine just drinkable. Two bottles disappeared. We then took to the easy chairs. Redmayne asked what we had to drink. I said we had no Drambuie. The only liqueur was Goldwasser, some sort of schnapps that had bits of gold leaf floating in it. It had been left by Nigel. 'Woman's drink.' Redmayne pronounced.

'I have whiskey,' I offered nervously.

'What sort?'

'Jameson and Black Label.'

'Ah, things are looking up. Now fathers, which would you prefer?'

'May I suggest, we do a little comparison. Call it research,' said Father Daniel.

'Brilliant.'

I sat back. The General produced whiskies and a jug of water, then saluted and said goodnight. The whisky levels lowered. Their faces beamed. Redmayne laughed a lot and the Fathers full of their favourite tipple 'free', were abandoned with their stories. At two Redmayne announced that he had better turn in as he would be departing early. The fathers went home. We brushed our teeth and went to bed.

Next morning I was up early, having consumed almost no alcohol the night before. Redmayne was up early too. We had to be at the ferry by 10.00.

On the journey, he apologised for his behaviour of yesterday. 'Good show. Not easy living out here in the bush. How old are you?'

'Twenty-two next month.'

'Well, good luck. Take care of yourself. Last night, don't know when I have enjoyed myself so much. Brilliant evening. Thank you.'

We shook hands. As he stepped on the ferry, I turned the car and drove home elated, giving up a long sigh of relief.

There was one family, the Assafs, Christian and educated, who were a cut above the rest amongst the Lebanese. He was the most business like and energetic of the traders and I wondered why they were there. It transpired that he was wanted for terrorism against the Moslems in Beirut, and had banished himself to Africa. His wife was the only Lebanese woman who could speak to me about anything other than the most limited of women's subjects. They were a lovely couple.

In Freetown I'd had my civet cat, not a cat at all, but a relative of the mongoose family. It had been given me as a kitten, some six inches from tip of the tail to its sharp little nose. Dai Evans from whom I bought my Hillman Minx before he went home to the UK, gave it to me. Dai painted a picture of his lonely wife awaiting him. Alas it was not so. While Dai was away, the wife was at play and poor Dai in traditional manner returned to Africa to forget. He was devastated and clung to me as he suffered a breakdown. It was a strange sensation, at twenty-one, to be the confidante and comforter of a thirty eight-year-old man in such distress. It was the first time I had come up against such mental trauma in another, and it sapped what little energy I had. I was also embarrassingly put on the spot to be his carer by our chief accountant, simply because I knew him slightly. It was a burden on top of all the others I had to carry. I am ashamed to say, that having to visit Dai in hospital everyday made me feel feminine and I was terrified that I would show my real self. He was eventually repatriated; back to I knew not what, poor soul.

Manky my civet, as Pete christened the little creature, adopted me from the start, loving to cling to my shoulder as I walked about the house, or to fall asleep there if I sat. He was a nice little pet, and I adored him. He was very much a one-person animal. That meant he practically ignored everyone else and treated them with utter disdain. What was remarkable was how tame he was with me. He loved me to distraction, trying to follow me out of the door, running to meet me when I returned. He slept on the top of my mosquito net, making a dip in it like a hammock. As I awoke, he would come to life too, shoot down the net headfirst as if it was a ladder and wait for me to let him into the bed. He would also race up my nude body, a painful but bearable experience, his sharp little claws moving so fast that they did not puncture my skin, then he would sit on my shoulder and given a chance, investigate my ear with his bristly and wet little nose. He ate insects, moths and cockroaches as well as geckos. One day he just went missing. I suspected the boys had done away with him, but I could prove nothing. I missed the little fellow a lot.

Port Loko offered me an antelope, a kid that I bottle-fed and kept in the flat. She was quite clean using the veranda for her toilet, which I thought quite extraordinary. She did a fair imitation of Bambi on the polished floors, until she learned to cope with them, taking tiny steps like some mannequin on a catwalk. She and her companions, my cat and a water python rescued when it was cut by a scythe by accident, all lived amicably around me for the three months I was there, then they were passed on to new homes. An An the antelope went to live in the grounds of the first secretary of the High Commission and grew into a fine animal until one day it just took off, never to be seen again. Likewise the Python, the wound healed, just disappeared.

When I moved on to Pendembu I had a scaly anteater, but he was not very sociable, so he won his freedom quickly. That was followed by a half-bred Siamese cat, which looked the real thing. She was a lovely animal, with one really bad habit, eating rats beneath my bed. She had kittens, a litter of four, which had to be put down unfortunately, for I could not find homes with Europeans and I would not trust them to the hands of anyone else. Mitzi survived my leave, and won the heart of my successor there, Pete, who would then not give her back.

After all the hunting in the savannah bush of Port Loko, there was none to be had in the thick jungle of Pendembu. It was just too arduous, cutting one's way through bush and then never seeing more than a dozen feet in front of one. I was somewhat at a loss for entertainment.

Apart from the Fathers the only Europeans were David and Pauline Bick. David was the Agricultural Officer. They were in their mid twenties and Pauline was pregnant. I spent many afternoons with Pauline while David was working, surveying coffee and cocao plantations which were the main crop of the area. David didn't drive, so I was on standby should Pauline need an urgent visit to hospital 50 miles away at Segbwema.

The military training ground in Segbwema was one attraction. There was a curry in the mess every Sunday and a swimming pool, built and paid for by the commercial companies. The major who was officer commanding, had brought his Labrador out with him, that alone proving him to be a fool. He allowed it to swim in the pool, until I protested. There was also a film on Saturday night; worth going to when company was so scarce and the round trip of a hundred miles on bad dirt roads was nothing to me then.

I went one night in smart shorts and knee socks, good shoes and a good white shirt, but no tie. My companion, one with the fitting name of Livingstone, also had no tie. We had another run-in with the pompous major Labrador owner, who told us that we were unwelcome without ties 'out of respect for the Queen'. He was on secondment from the British Army. Just to annoy him, I asked what the purpose of the camp was, knowing already that they took boys from the bush and taught them that they had two feet, a left and a right. 'Watching the border,' was his reply, 'strategic.' I could not resist pointing out that they were in fact fifty miles further from the border than me, and that they were on the wrong bank of the river to launch an attack on any insurgent army advancing down the main road from either Liberia or Senegal. They were there to recruit from the Mende tribe, from which most of the army came, while the police to balance power in the country, came from the Temne. A cunning British plan!

This was diamond country. The mines at Koidu run by de Beers produced mainly industrial stones, but there were occasional gem finds. Illicit digging and dealing was rife. A house would be built for the sole purpose of hiding a mine beneath. There was a whole industry trying to stamp out these pursuits and the mining company maintained its own security force. It was rumoured that they could be quite ruthless when finding illicit mines or dealers. Many packages stayed in my safe for a short time, of which I would know nothing. That was the Bank's rule. Packets were brought in, sealed in the presence of the owner and a receipt given for 'one packet, contents unknown'.

The Lebanese would tell me that it was a gold ring for the wife, or some other story. They usually wanted to stash the stones while they thought the security guards were on to them, but their fears were largely imaginary.

On my second tour, I was offered stones to buy, which I knew to be glass. Buying real stones would have been a crime, as I had no licence as a dealer. It was also illegal for them to sell me diamonds. The two Senegalese who tried this trick, may have thought they had real stones or they may have just been looking for a sucker. Either way, I had them arrested at the point of a .303 hunting rifle, and the police loved arresting such bad men. The following court case was a fiasco and took up several days of my life. The police charged them with illegal dealing, when they had not had diamonds at all but paste out of a cheap ring, so how could they have been dealing in stones? The police recharged them, this time for illegal mining of which they had no proof. The defence lawyer accused me of entrapment, which I objected to, and the judge, one of the last British judges in the country, obtained an apology for me, then threw the case out of court, saying that the police charges were incompetent. They should of course have been charged with deception if anything, but even that would have been difficult to prove.

Pendembu was a good farming area, producing coffee, cocoa beans, and oranges. The smell of the orange blossom was as the Yanks say, awesome, and on the journey to Segbwema I travelled through twenty miles of orange farms, breathing in the sweet loveliness.

It was also extremely hot. In the middle of the bush, there was no air. At night, the full moon seemed to be so close and large, that it appeared to radiate heat like the sun. The Bank was a long low bungalow, my quarters at one end, the Bank in the middle, with a produce store at the far end. The water came from a well, bucket by bucket and was boiled and filtered before being fit to drink. My bath water was heated each night in a large black pot, which a cannibal would have envied, then transferred by the night watchman to my bath in two gallon buckets, often with charcoal floating upon the top. The lights were Tilley pressure lamps, and buzzed and roared and threw out heat and a faint smell of paraffin, but they gave a good light. There was no mosquito screening, and long trousers and sleeves and knee length mosquito boots to protect from bites, were necessary. Night came early; it was dark by 18.30. I would bath then, the Tilley lamps sizzling, change into fresh clothes before sitting down to dinner cooked by my old retainer, 'the General'.

My evenings were spent in reading and listening to radio Liberia on my little battery set. The voice of Sam Cooke came over the air, sometimes clearly, sometimes distorted by the short wave atmospheric interference. 'Cupid' has remained one of my all time favourites, and reminds me of those long lonely tropical evenings even now. Ben E. King and 'Stand by Me', is another.

I learned to dress make, teaching myself from what books were available, and making my own patterns. I hand stitched everything. In this lonely and male dominated environment, it was one way that my femininity could express itself. I was to do more when I returned to Port Loko the next tour.

There were times when I feared for my sanity, a fear that was to become stronger as I grew older. Long, lonely nights under that damned burning moon, surrounded by an alien culture, in an alien body, the silence and isolation, was a torture; the denial of my real self, a burden, too full of fear to be born. I was so worried by this that I determined to try to do something about my sexuality when I returned to the UK on leave. I could not wait to leave that lonely station. My only friends were the young agricultural officer and his wife, David and Jan, but their nights were their own and not to be shared by me, so wrapped up in themselves were they. The tour was supposed to be eighteen months; after twenty I was finally relieved to return to the UK for a four and a half-month leave. I needed it badly, and raced down to the coast in one long hop, three hundred and fifty miles, all except sixty of them on dirt roads, nearly falling asleep at the wheel after three hundred miles. I carried a chief's bone and horn walking stick presented to me by a good African trader and friend, which was much admired on the plane.

CHAPTER 7.

It was some leave. I was twenty-two, money in my bank account. The world was mine, some of it at least. I had wanted to go skiing, but by the time I was relieved of my duties in Pendembu, the season was over.

Had I been a hot-blooded young man, I would have been out and about trying to pull the girls. Did I want to? Maybe, even now I am uncertain about the correct answer, but for what reason would I have wanted to? To lay them? Almost certainly not. To love them, without sex? Maybe. For their company? Certainly! Because it was expected of me? Probably. I have always wanted to conform and that has made life the more difficult, created more problems than it solved.

I lived in a sort of dream world. I moved between the sexes. I was outwardly female or male, but inside neither one. Whatever role I took, it had no permanence. I noticed girls. I looked at them, admired them. I was also comparing them to me. Learning how they wore their clothes, what jewellery they had, observing the fashions. I was more interested in being them and being with them, than having them on my arm.

I went to London twice as a woman, and carried it off. I stayed in a five star hotel on the south Devon coast and was pestered by an over attentive under manager. I stayed in Cambridge at the best hotel, and saw the town that had been home when at boarding school, in a new light. It made up for all those years there when I frankly didn't know who I was. I knew now, but not how to get where I wanted to be.

The more I investigated the female world in this way, the more I learned of the different emphasis on life and the view from the other side seemed as good as I knew it would. Automatically, seventy per cent of the population adopted a gentler more loving attitude to me when I was 'female.' Most men and many women, showed this different emphasis. I experienced that same sweetness that people showed me as a child when they confused my sex. And this attention was thrilling. I knew that had Redmayne known me only as a woman, he would not have been so disagreeable. If he had known of my inner turmoil however, he might have sacked me on the spot. I was riding a tightrope. The last thing I wanted was to be exposed in the tabloid press as sometimes happened then.

I was lucky. I was not tall as some transsexuals are, being only five and a half feet. My features were not particularly male, in that I didn't possess a thrusting jaw or protruding brows. I was slim, particularly after my illness abroad, and slipped into a size 10 easily. I was not very hairy and had no stubble shadow. In fact Pete in Africa had laughed at me, saying that I had less facial hair than Eumig as he called Dick's fiancee, Eunice. I seemed to fall into the role so naturally, that it wasn't a strain. I never experienced a bad moment when I feared discovery. As a female if confronted it was easy to fall into the helpless shyness that made men gentle and made me believable. It was a delightful world of gentleness and beauty, even though it was of necessity, very lonely. For example, leaving the University Arms Hotel in Cambridge one morning, the porter saluted, asked if I was taking my car and then brought it round to the front door for me. This extraordinary attention made me feel like a star, but was also potentially dangerous. Still, it gave me the adrenalin rush I needed and no doubt released endorphins that kept me from depression.

The worst time was coming out of it, back into a male reality, into a world that for me was filled with a self-loathing and a heaviness of heart, which at times filled me with utter despair. It was like walking from sunlight into the shade of a black cloud. I felt unclean and loathed myself both for being male, and for indulging in what anyone else would see as bizarre behaviour.

One of the worst facets of my male life was that I could not share my inner thoughts with anyone. Therefore, I remained aloof, apart, out of things, a watcher, and seldom the player. It was a cliché that, in a room full of people, I would be alone even if people were talking to me. Half my mind was away in that other world. It was uncanny; there was this barrier around me, like the Mekon's capsule in Dan Dare, insulating me from the world. That was due partly to the doubt I had in my mind about my sanity. I could not come to terms with the obsession I had with femininity and had no idea that many others shared the way I felt. No doctor that I had so far spoken to, gave me any understanding of myself and the position I occupied in society. Not one, apart from the RAF selection doctor who seemed a complete idiot, had said 'it is a known syndrome'. Of course I had read of cases in the papers. I knew that sex change had been a possibility for some, so could not understand why it was denied to me. The perverse argument was therefore, that I was different to transsexuals and, that worried me. Would I turn into some other kind of deviant, perhaps a child molester? I had no tendencies towards that, but what then would I be? What damage would this mental agony cause? What would happen to me when mentally I could no longer carry this burden? It was extremely worrying. Cut off from the rest of humanity, the insane asylum seemed to beckon. I started to self mutilate again, usually with needles and piercing, sometimes burning myself with a cigarette. I accepted danger, deliberately sought danger, for example driving to the limit. I had some close shaves which only quick reactions saved me from. It was another facet of my troubled mind. Adrenalin became a drug that I needed, and to raise the adrenalin I needed danger. It would be a further fourteen years before a doctor would put the whole thing in perspective and the medical profession would at last show compassion and begin to treat me.

There was therefore unquenchable loneliness and sadness with intervals of extreme pleasure like sunbeams in a stormy sky. I managed the downs in that leave by treating myself well and an analogy would be retail therapy. I had a car on hire for the whole time, bar the two weeks when the family all went to Spain.

Sitges, south of Barcelona, was a much nicer place then, but no real thrill, because I was having difficulty relating to my family, having been apart from them for twenty-one months and having this awful secret within me.

We stayed in a town villa of some three storeys, just a few metres from the north beach. The English tenant had been a minor racing driver and car tester for Jaguar. His wife was rather blowsy, and had the look of the gin bottle about her, that bloating and puffiness that is usually a give-away. They were a pleasant family though. Their daughter was thrust towards me, but I did not bite the bait. My brother was faintly puzzled. He would have 'given her one,' not the phrase then, but the meaning was the same, and my father thought she was wonderful. I didn't. She was plump, slightly ungainly, but for all that, was a nice looking and well-mannered girl. We had little in common, not even lust to light the spark. I sensed that she wanted something that I knew I could not provide. She could have been the most beautiful woman, with the most wonderful personality and intellect, but I would still not have lusted after her. I would have wanted to be her. The highlight was the flower festival, when certain streets decorated the roads with carpets of flower heads. We entered into this and made a creditable design.

Back in England, with the freedom a thick wallet and a car could give me, I had a better time. I visited friends, those I had known before Africa, and some I had made over there who were on leave too. I would drive from Surrey to Devon and back in a day, or go off for a few days at a time. Motoring was still an utter joy. There were few jams, hardly ever a convoy of more than two or three cars, even on trunk routes, single carriageways then. The A303 a dreadful road now, was then an absolute joy. A speeding fine was a rarity especially if you kept an eye on the mirror, for that was the only way the police could catch you. Sometimes I would surprise mother with a shopping trip, the theatre, or a visit to the seaside. I introduced my widowed aunt at Runfold to the Mini car. She loved it, having given up motoring years before. In the small circle of her drive, she sat in the driver's seat, found reverse and did half a dozen circuits at high speed backwards. I suggested that she now try a bit of more normal forwards driving or some manoeuvres, but she declined. 'No, I think I have done enough,' she said. I was relieved. Six months later she had bought her own Mini and set herself free much to the consternation of her sons and other motorists. It was some small payment for her hospitality when I was convalescent 15 years earlier.

My GP referred me to a Harley Street psychiatrist, who proved more afraid of me, than I was of unburdening to him. He sported a fancy French name and may have come from the Channel Islands. He asked me lots of questions, was clearly unsympathetic and offered nothing. He asked whether I had been in public as a woman and I confessed that I had. He advised me that it was a crime, that I could be arrested and sent to prison, all of which I knew, though why it should not apply to women who dressed as men, I could not understand. He forbade me to ever appear before him cross-dressed. I asked why, and he admitted he would 'suffer embarrassment.' I wondered why he was in the business and why I had been referred to him. He was a wimp, ill suited to the trade. I would not call psychiatry a calling or a career, nor yet a science. I believe it to be filled with too many theorists, experimenters with human suffering, or else out and out charlatans, to be granted anymore than that status.

Chaucer living now, would have a 'psychiatrists tale' along with an 'estate agents' and a 'motor traders'. There are good practitioners of the art, but it is a matter of luck whether one finds the right one. The corpses of those this 'science' has failed, pave its way. I never went back. Even now, the quasi psychiatrists, those who set themselves up as counsellors, prey on the vulnerable and often do as much damage as good. I shudder, every time I hear the words psychiatry or counselling. I shake my head, every time counselling is offered after some public or private trauma. We never had that in the Second World War. It is the nature of the human being that the more it receives, the more it desires, whether it be money, sex, learning or the support of others. For example, sympathy given, can suck all the resilience out of a person, and turn them into 'a victim'.

I received the bill for my Harley St. consultation, after I had returned to Africa, twenty-five pounds, which at that time was money. I paid it, thanked him for nothing, and settled back into my limbo life. It is only lately that Harley St. has been exposed for harbouring all sorts of charlatans.

It was 1962 and swinging London excited me, the shops the theatres, the bustle, more than it does now. As it has become cosmopolitan, it has become less friendly. Then it was the capital of Britain, now it is a World City. I walked past St Martin's in the Field one night, having been to see 'The Mousetrap', still running even now in the new millennium. I lingered on the steps just watching the passers-by, the traffic around Trafalgar Square, people walking down towards the Thames on a fine evening and was nearly picked up by a young priest who thought I had come to help. At that time, there was a soup kitchen, a few beds in the crypt, but now we would need Westminster Abbey and St. Paul's to house the homeless, mainly fostered children from broken homes, who live on our streets.

The anonymity of the great city suited me. There I was like all the rest, alone and friendless, or so it seemed and amongst the mass, safe from eyes that would see too much. Thirty years later, I would again find this same freedom just a stone's throw from where I then stood.

I spent time with David and Pauline, my Pendembu friends, at their parents home in Poole and in Perranporth. I had become more a friend of Pauline rather than David. I suppose a natural affinity brought us together, just as women tend to make friends of other women. After a night out and while David was parking the car, she tried to seduce me. I was really quite shocked and completely froze. I wondered afterwards whether she was merely testing out this strange male friend. They later went off to Australasia.

At last I had to go back to Africa. I went to head office in Gracechurch Street in the City of London, to get my posting and to be told what they expected of me once I was back in the Dark Continent. I was surprised to find that the posting would be Port Loko again. There were worse places, Pendembu for one and I had friends in Port Loko. It was a bit like going home therefore. They wanted me to get the overdrafts into order. That was easily said, but not so easily done, not when your customers had less ethics than a bunch of pirates.

The unpalatable truth that the Bank would not accept, was that ninety per cent of our esteemed customers, should never have had overdrafts in the first place, but a bank makes its money by giving overdrafts and loans. We had given overdrafts, a working fluid loan, when we should really have given loans proper. In a loan, the customer borrows money for business development, and repays at a set rate. There is a psychological difference. An overdraft becomes part of a person's own finance in the mind of a borrower, while a loan is a debt to be repaid. Credit cards today, have the same effect as overdrafts. They are dangerous, even for intelligent people, and should only be given to long established and trusted customers. The Chairman of Barclays Bank has advised his children never to use credit on a credit card. But of course, the credit card companies do not make a profit out of the sane who repay on time, they make a profit from the profligate who use their credit to the limit and repay the minimum.

Port Loko was a microcosm of the banking world. Most of the bank's debtors, were untrustworthy, poor and bad traders, in a place with no profitable future. An overdraft has to be repaid, usually monthly; the bank manager may then give a further overdraft if he or she considers the borrower a good risk. The other rule observed by the bank was, any overdraft that remained on the books for a continual twelve months, i.e., never fully repaid, became a bad debt. That could lead on to seizure of stocks, bankruptcy proceedings and all the other ways of recovering an advance.

How these Lebanese managed it, was to repay by temporarily borrowing from their friends. They would then draw money on their new overdraft to repay them. It was a reciprocal arrangement, and they all played it. Other managers turned a blind eye to this chicanery, I tried to do something about it. I was warned off by Khalil. He sat in my office, as oily as only he could be, wheedling like a kindly uncle with a demanding child, and told me that they would leave the bank en masse if I persisted. Trying to bring these customers into line could spell disaster and a whole bundle of bad debts in a close knit Lebanese expatriate society. It was then, like walking a tightrope, trying to get all these Levantine pirates to play by the rules and to make the bank show a profit. Realistically, as long as they paid the interest, our branch losses were minimal and may have resulted in spin off benefits elsewhere in the network.

Port Loko never did make a profit, nor would it ever, I said in my first quarterly report, until African man got out of his hammock, stopped playing draughts, the male national pastime, played at a furious speed and very skilfully, and go instead to the fields with number three wife to work the land. African man, was like the male lion, lazy and a leach upon the efforts of his women, who worked the fields, marketed the produce, brought up the children, cooked, cleaned, carried the wood for the fire, the water to drink. The report was like a bomb, ready to explode should it have got into the wrong hands. If the mail had been intercepted and, after Independence, anything would soon become possible, the government might have seized the bank and all its assets, glad of an excuse. All this was explained to me in a letter from HO., but they added that I had summed up the problem of Africa in a few lines.

This time there was no Bob to amuse me, but there was John Oliphant. He was the Agriculture Officer, and a 'coaster' of some years. He liked to boast of his time in the desert, capturing a platoon of Italians single-handed. He was an ebullient character with a commanding manner that upset some. I liked him. With John I did different things, helped make a boat, went to the cinema at the iron mine, drank a few beers, listened to music, and we read quietly together in the cooling heat of the evening.

When he went home, there was Tim Marks to take his place. We did other things, tore his VW Beetle apart, and rebuilt it, walked, ate black pudding, peanut butter for tea, and smoked. Tim was a good guy, but was soon in difficulties with corrupt staff. I recognised that his chief clerk was depositing far more than his salary and mentioned it to Tim. I was proved right when the books were examined in the Department. There was fraud and cash missing.

This meant an endless court case, and threats on my life. The clerk, out on bail, stopped me in the street and said he would kill me. I told him I would shoot him with the twelve bore. Nothing happened. In the end he was found guilty and sent to prison.

Before Tim went home, he had to dispose of his spaniel. The poor creature was slightly demented, tormented in the extreme by ticks. As soon as we rid it of these revolting blood suckers, their bodies a dark purple filled with their host's blood, more would appear. There was nothing to do but shoot the poor thing and Tim asked me whether I would do it? Because he was a good friend, and because I knew that someone had to do this for him, I agreed. There was no one else. My reply was made without hesitation, but my heart pounded as I assented. Rocky was a typical spaniel, affectionate, nervous and slightly dotty. He treated me with the same love he had for Tim, so it was as much of a blow to me in many ways. I stood with the poor animal in Tim's bungalow garden, in the silence of the afternoon, as Tim walked away into the house. In the shade, atop the bluff on which the bungalow stood, the animal sat looking up at me with eyes like brown marbles. It was cool; the sun that penetrated the bamboo had lost its power, the light restful with all the quality of a sunlit cathedral. Rocky had complete trust in me, indeed sometimes seemed to love me more than his master. His silky ears fell at the side of his head and I touched them just once more. I put the .22 to his head and pulled the trigger. Death was instantaneous. Poor Rocky dropped like a stone without one twitch. I walked away, told Tim that it was done, then walked out into the sun of the front garden while Tim saw to the burial. I put the gun in the car, and sat in the sun upon the front stoop, chest heaving. My head was full of pain.

I returned to Tim's living room as he came in the French windows. We were both crying. I would dearly have liked to hold him and give him comfort, but instead, like true men of the British Raj we stood apart, gulped, took hold of our emotions and found something to occupy us. Life can be a bastard, especially when you can't off load your responsibilities elsewhere. I can see those trusting eyes still.

A few months later, the local padre who had left me quite alone once I had told him I was an atheist and that therefore, I would not be attending church, asked me to come to his compound. He had a big pit, into which he and the two missionary nurses threw all their waste. In the pit was a pye-dog, the local mongrel breed, emaciated and hairless. There was no helping it; it just had to be put down. The padre deserted the scene, leaving the atheist to do God's work. The shot from about twenty feet was not difficult, but I wanted to make sure that the first shot counted. The animal was in so much distress that it remained stock still making an easy target. The bullet hit accurately. The animal collapsed, a neat hole between the eyes, but the hollow bullet would have destroyed its brain. For good measure, I put two more shots into the head. Sure that the job was done, I was leaving as the padre reappeared.

'Will you dispose of it for us?'

'Haven't I done enough?' I retorted. I was really angry. Did he think that I liked doing this? Cur it may have been, but it was a creature, shot in cold blood and doing it drained me. I got into my car and drove away. Who better was there anyway, than a priest to attend to a burial? He could dig a grave as well as I. He was as susceptible to disease as I. We never spoke again. I have little respect for those who take the easy way and don't get to grips with the sordid affairs of life.

We went shooting; wild duck, the shooters sitting in dugout canoes poled by Africans standing up in the stern. It was a precarious craft and it did not do to rock the boat. Abdul Khalil, the bank's landlord had wanted to come for months and reluctantly, I agreed to take him. While not fat, he was portly. He squeezed himself into the narrow boat with difficulty and some fear. He had expected a proper boat, propelled by a bank of oars. The swamps were much like the Norfolk Broads, but hotter, cleaner and with crocodiles and snakes. The game was plentiful and one could soon get a good bag.

Abdul could not believe his fortune in having access to all this free meat. The dark, sly little eyes were alight with excitement. Unfortunately, Abdul chose to fire a broad side, rather than the bow shot he had been told to do. The kick was enough to capsize the craft, tipping out the canoe man and old Abdul. There was a yell of dismay. A terrorised landlord was floundering around expecting to be seized by jaws filled with rows of jagged teeth. He yelled abuse at the boatman, which the African returned with hurt dignity. To complete his tribulation, my friends laughed.

I could see as I approached in my canoe, just how distressed he was. He had fear, but he had also lost his dignity and although he was one of the biggest rogues in the district, I felt for him. I helped him to the bank, which meant that first I had to land and wade out to him. There was of course some risk. These swamplands were home to many snakes and in particular, poisonous water snakes. I had also seen one or two crocodile. My show of bravado struck awe in my companions and I enjoyed their admiration for my gay abandon as I lead a distraught Abdul to the shore.

We called it a day. We had enough birds anyway. Poor Khalil. He had long wanted to join our European shooting parties, but it had ended in disaster. I don't think he ever forgave me. Somerset Maughan would have had him reek a subtle and terrible revenge. The meal that he would later give for me, proved to be revenge indeed.

Guns are extremely dangerous. I had found that out earlier when Bob and I were walking through the bush. I had a five shot repeater on a sling over my shoulder. This is a terrible weapon, good for gangster movies and armed robbery, but little use for shooting game. As I stepped across some ants on the march, the sling slipped from my shoulder, the gun fell to the ground on the butt and as we both dived to the ground, went off with the shock of the fall. Luckily it only fired once. I learned the lesson, never walk with a shell in the breach.

On another occasion, an acquaintance who told us he had been a small arms instructor in the army, carried a gun in the same way while on a river launch. I asked whether the safety catch was on, and he said it was. I was relieved, as he steadied it with his thumb in the trigger guard. A few minutes later, the gun exploded, almost parting his hair at the back of his head and blew a hole through the roof right behind the cox. We were not impressed.

I shudder now at those shooting parties, regret my involvement in a blood sport, but I cannot undo what is done. Were I a Christian, particularly a Catholic, I would ask God's forgiveness and my conscience would be salved. As an athiest, I hold that hurt still. It was part of my camouflage, the daring white hunter, a bit of an odd ball, but wanting to be female? Absurd!

Abdul's wife was a smiling Moslem woman, who always bustled away when I visited his shop, to return with thick Arabic coffee or a beer or some sticky and incredibly sweet cake. There was no doubt, that whereas Khalil tolerated and toadied to me because he owed us money, she actually liked me. Consequently, when Khalil was away in Freetown doing 'the business', which I believe involved a few of the street girls, she relied on me if there was any emergency although her brothers-in-law were close by. I sometimes wondered whether she made problems so that I would visit, like asking me to collect the day's takings, which could have awaited Abdul's return.

One morning, I was in the office, checking the books, when in burst the Khalil's head boy. 'Missy Khalil, say come quick, some bad ting.' He had gone before I could reply. I chased up the street, leaving the safe open, and shouting at my messenger, Daramy Mansaray, to guard it.

Arriving at the shop, I found the place deserted, then the boy reappeared, beckoning me through to the Khalil compound that lay behind the shop. Arriving there, I found Mrs K her head swathed as usual in the headscarf, with the double barrel shot gun in her hands. It was a strange sight, and I wondered what was going on. She thrust it at me.

'Bad beef, in lavatory, you shoot.'

'What bad beef?' I asked sensibly.

'Bad bad beef.' The answer came back like a Greek chorus from the three or four with her.

Deciding that I would have to see for myself, I took the gun and made for the tin khazi. Reaching the door, I took in the scene, the expectant audience, some peeping over the corrugated iron fence. Sun filled the compound, lighting the rust and dust, the open cooking fire I would crouch round a few weeks later, the cur lying quietly in the shade and wondered what the hell could be inside. This part of Africa was not known for large game. There were no lions, though in the east there were leopards. There were a few elephant fifty miles north, but there was certainly no elephant in this small and rusting thunder box. There were a few bush buffaloes, like a water buffalo but smaller and very dangerous indeed. Hunting them, one could become the hunted, for they would circle around behind you and attack, but it could not be one of them. It could only be a snake and I was confident of dealing with any snake, especially with a shotgun in my hands.

Fearlessly the great white hunter, clad in black shoes, smart white knee socks, white shorts and white shirt, blonde hair shining beneath the strong sunlight, kicked open the door of the hut in true commando fashion. Before me, rising on its coil from the floor in front of the seat was a cobra, its neck fanned out in threat, head swaying and hissing. The head was at my chest height and I reckoned the beautiful specimen to be about ten feet long. The hood was almost six inches wide. It was a very frightening animal. Its long black tongue flicked out, savouring my scent. I was at the ready, feet spread, weapon to my shoulder and it seemed we were eyeball to eyeball. I fired number one barrel and the snake appeared to dodge the shot, its head swaying off to one side by about twelve inches, a way they have as do owls, of assessing range. I believed it was just about to spit poison into my eyes. I swear it actually moved again, as I fired. Realising that it was now very angry, who wouldn't be, being shot at on the loo, I pulled trigger number two with no result.

I retreated to examine the weapon and when I broke open the chamber, found that only one barrel had been loaded. By the time I had reloaded and returned to the front, kicking open the door again, the enemy had evacuated the battlefield, never to be seen again. The lesson was, with guns trust no one but yourself.

On another day, on my way to get a few bush fowl for the larder, I heard firing as I passed by the chief's barri, the open sided meetinghouse. The chief's hunter was shooting at something in the trees and I stopped to investigate. They pointed out a large green snake about twenty feet up, which the chief had demanded killed. He invited me to have a shot. With one shell, the poor creature landed at his feet in three pieces, cut in two places by the bird shot fired at short range. It was a spectacular demonstration of my prowess. A few days later, a present of fruit arrived at my flat, the chief's thanks for my services and he invited me to be one of the judges in the Miss Port Loko competition, which would be a preliminary to Miss World. Fame at last.

The great night came. The grand event took place in the barri, the elite sitting around the walls inside and the whole town standing outside peering into the poorly lit interior. There was much excitement. Africans love an event. They have in their nature, a curious mixture of deference and delight at people's discomfiture. At one moment they would be offended if the chief were not shown deference, but if the same chief slid on a slug of which there were many, there would be delighted sniggers.

None of the girls I was to see, would have stood an earthly, let alone a Worldly, but we picked one. None of them could understand any of my questions that were meant to elucidate whether they liked horses, helped old people, or wanted to feed the starving. Probably none of them had ever spoken to a European before. They were as embarrassed by me, as I was by them. It was a night to forget, I thought then. I would not have missed it for the world, now.

No great tennis player, I was however inveigled into being captain of the expatriate team. Our worst match was playing the local Africans, made up of the by now, black District Officer, the local Public Works manager, and several other local civil servants. Half the town had turned out to watch the show that took place on the town court, right in the centre, shaded by tulip trees. Of course, they were all baying for our defeat, but we managed to win, much to our satisfaction. They took it very well, saying 'We will beat you next time, old boy,' in true British fashion. We bought drinks for their side that had soon swelled by the addition of ball boys, umpires and non-playing captains.

We played the iron mine at Marampa, an all white affair. As captain I had to play the opposing captain, a very aggressive character, thin and bearded. The game was very well balanced, and the final set stood at 27 - 28 when the rest of my team came to cheer me on. With their coaching from the side lines, much to my opponents indignation, I finally won at 38 - 36. At the get together afterwards, he would not speak to me. I accused him of being a poor looser and of not showing British sportsmanship. We didn't bother with a return match.

I was hit by sickness. I'd had a small scratch on my ankle that I ignored. It seemed to heal, the skin forming across the top, but it itched like the devil, then turned an angry red. I decided to lance it, and found that there was now a cavity quarter of an inch round and deep, filled with maggots. I cleaned it out, filled it with some antiseptic and it healed again, only to break out some days later. The maggots were back, and not far off the bone. I sought out the doctor, who told me to take better care of myself, ordered me to soak my foot in hot brine three times a day and to fill the cavity with salt. It hurt. It was a constant smarting sore for three days, but then suddenly it started to get better. The cavity grew smaller, and the pain diminished. In a week it had healed. I watched anxiously for the thing to break out again, but this time all was well.

I contracted a foot fungus, not athletes foot, something far more sinister and violent that soon covered a quarter of my foot. It was a hot and itching rash. The doctor, an old coaster of many years experience, made up some ointment that cured it quite quickly. He admonished me for going without socks, or stockings as he called the traditional expat knee socks. These old coasters were very hard unforgiving men. In the old days they had to be to survive. Sickness was not easily cured before new drugs were found, so one was careful with hygiene and lifestyle in their day.

The natives were restless, so one showed them who was master, dignity was maintained, respect demanded. What we now see as an arrogance was as much a defence. Dress mattered, to show the natives that we were invincible and to preserve our own health. After that, I made sure my feet were properly clad and cosseted.

A week later, I stabbed my wrist with the filing spike, so that as I raised my arm, the spike rose with it. I pulled the spike out from a depth of about half an inch, and blood spurted in a stream. I closed the wound with a thumb, went up stairs and washed. The bleeding stopped. After six days I was aware of a throbbing in my wrist and on examining my arm, found that my veins from wrist to above the elbow had turned greeny-black. I did nothing until by chance bumping into the mission nurses, they noticed and told me to go to hospital, saying that if it reached my armpit it would be too late.

The Doctor had gone to Freetown, but the dispenser gave me a shot of antibiotics and some pills to take, followed by a shot of anti-tetanus. Everything seemed well again until one night I awoke, my whole body itching. If I touched my face, a blister would appear. I was frightened. At eight in the morning, I went to the Doctor's house. She was a charming and good looking Creole married to Mr Williams, the Creole Public Works Officer. When she opened the door and saw me, she knew at once what had happened, I had been given the wrong tetanus jab.

'Go to the hospital with this,' she wrote a prescription, 'see the dispenser. He will give you two injections, antihistamine and adrenaline. You will have five minutes only to get home before the adrenaline hits, then you will pass out, so you better move quickly. Can you do that?'

This all seemed to be turning into a drama, I thought, and she was exaggerating. I had the necessary at the hospital, exposing the bum of the British Raj to the natives once more, returned to the car and simply whizzed down to the bank. As I parked, my breathing rate had increased. I walked into the bank, twiddled the combinations and told the clerk to close up. Daramy would stay to tell people to come back tomorrow, and then I walked up the stairs to the flat, pulling myself up on the banister the last few steps. I told the steward to cancel lunch, staggered into the bedroom, let my clothes fall to the floor, clambered underneath the sheet and was gone, completely knocked out.

I was aware later that John stood in the door of the bedroom, someone else hovering behind him. He spoke, then whatever reply I gave made him laugh. I just turned over and slept again. He came back in the evening after tennis, just as I was coming round. I was better, the blisters gone, though there were red wheals. He stayed with me an hour, then I slept again till daybreak.

Over the next year, I suffered from boils, sometimes three at a time, on face, legs and neck, all as a result of that damned filing spike. They lasted till well after I was back in the UK permanently.

I was I in Port Loko when President Kennedy died. I heard the news via the overseas service, in the early morning of a November day, which broke there clean and fresh, the sky a clear blue stretching to meet the mangrove swamps away in the distance. I was leaning on the red painted balustrade, watching smoke spirals rising from the Bangura's cooking fires, next door. One of the wives was already pounding cassava with a large pole and a huge wooden mortar. The women sometimes spent an hour at a time pounding these roots to a pulp, sometimes two using one mortar. The product would then be used in thickening stews or could be left to ferment when it gave off a terrible lavatorial smell.

I savoured the morning, like a disturbed leopard, listened to the sound of distance, flared my nostrils, sucking in the scent of early morning Africa. Wood smoke, that so evocative scent, a faint smell of oranges from the wagon unloading at the market, all overladen with the decaying tropical forest smell of Africa. One could sometimes shiver in the comparative cool of morning. I shivered now. I could not believe the news. It was as if my heart stopped. I staggered. Tears filled my eyes for a man I had never known, and of whom I knew little. I had seen film of his 'Ich bin ein Berliner' speech, so inspiring, no matter that it actually translated as 'I am a doughnut', which fact the Germans had very politely ignored. They and the world accepted the sentiment.

I raised the flag to half-mast and wondered why someone had assassinated him? We still don't know. One of the boys from the 'Peace Corps', Kennedy's organisation which was to sow the seed of a new caring USA, mistook my half mast flag, for one of celebration because I had expressed some anti American sentiments. Another pointed out to this Rifle Association, shit kicker from Ohio, that it was a sign of respect.

The Americans didn't take criticism very well, but liked to make it of others, particularly Imperialist Limeys. That morning is still clear as a bell in my memory, as it is in the memory of many others, and it is a matter of wonder to me that so many were so affected by an intense sense of loss for someone so remote, so flawed, and so untested. It happened again with Princess Diana, but she was a living victim of all those fairy tales in which the beautiful princess is persecuted by the wicked Royal Family.

I liked the Americans. They were nice boys and a welcome addition to our little western community. However, some of their views of the world struck me as extremely naive. They propounded the view that Africa was a dump, and that as its custodians for nearly two hundred years, we British were culpable. That sort of statement was all I needed to launch forth into a counter attack. I pointed out, that we British had ended the slave trade, landing many freed slaves at Freetown, from whence the place gets its name, many years before their bloody civil war and the Gettysburg address. It was also a fact, that life expectancy in Africa for the native population and even more so, Europeans, had been a very short time indeed. In 1900 there had been no less than five Governors of the colony, three of whom had died in the post. The country was 'the white man's grave', and it was therefore not until medicine improved after the First World war, that any real progress was made in developing the country. Unlike other foreign stations, West Africa possessed no hill station with a more temperate climate for Europeans to retire to and recuperate in. I also said that unlike the whites in America, we had not killed off most of the indigenous population, committing an unforgivable genocide, nor driven the remainder from their homes. They had destroyed the 'human beings' culture of the Native American that recognised each being as a temporary resident of the planet, whose duty it was to leave it as he found it. They killed off all the game, as they had done with the Native Americans. There were other accusations too, of Empire. I pointed out that they too had colonies, Puerto Rico, Philippines, Panama, Costa Rica, and until Castro, Cuba governed by a Dictator financed by the American Mafia. Indeed, the continent of North America could be considered one large Empire, like the USSR was at that time. I added that but for the Europeans, there would never have been Americans. It was a surprise how little they knew of the atrocities they had committed in subjugating the Philippines, or against the Spanish in Mexico, their savage and brutal genocide of the Indian, and even of their fellow Americans in the Civil war and after.

They had, I said, committed these crimes in what were more enlightened times than when Britain had made its acquisitions of Canada, India, the East and West Indies, the Antipodes and our toe holds in Africa. I gave them a good history lesson, even lent them back their own books to read, supplied by the Peace Corps for their R and R, but left unread, where much of this could be found. Then there was much mileage in two world wars, when they had waited until the last minute to recognise the evil, and to engage the enemy. It was I said, not until mighty America was itself attacked that it joined forces against the evils of Hitler and the rampant Japanese Empire.

As a final insult, answering their challenges, we beat them at tennis. They then chose a sport that they assumed we would not play, basketball, but were amazed to find that we beat them at that too, and I personally scored five goals or whatever they call them. My impression was that they were soft, completely lacking in the frontier spirit that they deluded themselves they possessed. They were also extremely parochial, an Ohioan knowing nothing of New York or Tennessee. Reading Bill Bryson's essays on his own people, thirty years later, he confirms my views of his American brothers.

In spite of my disputatious nature, we actually got on very well, and though these boys were ill informed, they were not unintelligent. It was a surprise to me that they knew so little history, even their own. They had been taught that they were a 'brave people' full of 'frontier spirit'. They knew that God was on their side and America was God's own country. They knew of events like 'Custer's last stand, saw the man as a hero, rather than as the fool with delusions of grandeur, knew of the 'Alamo', but not of the Imperialist policies that had promoted the battle. It was the same with the world wars, they only knew of the 'feats of arms' of their nation, not the struggle that had lead up to their point of entry.

They lived in a world of make believe, and I think they still do. They boasted that they had never been defeated, but a new realism, a crushing blow, a supreme defeat was just around history's corner in the form of the Vietnam war, that delivered a lesson necessary to bring them to adulthood as citizens of the world. Disney time would soon be over. Reality was dawning but would not be permanent. Nor would America learn anymore about the World outside its shores. Iraq and Afghanistan has shown that they have still learned nothing. It has been a relief to me that in 2013 this nation, the United Kingdom voted in Parliament to stay out of the Syrian conflict and that resulted in the US deciding also to stand and watch. It maybe, that the US and the UK are learning at last, not to interfere. We only make things worse.

I descended to the bank and Daramy helped open up. I went back for breakfast. If I were lucky I would eat pawpaw with lime juice, then some toast with marmalade or Marmite.

The town was a Somerset Maugham set. There were all his characters living there and I could have been an excellent one myself. The place had a feel to it, the atmosphere of the tropical world of long ago. You could drift down the river and see the old slave stations, ships' muzzle loading cannons still to be seen. I bought a fast riverboat and explored, then allowed Daramy a month away with it as captain, to make his fortune. Whether he did or not, I don't know, he said that business was really bad, but others said he had made plenty. I did not mind.

Daramy was a special friend, very loyal, a retainer but money would have been too much of a temptation for him to resist. He paid me just enough to cover running expenses. We had many good moments together, hunting, on long car journeys and together in the bank, where he was the one person more or less trustworthy. He liked to laugh and we laughed together. If I had trouble on the road with an African driver, he would sort it out so that the driver and I parted friends. He had a trust in me and I in him. We were the fastest things on the road and he loved it. The adrenaline of chasing down a lorry, the dust from its wake thicker than any London fog, would make him tense up, his eyes wide, his mouth agape and as we burst by, bumping the ruts, skidding our way out of the unmarked edge of the dirt road into sunlight and clarity once more, he would burst into laughter, wind down his window and then assume a look of intense superiority over the defeat of the lorry driver. I think of him still.

Alas, poor Sierra Leone. Its beautiful name has now taken on another sinister connotation. Its rulers have filched the riches it possesses. Corruption has infected its people as in the rest of the continent. The laws we gave them have not succeeded in protecting the innocent from mutilation, slavery, rape, and murder. It could be one of the stars of Africa, but greed has made it a place of cruelty and shame, so much so that the people pray for the British to return. Daramy always told me it would turn out this way, but I, not knowing the African psyche so well, would not believe him. That same river that I explored, became the lair of the West End Boys, the infamous, drug crazed bandits who later captured British soldiers. Thankfully a brilliant rescue was performed by our own forces, killing most of the hostage takers.

Africa then, in the early 1960s, was a place of hope. The colonial Governments had taken people from the bronze age to the 20th Century and given every man and woman rights. Unfortunately the dawn was followed all too soon by an eclipse and darkness descended. This darkness fifty years later is still flitting across the continent and savagery persists.

CHAPTER 8.

Driving in the dry season was hell. Imagine more heat than on the hottest English summer day, add to this liberal supplies of flour fine, red laterite dust, a road full of gravel and bumps, African lorry drivers screaming towards you rocking and swerving on twisting roads, trailing clouds of impenetrable dust in their wake. Deep bush often lies on either side, so that the only visible sky is a narrow strip directly above the roadway. There is dark shadow in the thick undergrowth. The jungle on each side of the road is no longer green; dust has coloured all the plants terracotta red. The rushing air is laden with the smell of the rain forest, pungent, decaying; the detritus of the natural world gradually festering into compost to feed the luxuriant growth.

It can appear an alien and frightening place, yet at this time, just before and a few years after Independence, there is no need to fear. The natives, particularly in the bush are friendly, still in awe of the white man, who represents peace, authority and justice. There are few dangerous carnivores. There are noxious insects, tsetse fly, mosquitos and a thousand more unknown biting creatures that will poison your system but modern drugs take care of most infections. Snakes were the most visible danger, feared by many, but with care they were harmless unless threatened by a misplaced boot. Even then, if they hear you coming, they will usually move away.

But there is loneliness, there are sounds of unknown animals and, as in the entire world, mankind always presents the possibility of danger. It is still a mysterious continent. There had been cases in the local paper of leopard and crocodile societies killing, mutilating and supposedly eating victims. Indeed Daramy will not go to certain areas where cases have occurred, to the North of Port Loko and where thirty years later rebels emerge, bloody and cruel, with it is said, cannibalistic tendencies. They believe that by eating the heart of a respected victim, they will become stronger. Mulai, our junior boy in Freetown has the filed front teeth of the cannibal, the practise of his tribe in the East of the country. We tease him about it, and hope he won't eat us.

Part of my duty was to fetch the bullion. My branch tended to pay out, rather than take in money, because my customers were mostly small farmers and traders whose produce was purchased by large organisations with headquarters in Freetown. They have labour to pay and purchase palm oil and rice around Port Loko, coffee and cocao beans around Pendembu. The iron mine of Marampa and the diamond mines of Koidu are also wealth creators. Large amounts were therefore transferred, much of it in coin, because the Africans do not like notes that are too easily eaten by termites. I could have let someone else fetch the bullion for me, one or other of the expats, but it paid well and was a handy addition to my salary. Anyway, it gave me a chance to see someone else in another district, and relieved the monotony. Going to Freetown, I could also do essential shopping for food items not available locally, drink for entertaining or clothes, records and other luxuries. I usually took Daramy and carried the .22 rifle.

The unmettled roads form ridges which run across the track at right angles to the traffic direction. These ridges are called corrugations and make a surface very similar to corrugated iron. They can be large or small and no one quite understands the mechanics of how they form. They are straight, even at the sides where less traffic occurs. At ten miles an hour, they were bearable, between fifteen and fifty, the car felt as though it would shake to bits, so I tried to go everywhere at sixty or seventy. Daramy said I 'savvy drive fine', and told a lorry driver when we stopped at a wayside bar, that 'the Massa savvy corner, like no udder'.

In Pendembu I was lent a Jeep by Assaf to fetch the bullion, when my car was off the road. It was the end of the dry, the roads never dustier. The vehicle was open sided, no top. The floor proved to be full of holes. Dust poured in all over me, and I arrived home completely red, from top to bottom, white shorts turned red, socks turned red, only my shoes were a peculiar shade of black. I had tied a handkerchief across my nose and mouth to keep the dust out and when I removed it there was a patch of skin reasonably clean. I would wait for the rains before I used the jeep again. Mrs Assaf, who was also my next door neighbour, thought it very funny.

At the end of May the rains began. They were first heralded by the 4pm storm. Clouds would suddenly gather out of a clear sky. The humidity rose into the nineties and the clouds within half an hour had changed from cream to deep purple. A flash, a clap of thunder and spots of rain, then a torrent, sometimes hail, huge hailstones. The roads still hot from the burning sun would turn the rain to steam. People would stand in the rain, welcoming the deluge that had ended a six or seven month drought. Leaks would appear in previously sound roofs. The monsoon drains would fill, overflow, choked by the dry season's debris, bottles, orange peel, sticks and paper. The road ran red with the tide of laterite dust and then just as suddenly the rain had stopped. Clouds disappeared as though having emptied and done their duty. The sun warmed the soil again. Clothes dried on ones body. The birds sang and people moved about. All was clean, the atmosphere fresh, the air smelled pure and was clear to the horizon. If one had stayed out in the rain, ones skin lost the usual stickiness caused by living in a perpetual Turkish bath.

In the rainy season, the roads could turn into rivers, or a sea of mud. Vehicles became stuck in the ruts or slewed across the road. Mud would cling to the bottom and any cavity, increasing the weight of the vehicle by half its own weight, as someone at the mine had calculated. Boredom makes people there, take up all sorts of weird pastimes, mud calculation being one. The most popular one was of course, total oblivion, played with a bottle of whisky and a glass. You could have as many players as you pleased, but one rule had to be followed, supply your own whisky or take your turn at being host. It was no hobby of mine. Alcohol was poison to my system, just as well, for I could not use it as a refuge from my problems. None of my friends drank to excess either, and compared to the UK now, binge drinking was only in its infancy. It was a matter of pride among the expatriates that one held one's liquor, along with one's emotions.

Daramy was my henchman, always willing for a trip, a new experience. He would have been in his thirties and had a typical African lifestyle, except that he had a steady job. With three wives and four children, a house of three rooms, in which he lived with his mother, a small plot where he grew local vegetables and fruit and, a permanent job, he must have been considered reasonably wealthy. Ostensibly he was Moslem. He wanted to make the pilgrimage to Mecca so that he could wear the red fez and take the title, Hadji. He also laughed at the daily procession from the mosque, pointing out the rogues, telling me how cruel the mullah was to the children who chanted the Koran nightly under his tuition.

The American Peace Corps boys considered the .22 to be a toy, incapable of doing any damage. They talked wisely of guns. The gun lobby in the States is very powerful and the right to carry arms is enshrined in the Constitution. They attribute the reason for their army's prowess at arms, (in their view) being partly due to this right and, even now this late in the century, the 'frontier spirit.' They were convinced that they could, like any neighbourhood bully, 'beat the hell out of any nation on this earth'. Guns were in their blood, they said, though most had chosen the Peace Corps rather than the Forces of the USA and a trip to Vietnam. Humility in national pride was not a strong suit. I wondered who they had beaten of note, unaided, to prove that statement. My history books must have left out some important conflicts somewhere and I asked if that was the case? They didn't understand what I was getting at. They pointed to the world wars and the Korean War as if they had been the sole defenders of Liberty, a view challenged vigorously by me.

Uncle Sam was about to find out just how far removed they were from the Indian Wars when repeating rifles and cannon had beaten a defensive and oppressed, poorly armed Indian Nation. In ten years from when we sat talking in my lounge, they would have suffered a defeat that brought the nation to its knees. Vietnam showed up their weaknesses. Might does not mean right. You cannot make people like you by shooting and bombing them. The bomber cannot win a war. Yet they persist in the belief that technology will prevail. In Iraq, they have found that an invisible enemy, armed with explosives and grenade launchers is more than a match for their armoury. Yet I doubt the lesson has yet been learned because there is such a strong belief by the Americans in their own myth.

The boys from America arrived unannounced one night as I sat cleaning the small-bore rifle in my living room. They of course knew all about guns, talking of .45s, .38s, 32s, magnums, but never of a little .22. As I put it back together, I argued in favour of the little gun, light and easy to use, accurate because it doesn't kick like a mule and throw one's aim off. They asked for a demonstration and I slipped in the loaded magazine that held six shots, then worked the bolt to put a shell in the chamber. There was a box in the spare room, its sides one-inch thick. I aimed and let fly, frightening them all, then invited them to inspect the box. They found the bullet had passed through both sides of the box and buried itself in the soft concrete of the wall. Point proved. I had a hunting .303 also, which did kick, which would have been better for buffalo or deer, but for accuracy you can't beat the .22. At close quarters, the twelve bore is king loaded with the right shot.

This demonstration was because they disputed my plan in the event of a hold up on the road. There had been two robberies, neither on a bank vehicle, but on the mine payrolls, which were run to schedule. My plan was that I would abandon the car and the money, take to the bush with the rifle and pick the villains off from a distance. These robbers were usually armed with machetes and I did not want to lose an arm at close quarters. I figured that after I had shot one, the others would run for it. I was confident that I could hit them at will. I was a crack shot. The Yanks are suitably impressed, except for Joe, who despises everything British. On the whole though, I think the 'Limeys' won the argument.

Daramy tells me that the Americans challenged the Africans at draughts or checkers as they called it. They lost all ten games. Daramy giggles as he tells me. He had a sense of humour, more so than any other African I met and would rock with laughter, tears in his eyes. His ambition was to possess a cuckoo clock and hoped that if I went to Switzerland I would send him one. Alas, I never did. He would not have received it anyway. The postmaster would probably have taken it, as happened to my Christmas parcel.

The theft of my parcel was extraordinary. They ate the jam, marmalade, mincemeat and the cake, then replaced the empty jars and containers in the parcel and I was allowed to collect this from the office. Strange people.

Daramy and I would take to the bush in the rain, walking soaked to the skin. We ranged over the savannah plains and swamps for miles, without a map, without food, just carrying the guns, normally a couple of twelve bores. Direction became instinctive and has stayed with me even in the urban jungle of the UK. We were very close, for two people of such different backgrounds, he from the bush, could hardly write his name, a Moslem of sorts; me white, naive, reasonably educated, a lost soul wandering the world as map less of any direction in life as we two were wandering the bush. There was a bond between us, which was more than master and servant, employer and employee. We never spoke of it, but we were fiercely loyal of each other. He also had insight as to my real persona and one day as we sat in a tree overhanging a river, shooting carp with the guns for our lunch, asked if I would like to be 'oman? He added that he thought it a bad idea, 'work too much', being his reason, undoubtedly true for the burdened women of Africa.

The second tour, I bought a new Beetle. Hans, the German manager of the VW agency had threatened to visit me for some time, in fact ever since his garage forgot to put any oil in my engine. He turned up one day, complete with two twelve bores, a hunting rifle and a Luger. God knows where he got the latter. He wanted to go shooting with me. Hans was about five feet ten, thickset and extremely strong. He was a good mechanic. When his engine seized in the bush; he dismantled it and filed down the piston rings until he could drive back to his garage. He was as gentle as a nurse when working on an engine, but there his gentleness ended.

As we drove down the road to the swamps, a figure appeared in the road, weaving across it on foot in such a manner that we couldn't pass. Hans was furious, he hooted, scrunched his brakes, stood up in his Beetle convertible like Rommel in the desert and shouted abuse in his booming voice. I explained that the woman was crazy, one of the local beggars and that she would only move over when she felt like it. I watched in horror as Hans vacated the car, marched after her, aimed his size ten at her backside and booted her into the ditch. The argument that followed put a damper on the day.

There was a fellow called Joe. He was the Public Works manager before the Williams. He came from Malta and had hidden talents. He had a short story read on radio and we listened to it together on the World Service. For a few weeks we saw quite a lot of each other. One afternoon, he caressed my bum; there was no mistake. I just turned and said, 'No thanks Joe.' He said nothing, but after that, I hardly saw him. Whether he found someone else, or was just shy of me I don't know, but I bore him no grudge and would have treated him just the same. Sex can spoil relationships.

One of the compensations of Africa was that there were no women, well hardly any European women, so the pressure was off me to date them. On the other hand, I lacked female company. It was a strange existence, in its way just as artificial as the military would have been and, almost as strange as boarding school. I had come to the conclusion that perhaps it was the wrong place to be. I had an increasing fear of mental illness, I would hardly sleep at times, worrying about myself, worrying about not sleeping, and worrying that this would all lead to a breakdown. It seemed to be a vicious circle from which I would have to escape.

I was experimenting with cosmetics. There was plenty of time to think, more than enough time to be bored. Four or five nights a week in Port Loko, six nights in Pendembu, I was on my own all evening, with only books, a few records and the radio for company. I tried painting in oils on the canvas I had bought, but could not concentrate on it. I needed adrenalin more than anything, to take my mind off my inner turmoil.

Sometimes I would have a war with the Highlife bar, fighting their Afro rhythms with Tchaikovsky or Beethoven, when I could stand their racket no longer. Now I look back on their music with affectionate nostalgia and when I hear it, there is immediate joy. But there was just too much time, not to dwell on life as I would have had it. I would read, sometimes for four or five hours, but my mind would wander off to my problem. I would have to read even a whole chapter again, to take it in.

I knew that sex change was possible, there were several documented cases and I could not make out why the idiot psychiatrists I saw, would not help me. If they had, it would have saved a lot of heartache later. Had I paid the right ones it would all have happened sooner.

I sat reading in my flat one day. The rain fell from an endlessly grey sky and hammered on the tin roofs, from where it descended gurgling down the monsoon drains. I was surprised when a figure appeared on the veranda. He was European, but unknown to me. His cream mackintosh and brown trilby were incongruous with the surroundings. He looked as though he had descended from the afternoon train from Victoria after a day in London. Having invited him in, he announced himself as James -----, the third secretary from the High Commissioners office in Freetown. We had tea and biscuits, a rare treat for me, for when alone I would not bother to eat tea. Fresh company was almost always welcome. We talked of this and that. What it was like to be so far up country on my own? Had I many friends? Did I know the local situation regarding the Chiefs? Did I know a Chief who ran a contracting business fifty miles away? Had he an account? If he should suddenly receive large funds would I let him know? What was the situation on the Guinea border? If anything significant or interesting came up, would I please be in touch? I agreed to, though like a real banker, reminded him that I could not disclose details of customer's accounts. After this first meeting, he would appear unannounced every couple of months to hear the gossip. It was evident that there was more to this trade secretary than mere commercial information. He was very different to the happy go lucky expatriates I usually ran into. He was a real city dweller set down in Hicksville. He seemed a quiet, almost remote character. He was perceptive and intelligent, that much was evident. I learnt that he had a Cambridge degree, and we swapped reminiscences about that city. After the second visit I concluded that I was, like so many expatriates, an unpaid member of the intelligence services. James hinted that he expected a power struggle that would not necessarily be democratic.

Later I had lunch at his home in Freetown, having given my fawn to him at his request, as a present for his wife. He lived up the hill where all the ministers, senior managers and diplomatic staff lived, with views across the distant golf course and beach. The house could have been set in Surrey. It was quiet, and so was his wife. They kept no house servants, he said, for the sake of privacy. She was pleasant, a cool blonde, good looking in the Scandinavian way, but perilously thin. I understood that she had been ill. She seemed withdrawn if not depressed. Her unhappiness was palpable even before she spoke of it. While he was out of the room she confided that she hated Freetown. She felt isolated. She was lonely and insecure. She thanked me for the fawn that now stood about twelve hands, and lived in a little paddock. It seemed to be her only friend apart from their cat.

It is as easy as that to become embroiled in harmless information gathering that in times of trouble can escalate into arrest for espionage. There have been countless numbers of trade representatives who have found themselves in deep distress through such actions. I was fortunate. I knew little of a sensitive nature, and in truth at that time there was little occurring other than the democratic actions of a corrupt government. However, he did tell me to say should anyone enquire regarding his visit, that he was asking what the situation was likely to be for the rice harvest. The real subversion was embryonic. It would appear a few years later and gradually brought about the collapse of the whole social structure, government, army, police and judiciary. In the late 1990s Sierra Leone was a ruined country, taken over by bandits who with the gun took what they wanted, money, slaves, women, sex and even ministerial powers. Every sin was committed there and what was a sort of paradise became a hell.

The British legacy of democracy, peace, law and order, an incorruptible police force and a loyal army, had been swept aside by selfish and avaricious politicians and people who are no more than bandits. Sandhurst training, school or university in the UK count for nothing. Rank or learning is usually power, but power in Africa it seems, is in the hands of the ruthless. One takes but does not give would seem to be the motto of many, though there are many excellent exceptions who unfortunately are probably the first victims of the bullies who now hold power.

In the 1990s children with AK47s swagger down the street. They are the most dangerous, for they have no idea of right or wrong, no compassion and have been brought up on torture, killing and drugs. The innocent men women and even babies, had arms cut off with a panga, as an example to others. It was a cruel and sadistic nation now at the beginning of the 21st century. Thankfully, the British Army put an end to that misrule and now in 2012 elections are declared free and fair and peace rules again and the country is becoming more prosperous.

Three months after my accident with the filing spike, I was still getting boils, but otherwise I was reasonably well. I became ill again. I had gone to Khalil's for dinner, having run out of excuses not to. It was a male bonding evening of course. The Moslem world is so male dominated. The women were gathered in a dark corner, as the men sat round a fire on which most of a sheep was stewing in a large pot. This stew was the colour of tomato soup, but clear. The sheep had been cooked with tomatoes, peppers and chillies and with palm oil, so it was very oily and red. It was washed down with liberal amounts of whisky, neat. I asked if the dish had a name? 'Red stew', one of the Khalils told me, and after they had translated it, they all laughed uproariously. 'We put anything red', they explained. 'Except the sheep,' I countered, and they cracked their sides again. 'No,' Abdul said, 'We do not put the hair, only the red flesh.' More laughter, and Ahmed Khalil, Abdul Ahmed's brother, fell from his log, clutching his aching sides.

This was how the boys lived. It was a very macho world. Men drank and deeply, but were expected to hold their liquor. The teaching of the Koran on alcohol, meant nothing. To abstain would not only be impolite but would involve a loss of face not only for me but also for the bank. All the Khalil men were there, all trying to outdo each other looking after me, fishing out choice bits to eat, even an eye which I turned down, polite or not.

When I finally staggered home, it was half past one. It had been one of the worst nights of my life and was to continue to be so. I was ill all night. My kidneys, weakened by the dengue fever, could not take the whisky. In addition, I must have eaten a pint of palm oil and a pound of sheep fat. The stew had indeed tasted extra good and I like them, mopped up the fat with a handful of rice, then with some bread. After two weeks, I was still being sick. Any soft fizzy drink would send me rushing to the loo. The headmaster of the local boarding school, a Brit and gay as I found out by accident, came round with his pet cure, Collis-Browne and a shot of brandy. I was sick after his remedy. He took that as a personal affront. Extraordinary!

In the end, I went to the Roman Catholic hospital twenty miles away, an imposing brick built place with a front door that looked like oak and was adorned with hand made nails, just like a Church door anywhere in Europe. I rang the bell and waited. The doctor priest had a good reputation, but I had never met him. He answered the door himself, clad in a white habit and sandals, looked at me and stepped back.

'An angel,' he said, in Italian and then in English.

I was immediately embarrassed. He beckoned me in continuing in the same vein. He explained that with the sun shining from behind, my hair looked like a halo and he was paraphrasing St. Augustine who had called the Angles, angels because of the colour of their hair. Had I not had my secret, I could have enjoyed the joke, but his attention confused me extremely. I blushed. He asked a lot of questions, told me what to eat and what to avoid, then gave me some red pills, enough for two months.

'The cure is slow, but it will be complete, it is the only way,' he said.

I did indeed recover. It was to be a long time before I could drink alcohol at all.

Then there was Mike. He was on a short-term contract, surveying the bush and looking for minerals. He lived on site; miles from anywhere, cooked for himself, corned beef curry every day of every week! He came into the Bank one day to cash a cheque, and I followed procedure, refusing payment until confirmation of clearance. I liked him immediately, a manly but gentle and humorous soul. He invited himself for dinner and when I enquired what he would like to eat as a change from the corned beef curry, he said fried egg and bacon sandwiches. There was little time to become real friends. When he moved to Freetown, back to his wife, I was invited to dinner and spent the weekend with them, in a relaxed and affectionate atmosphere. Their care of me was extraordinary, and I wondered whether they had some understanding of my mental state.

Illness and two more fraud cases made Africa seem altogether the wrong place for me. I went home with all my belongings. The last night was spent with Mike and his dear wife and they picked me up the next day to transport me to the harbour. I bequeathed him my .303 and later received a letter from Australia in which he said they had two children and the .303. They hoped that I was well. I was not, I did not reply, but wish now that I had. I hate losing contact with friends.

I left behind a cat that I loved, with someone who was not to take care of it. It was a dear and loving animal. I regret that to this day, feeling that I have betrayed a friend.

CHAPTER 9.

I arrived home from Africa in March. The MV Accra, a ten thousand tonne passenger cargo boat, sailed into Liverpool early on a bleak grey Monday morning. It had been a ten-day cruise from the heat and sun of the West African coast to the snow lying on the dilapidated Liverpool dock. There was a cold wind blowing and the warmest thing I had was a tropical suit and a sweater that I had bought in the ship's meagrely stocked shop.

Those old coasters, and I suppose most passenger liners, were very class conscious. You had to be someone for the Captain to notice you, someone else for the Purser to notice you, etc. There were not enough seats in the main saloon, the only really comfortable place to sit in the evening after dinner, for all passengers to sit at once. It began to dawn on a few of us passengers that, no matter what, the Captain and his table guests always had seats and like good revolutionaries should, we plotted to overturn the regime. After all, there was nothing on our tickets, also first class, which said no saloon seating. We were just as entitled to comfort as the Captain.

We had observed that every night while we were all at dinner, a steward took a tray of cups to the large table in the saloon, much as the Germans supposedly rush out to bag their sun beds at midnight. Then we would all dutifully avoid the table, since it had obviously been reserved. About the fourth night out, when the passengers had started to talk to each other and our patience was exhausted, we took possession of the table. It was convenient. A long couch on two sides and had chairs on the open side. We made ourselves comfortable, talked, read our books and ignored the tray of coffee cups. When the steward appeared with the coffee prior to the Captain's arrival, he was completely thrown, stammered that the table was reserved and what's more, for the Captain. No one, we said, could reserve tables in the saloon. Just then the Captain and hangers on appeared. The rest of the saloon watched the fun. He asked us to vacate, we asked him to find somewhere else. One among us, the born revolutionary asked whether there was something wrong with our tickets.

'Should they say not allowed to sit in the saloon?' he wanted to know.

It was a stand off for a time, then not wanting to lose more face or dignity than he had already, he sent the steward to see whether there was room in the library. When the steward said there was, they all departed. Someone blew a large raspberry at their departing backs, and the saloon battle was over. Thereafter, the Captain always went to the library. The chairs were not comfortable, but at least, they were free, and no mutinous passengers were there to challenge him.

When we reached the Bay of Biscay, a storm blew up. The ship rocked and rolled across twenty-foot waves. Suddenly the ship was deserted, most of the passengers taking to their cabins. I went to dinner; the dining room was only a quarter full. Half way through the meal, there was a terrific lurch and the baby grand piano took off across the dining room, with three stewards in hot pursuit. Luckily they secured it before anyone was flattened.

I went for a walk on deck. The nearer the bow one got, the more the effect of the waves, until it was actually throwing me into the air as the bow rose. The deck then came up to meet me as I came down. It was like jumping off a ten-foot high wall. I retreated to the middle of the ship. Later I too felt queasy, though I was not sick.

I lay in my bed, the ship rocking, engines humming steadily. It was a restful place to be, the steady drone was soporific. I was cut off with nothing to do and nowhere to go, with no one to call upon me. For a rare moment in my life, I was free to be just who I wanted to be, no character to act out, no one to please or shock or disappoint, even though restricted by the confines of my cabin. Rest came easily. I relaxed for the first time in my life. When the rich were ill in the old days, they took a cruise and I could see why. It is a most restful way of passing time.

I slept. Then I would wake, read a book, or go to eat. A little air on the deck, maybe words with one of the few passengers still about, then back to the cabin. I could experiment with my appearance without fear of discovery or interruption. That was my routine for two days. After the second day of this, I could sleep no more. I went up on deck with the portable radio out of my car. I tuned in to 'Top of the Pops' with Alan Freeman. I remember hearing the Searchers 'Needles and Pins', and Cilla Black 'Anyone who had a Heart'. I thought of the future, but there was none. I had no idea what I was going to do, or even who I really was. The whole future was so confused that I could not think clearly.

Next morning I awoke to find that we were coming into the dock at Liverpool. I just wanted to get off the boat. The only warm place was my cabin, but after ten days I had seen enough of it.

Customs came aboard, asked a lot of questions about the amount of luggage I had and I lied that I was going back to Nigeria and because of the thieving problems on the coast, it had been safer to bring it all home. By ten we were off the boat. I found a hotel and holed up in the lounge till I could collect my car at three in the afternoon.

Even the taxi was freezing. I found my car waiting, battery disconnected as it was considered a fire risk to have possible ignition at sea. An engineer connected the strap, and then I was away, bulky luggage to follow.

Having filled up with fuel, I headed through the Mersey tunnel, made for Chester, then eventually picked up the new M6 that was still being built, and then the M1. There was snow beside the motorway. The heaters, never used in Africa, pumped out a nice mixture of hot air and oil. Still I was warm, on the move and in five hours, I was home.

Welcomes in our household were unemotional affairs. I felt the loss of a show of welcoming love. The house seemed quiet and dull and small. The best room was the kitchen, a Rayburn cooker making it a cosy place. It was my brother who took most interest in me and the things I had brought home. The next day, I was on my own; everyone had gone to work. I had no friends, nothing much to do, a bit of unpacking, but other than that, there was nothing. I decided to go skiing as soon as I could get away.

There were package holidays then, but I was more an à la carte person, not having any specific plan other than to see Melchsee Frut where I had gone skiing with the school. I bought a plane ticket to Zurich where I had a bank account, but didn't bother to pause there to draw any money. That would have delayed getting to the slopes. I arrived at the hotel at five in the afternoon and luckily they had a room, for they would soon be full. I had dinner and then left to go to my room. As I passed through the door of the dining room, some Brits who had been at a table next to me said 'Guten Abend'. I replied, 'Abend', and was soon in my room, bathed and in bed by eight-thirty. I was very tired, more tired than I think I had ever been. I went to sleep immediately.

The knocking woke me. Daylight was gleaming round the curtains, but it looked like faint early morning light. I looked at my watch and saw it was six thirty. I was really annoyed, tired as I was, being awoken so early. Putting on my silk dressing gown, I opened the door to find the receptionist there.

'Yes?'

'Everything is all right?'

'Thank you.'

'You are coming down for dinner?' She seemed an extremely confused girl.

'I should think so.'

'Good. We see you later.'

Then she turned and went down the dark staircase.

I was pretty puzzled. I pulled back the curtains and looked out at the snowy scene. For early morning, there seemed to be a lot of people about. They also seemed to be dressed strangely for the time of day. My mind worked slowly, putting the clues together and I finally concluded that it was in fact evening. I had slept for twenty-two hours. When I finally went down to the dining room, there was a slight stir as I entered. The Brits who had said good evening the night before asked me to join them at their table. They soon told me that the hotel had been speculating about me and the management was worried that I had taken my life or died or was ill. There was much mirth, and glasses raised to me. That was why the girl from reception had come knocking at the door. Apparently, they thought I looked so ill when I arrived, that any of those possibilities had occurred to them. It was quite embarrassing. I assured them of my good health and we sat talking and drinking all evening.

Skiing next day, I found out just how unfit I was. At five thousand feet, I was puffing and blowing, felt weak, and tired. I was glad when the lesson was over at three-thirty, and I could go to bed. This time I did wake in time for dinner.

I sat with the same people for a week before I found out that they thought I was Austrian. Apparently my gold teeth, and a little habit I had of inclining my head in a little nod, had made them think I was from central Europe. They had complimented me on my excellent English and asked where I had learned to speak it so well! They wouldn't believe that I was English. Fifteen years later, skiing on the Edinburgh dry slope as a female, I was again accused of being a 'central European', and my teeth and my skiing style given as the reasons. On that occasion I finally admitted that I was Austrian, making them very happy that they had uncovered my real identity. Little did they know how much more there was to uncover.

I stayed there another week, then the hotel asked me to leave, as they were fully booked for Easter. I decided to go to Austria, to Obergurgl. The snow in Switzerland wasn't that good, and Obergurgl being very high, was thought to be the place to be. The hotelier even phoned Obergurgl to check for me, a very kind action. Now there are higher resorts in France, but at the time Obergurgl and Hochgurgl were considered very high indeed, with snow guaranteed.

I hitched a lift with a woman and her crippled husband, in a taxi to Zurich, assisting them in the airport until they arrived at the desk and the airline took over. My duty done, I headed for Zurich and my bank. I found it, told them I wanted to draw my money out and to my surprise was invited to talk to the manager. He expressed astonishment that I should wish to have my money. It was after all, a good sum, about three month's salary and he thought I should leave it to accrue interest. I explained that it had only been sent so that I could have a holiday, and as I was now bound for Austria, I had come to get it.

We talked for quite a time, and it slowly dawned that they thought I was a diamond smuggler, diamonds being the only product they knew came from Sierra Leone. I insisted that I needed the money. They asked, 'Why not stay in Switzerland, there is very good skiing at Davos', but I told them I was set on seeing Austria. That didn't go down too well. Had I been going to spend my cash in Switzerland, I dare say they would not have minded, but Austria? They shook their heads in horror. Having agreed to leave five pounds in the account, about one hundred pounds in today's value, they let me have the balance.

I stayed the night in a hotel beside the lake, wandered the city, bought an American edition of Pride and Prejudice at a book shop, looked at lovely underwear in a shop window, and dresses in a smart shop, then by chance had dinner with a delightful old Swiss lady in the station buffet. It was, we both agreed, extremely good value and she said that I would always find good food in railway restaurants in Switzerland. I have found that to be true.

The journey to Austria was enchanting, always in sight of snow covered mountains, in a carriage full of people who spoke no

English, it felt like an adventure. We crossed the border into Austria, the mountains of Liechtenstein on our left and meandered down the valley filled with resorts such as St. Anton, where there seemed to be precious little snow. I left the train at a quiet stop, the only passenger to dismount, then travelled by post bus up the valley to Obergurgl.

The little village was very full. I managed to get a room in a pension, but only for a few nights, then I would have to find somewhere else. The skiing was challenging. The slopes were steep and icy and I was skiing on my own. I met a young American whose father was something diplomatic in Bonn and for a few days we skied together.

My boils all disappeared, as did a wound I had on my calf for about two months. I was really starting to feel well again.

I found a hotel at Untergurgl, 400 metres down the road and was pleased to find some nice Dutch girls and an English solicitor and his wife would be my companions. There was also a party from Charterhouse school and a band every night in the little hotel nightclub. It was a lively place and as long as we drank wine and not coffee, it was a cheap evening. We were up till one every night, and out of the hotel to the slopes by nine in the morning.

After a month, I'd had enough. I made my way home, had my ski sticks stolen in Zurich where I spent another night in a beautiful hotel beside the lake, then reached home in a taxi at three-thirty in the morning. When my parents awoke, they found I was back in the fold.

My parents' plan was to take a business in retirement and I was welcome to join them, as was my brother. If I were to stay in England, I would have to find a new job outside banking, for at that time the banks operated a bar on staff transferring from one to another. I was not sure anyway, that banking was exciting enough to be my career. After some time, I gave my notice into the Bank. In reply they summoned me to head office to discuss the matter.

'If you don't like Sierra Leone, we could send you to Nigeria. How would that suit you?'

'I don't think it would be any better. The climate really doesn't suit me. I seem to have had one illness after another.'

'Sometimes health settles down after one or two tours. Don't you think you should give it another try?'

'I'm tired of feeling ill.'

'We can't employ you here, we just don't do that, not for people of your age.' They meant my youth. Managers were usually middle aged.

'My mind is made up.'

'If you ever need a reference, just let us know, I can assure you we will give you a good one.'

That was it. Boats were burned. At twenty-four and a half, I seemed to have all the time in the world to make up my mind on another career, so I decided to join my parents in their new venture, at least for the time being. Maybe, I thought, I could sort out the matter that meant more than anything else, my sexuality. It was the worst decision of my life.

CHAPTER 10.

We moved from Surrey to Norfolk. At first it was enjoyable to be away from the bustle of the Home Counties, to have roads with little traffic, a sleepy and slow way of life. We settled into a coastal village, with local people but with local prejudice against 'newcomers'. This was displayed quite openly in the shop. We were quite unprepared for the amount of change from Surrey that we found. There were people in the village who had not been to Norwich, a mere twenty miles away, more than once or twice in their lives. London was even more remote, a completely alien land and culture, to be avoided at all costs. It was scoffed at and scorned, as one might have, Sodom and Gomorrah. It seems almost impossible to believe now, in these times of package holidays for everyone, and in a time when almost anyone goes away to college or university, that people could be so insular. Women ran the house, men went to work and maybe worked on their garden or allotment. The owner of a riding school complained that he had had to come into the village to get his tobacco, because his wife was looking after her mother. 'First time I been in a shop since I got married,' he complained.

They were insular. 'Ought to have a customs post at Thetford', they joked, but beneath this humour were many grains of truth. 'Shouldn't sell houses to foreigners.' They meant anyone from outside the county. But all the large houses in the village had once been owned by well to do Society and Royal hangers-on and the villagers still spoke in awe and respect of the people who had given them employment as cooks, maids and gardeners.

There was even semi-serious enmity between Cromer and Sheringham, adjacent resorts, 8 miles apart, involving fights between the youths. The local economy then was largely agricultural, far more so than today when new industries have been attracted into even the smallest of these tiny Norfolk towns. At the same time, labour has left the land now they have full mechanisation. The other occupations at that time were mostly local services and the holiday trade on the coast. Long-shore fishing and crabbing were prominent too. The fishermen did not make a fortune, but by paying full stamp, claimed unemployment benefit when conditions at sea were too hazardous. It was a hard life for what they made out of it. Even with the rivalry that existed between them as personalities, they remained a distinct class on their own. A boy who would later become a lifeboat coxwain, always wore a fisherman's jersey from the time he went to school and no amount of remonstrations from his teachers would get him into uniform

The blunt 'peasant class' were fiercely proud of their origins, aggressively defending their lack of education and, by this aggression I believe, trying to disguise a rural and provincial feeling of inferiority. They would show this fear in other ways too. Parents who had bright children would display a dichotomy of emotions, pride in the child's progress, fear that they would grow up to be superior and forget their origins and family. Indeed some actually regretted their children's success at the eleven plus, 'cos we don't want them to get too good for us'. Snobs. The word was used to describe anyone who spoke well or had learning, until they had proved their worth in some way. There was an innate distrust of the new, any departure from their old ways and a failure to recognise that change was not only inevitable but necessary, especially as fewer and fewer people would find a living on the land. There was still a feudalism about, local squires, in positions of influence, and some at least of the population, tugging their forelocks. One old squire, then in his eighties, would walk the middle of Cromer High Street, purely to impose his superiority and inviolability, it was said.

There was a feudal love-hate relationship with this local squirearchy. The family was old, well connected in the banking world, but with the manners that only such people can display. They were rude and overbearing to their tenants, treated their servants as servants, and showed a belief that this small area of North Norfolk was indeed their fiefdom. The servants had stories to denigrate them, of dog mess all over the house, curtains in rags, damp and decay, the children involved in drugs, spewing on the floors of the local hostelry. The local people despised them behind their backs and touched their forelocks in the street. All this was a far cry from the suburbs of Surrey, where you mowed the grass verges, trimmed your hedges and kept yourself to yourself.

Norfolk was also a place of retirement, with people coming from London and the Midlands to spend their last years. It was a mistake for many of them and increased the price of property beyond the means of some local people.

I soon realised that it had not been the right move for me. The confines of a family and their expectations and being far removed from London where I might possibly find some understanding, were added pressures. Wrongly, I resolved to put my problems behind me and lead a 'normal' life.

It was difficult to do. Every minute of every day, my real persona was tapping at the window of my mind, demanding to be let out. After the initial enthusiasm and the planning in the business, it all became rather a bore, nothing to stretch me, no good company other than my family. I became one of the local councillors on the rural district council, but soon found that my wish to serve the community would not be satisfied by that position. Between the vested interests of the farming fraternity on the one hand and the takers and changers on the other, I was pinched in the middle. It was in these years that I became disillusioned with politics and politicians and yet they have a great fascination for me. They are practically all out for one thing, power over others and the furtherment of their own egos and interests. I lasted the three-year term, assisted the community to the best of my ability, and then called it a day. When I announced to the chief executive that I would not stand again, he said, 'That's such a shame, now we have you tamed.' I was not tamed, simply disillusioned and could not bother to carry on charging a brick wall. There was no room for mavericks with a mind of their own. Parliament too, keeps from any meaningful power, those who are honest enough to state and live by their own views.

Meanwhile I tried again to get some help. My doctor was an amiable fellow, a handsome man and well respected. He had though, definite ideas about what was permissible and what was not. For example, child bearing was good, and a mother feeding her baby with her own milk was described as a good cow. He was a lay preacher. He took the bible seriously, as one day I would find. In the meantime, I consulted him about my problem and the result was a session with yet another psychiatrist.

This one was a really cold fish. He was without a trace of humour; not a smile of reassurance creased his face. His darkest blue suit was cold and I had the feeling that he was not human, merely an automaton. The skin stretched tightly across his face like flesh coloured cling film. His eyes hardly ever met mine from behind cold steel rimmed glasses. He had of course no experience of transsexualism, which at that time was much more of a mystery than it is now

I do know now, that this consultant and my doctor had cooked up what was to be said, before I ever entered the room. My doctor later confided this to me. They had decided that no matter what, I could not have the treatment I wished for. His objective was to disillusion me of this aspiration and thereby, return me to the fold of the 'normal'. Therefore he *was* an automaton, merely going through the motions. They could have set a recording up for me and left me in the room with it. He was quite severe with me and showed not a mote of human understanding nor compassion. He informed me that my beliefs about myself were self-delusion, that I would never change my sex and that I had to come to terms with being as I was. He suggested that I took up amateur theatricals, to satisfy my need to dress as a woman and marry to discover how good sex could be. He added that being a woman was a messy business and I wouldn't like it, a statement that my doctor also made later. I wondered as I sat with this idiot, why it was that all women were not trying to change into men if it was so unattractive being female. All in all, I came out feeling that I was a mental case and I believe that is how they considered me. Would they consider gays the same way I wondered? As for amateur theatricals, how many parts were there, that would allow me to express my femininity? Was that a means of developing my wish to be feminine anyway? I told him that his suggestions were inappropriate. I was not a transvestite, nor an aspiring drag artist. The mere association of my condition to those people, was just as obnoxious to me as it would have been to a natural born woman.

He gave me no comfort at all. Not only had he managed to insult me and belittle the way I felt, he had sentenced me to a life of unremitting misery. I went for a drive in my car, foot flat to the ground, fury in my heart, tears in my eyes. It was February and the day was cold. Wide steely grey Norfolk clouds cast further gloom upon my soul. The bleak open countryside with the wind blown oaks and open fields thrust agoraphobic pressure upon me, completing my sense of being alone and lost. I thought of just driving into the front of a lorry, discounted that and thought about a brick wall, an old railway bridge I knew, but was frightened that I would survive. Even as I write this, the tears are near. I feel the same hate for that psychiatrist I felt then. Instead of trying to find out about my condition, he and my doctor, in complete ignorance, had attempted to coerce me down another path. This was probably my most desperate time, the lowest ebb in my life to date. There was nowhere for me, no place to go, no future and a bleak past, no real joy of living, but an existence of slow death and denial. They had between them managed to take away that last glimmer of self-esteem, which I had stored within me in a secret place, knowing that I was really female and trapped. I had exposed my soul and had it spat upon.

At last I had to slow for traffic and found that I was not far off the sea. I sat above the beach on low cliffs, in just a sweater and slacks, watching the waves crash and suck hungrily upon the shore, battle ship grey and creamy spume in perpetual motion. The beach was pebble; the waves fell relentlessly drawing at the land, rattling the grey cobbles with cold monotony. I sat and cried for some time, rocking backwards and forwards in deep despair in time with the breaking waves, hiding my face as some walkers passed by, the chill slowly permeating my body.

It was the cold that seemed to bring me round, the discomfort seeping into me rousing the primeval instinct for self preservation and sending me at last for physical warmth. Like the suicide shocked to see blood welling from slashed wrists, self-preservation took over. I returned home. I had told my family that I was being examined for some tropical bug, bilhazia, a nasty little worm caught from walking in stagnant water in the tropics, a lie of course, just told as an excuse for my absence. I was good at hiding my feelings, just went a bit quiet and kept the tears for my loneliness.

My boils had come back. Up and down my legs they roved and my doctor said that I was in danger of septicaemia. He asked about my consultation with the psychiatrist, had it helped? No, I replied. Well, that is the only answer, he said. We can't have people changing sex all over the place, it isn't right, and where would we be if we all did it? He confided that they had deliberately taken this line with me. I thought he was more intelligent than that. He would prove later that he wasn't. He said he disagreed about marriage and thought it would present insurmountable problems. For the first time he was right, but without marriage and the reason to live it gave me later, I doubt I would have survived.

I took up riding, something I had always wanted to do and there was Margaret. She was at least a ray of sunshine in my life, someone to share with and to care for. We spent nearly every free hour together. She was not well educated, had hated and avoided school, but was an animal lover like me. One of my dreams had always been to farm and this was something she in part shared with her love of animals and horses. She raised my self-esteem again, gave me back some respect, made me feel useful and a part of another being's life. Companionship, that above all I have found, is the essential need in my life.

After eighteen months, we married in September, quite quietly, spending a week in London which Margaret had never seen, for our honeymoon. We did the sights, but she had little interest in town life. Even then, we had difficulty making love, I could not find the right place and she could not help me. On balance, the fault was as much hers as mine. I do believe, as she once said, I would have fared better with a different woman, one who could take the initiative more and who wasn't frightened to touch me. A different partner too, would not have put up with me for so long or might have understood my predicament. There would have been no children to complicate matters and I might have set off on the right road all the sooner. That does not mean that I attach any blame to her. She was just long suffering, a child abroad like me. Neither of us had the necessary strength to deal with my problems.

All was not bad. We worked well together. In the garden and the house, we achieved much that other couples never would. We enjoyed many of the same things, holidays, touring the UK, animals and horse riding, the cinema and when they came, the children. We kidded ourselves that we were happier than other couples and in many ways we were. The anomaly of this marriage was that she had a very good, loving, generous, helpful and sharing husband in all but one dimension. Looking at it from this distance, it was as if she had married a butch dyke. There was hardly anything, that I could not turn my hand to, in the house or out and at some time or other. I would be in turn, mother, housewife, cook, nurse, gardener, mechanic, bricklayer, electrician, carpenter, glazier, drain layer, plumber, tiler, furniture maker, dressmaker, designer and architect, lover and husband. I would come home from work, she would tell me that this or that didn't work, and I would fix it. If anyone came to dinner, then I would cook. Nothing was a problem, except sex and of course my own self image which blighted my life, sending me into the deepest depression from time to time, but even then, though somewhat withdrawn and in inner turmoil, I was never unkind or cruel. We never came to blows, hardly ever rowed. Perhaps we should have done.

We started off in a new two bedroomed bungalow that we could ill afford. To cut the costs, I painted the entire interior and exterior. I also designed and installed the central heating, built the garage and added a porch to the back door. Our doctor who was later to be so little help to me, said on one of his visits, 'You are really a good and talented chap.' There was a grudging tone to this patronising remark and I knew then that he would never understand for all his fine words.

The other problem was Margaret's mother. We would return from holiday to find the furniture rearranged, our pictures or ornaments removed from the wall to be replaced with some cast-offs of her own. When our son locked himself in the bathroom, she removed the lock. I replaced it, saying that the children had to learn to live in the world as it is, not rearranged for their benefit. This continued interference wasn't liked by either of us, but we never rowed about it, even with her. Mother-in-law was always ill too, and thirty years later she was still ill, complaining that no one goes to see her. It is not surprising. She was probably the greatest living hypochondriac. The odd thing is that when her second husband became ill in his eighties, she said that he was the hypochondriac. He was dying of terminal cancer.

I worked part time at a country club, so called, although it had none of the facilities usually associated with such places. It was really a restaurant, bar and dance floor. In the late sixties it had a reputation as the place to be on a Saturday night. There was a band and a set menu which was supposed to represent fine dining. It was well patronised, almost always fully booked. The owner Jimmy, was a devil. He had been a headwaiter at various hotels, a rough diamond with a certain amount of polish. He was assisted by his long-suffering wife who looked after the financial side, while he was front of house and ideas man. On party nights he was in his element, everyone's best friend, dancing with some lady patrons, singing a ballad, playing host and spreading bonhomie. He was also a man for the ladies. He would take them off to show them the renovations or extension or gardens and his plans for all of these. The summerhouse made an excellent refuge and ladies would reappear, flushed from the cold night air. A friend would come over on Saturday night or at other busy times, to help in the bar which I managed. He would make expensive cocktails at knock down prices, but refrain from assisting with the less agreeable tasks. He must have cost us no end of money. Meanwhile this poor deluded fellow's wife was easy meat for Jimmy. They romped together and met at other times too. Jimmy would say he was going to meet a friend or colleague, go to a trade fair, go to look at a car, and tip me a wink that he had a tryst again. At times he would make me a co-conspirator, priming me with a story of where he was. One time he told me he was going to meet her at his son's bungalow, then his wife also announced that she was going there too. Luckily for Jimmy, his wife fumbled finding the right key for the door, and when she entered Jimmy was found with his head in the cupboard under the sink, looking for a non existent 'leak in the plumbing'. The girl friend meanwhile was playing sardines by herself in the bedroom wardrobe. Two months later, it all came out. Swear words, tears and for the injured party the amateur barman, divorce from his cuckolding wife.

Jimmy had a winning way, but I could not hide my dislike and disapproval of his antics. He could also be quite violent and had been on a charge of GBH for throwing a waiter down a flight of stairs. When my own problems came to a head I parted company with Jimmy and his deceptions. The place began to go down hill and

Jimmy sold out. The clientele were moving on, clubs were springing up to attract the younger people and eating fashions were changing.

We visited some old friends of Margaret's who had a farm in Wales. They suggested that she should have a horse and had seen the very one. This was her passion. Before the children, she worked as a groom at the stables. Though we could ill afford it, the animal eventually arrived. It was a nice creature as horses go, a handsome half Arab, a chestnut gelding, which she had to break and school from scratch. We then looked for premises where we could keep him and lighted upon a cottage with a small paddock with other grazing nearby. The cottage we found, was a mess, cold, floorboards rotten, and worm in the rafters. Over a six month period I installed central heating, had the rafters treated, ripped up the floor and we both laid a solid floor instead. When the interior was reasonably snug, I turned to the outside and built a stable, rewired the street lamp in the drive and fenced in the paddock.

Meanwhile Margaret was having the children. First our son was born, a beautiful bonny boy, five months after we moved in. I could not get enough of him. He had grown into a loving child by the time our daughter was born fourteen months later. She was not the easy child that he was, destined never to be so until she was herself pregnant.

Later I would put a roof on the extension, doing all the woodwork construction on a second storey, and flashed the chimney. That leaked, but later I cured it, sitting up on the apex of the roof although heights have always terrified me. As I started down the ladder one day, my son's head appeared at the top. At the age of three, he had climbed twenty feet up the ladder to see what 'Daddy' was doing, a beaming smile upon his face. Quietly I greeted him, grabbed his arm and pulled him up, hugging him tightly to me. It had been a heart stopping moment. We came down together, one rung at a time, and I careful not to transmit my fear to him.

The pity was that by the time they were five and four, I would be gone, never to see them develop. Whether it was the added pressure of having children to support and money being even tighter or whether I was just a time bomb with my fuse running out. I could not go on with life as it was. My femininity had to be fulfilled somehow and I resented more and more the masculine side of my life, continually being Mr Fix-it, the provider, father, protector and do my duty by Margaret. But it was not my choice to leave. The thought of losing the three people dearest to me was unbearable. Inevitably,

Margaret looked for comfort elsewhere and gave me my marching orders.

There is no doubt that I loved her as a person, in spite of all the little niggly things my parents would mention about her. Even now, at this distance of time I can forgive her loud and slapdash ways, for there was a joy behind it and a childish innocence which I too shared. She was a good person, even though later she would assume a hard vindictiveness and homicidal wishes towards meHowever, my daughter now says that after my departure, her mother became selfish, a poor and neglectful mother. She ruined my son. Luckily my daughter is strong and has pulled through.

I went back to my doctor in distress. He could see just how down I was, although in life I was still functioning, working, playing with the children, keeping the place running. His answer this time was that I should go into the now defunct David Rice Psychiatric hospital. 'What for?' I asked.

'They'll put you to sleep, give your mind a chance to calm down and start working naturally again.'

'For how long? A few days?'

'Oh, I would expect it to be longer than that, probably a few weeks, months even. It's nothing to worry about. It's not an asylum. The patients are those who cannot cope, through stress of one sort or another.'

He was offering another painkiller instead of trying to treat the cause. It didn't take me long to make up my mind. I knew something of electro convulsive therapy and if they were to use that on me while I was drugged up, I would probably loose many qualities I possessed.

'I am not having a breakdown. I still work efficiently. While things at home are not ideal, we do not fight. I don't berate the children, nor do I beat them. I don't come home drunk, nor consume gin all the evening. I don't drink at all. I have a severe problem that is causing me distress. Sleeping in a drug induced stupor for three months or for the rest of my life, will not take that away, but it would take away the humanity that I have. I do not want to be a zombie, a half person reliant on a chemical cocktail. I am not going to voluntarily enter an institution that I believe will in the long run only harm me.'

'It's the best suggestion I have.' He seemed taken aback, bemused and stung. I should have found another GP then, but where in Norfolk?

The break up came after ten years of marriage, when she realised I would never come to terms with my masculinity. I had tried and I tried again. It is difficult to explain how awful it was playing the hated male role. For a start, sex was a balance between physical pleasure and mental disgust. The whole act filled me with dread, not the dread of failure, but every time it was an admission of that very masculinity which I so hated, a visitation of the actual which denied the belief I had in my real identity. It undermined my very excuse for existence. The fact that Margaret needed sex was a pressure too and my infrequent lovemaking became a guilt which was hard for me to bear, leaving also a gap in her existence. We seldom discussed it, even when she knew about my difficulties. Talking to our unsympathetic doctor formed her opinions. I too, was quite unable to talk to her about it, feeling insurmountable guilt, shame, embarrassment and humiliation. There was no hope for us therefore.

In the end, as the restraint I had used to control my desires drifted away and I became more and more feminine, she realised that this problem would not be rooted out, as my doctor, the lay preacher described his remedy, in almost Biblical terms. He was almost looking to cast out demons.

Margaret had endured enough and decided to release me, although I had not come to terms with that possibility at all. I still loved her, could not believe that she did not love me anymore and there were the children too, whom I adored. What would become of the three of them? Who would look after them? Would another replace me in the children's affections? Any displaced father or mother particularly knows the latter fear and I believe it to be the greatest weapon any spouse has, used by many in a most vindictive way. Even worse, I considered what would be if there was a stepfather who mistreated my children. Could I live with that? I believe I would have killed to defend them. Even though I had no choice in the matter by now, I still felt the responsibility of my actions and of my character. My mind could cope with none of it. These were decisions too great for me to make. I was too unselfish to make them, even to go off and be happy. I could not even discuss it. I was in a trap which my psyche, my mental being could not escape from. I was therefore at the mercy of others who could make decisions. I was catatonic again, yet still managed to work and to keep myself clean.

I drove Margaret to despair and onto hate and then to desperation. She has told me since, that she tried to poison me and that too is something that I have to take responsibility for, driving her to that excess. Part of the problem was, as Dannie said years later, I am an innocent child in my heart, whatever excesses come from my mouth and pen. In our relationship, I could not believe that she would not continue to love me, as I loved her. That is another familiar thought process suffered by those in broken relationships.

There had to be a solution. As in so many cases, it was the female partner who made the important ones. She left with the children, who were immediately made wards of court, in case I should try to snatch them, but with access to be agreed. Later, there would be no access, as reports by social workers, by psychiatrists and my holy Joe doctor all came down against me, even though none of them had any experience of transsexualism and of the effect or otherwise on children. What evidence there was, spoke to the contrary, from Dr Randall, who was soon to become my consultant, the most eminent expert in the United Kingdom; also from the U.S.A, where much more was known and a more liberal view was taken. It bore no weight in their decisions.

I lost the house and most of my possessions. I gave it up to Margaret and the children. What was worse, I lost the affection of Margaret and the love and joy of my children. For a time I struggled on in the house alone while they lived with her mother, hardly believing what was happening. Then as the noose seemed to be tightening about my throat, as all these possessions were being slowly withdrawn and it dawned upon me that there would be no more future with them, I at last managed to make my doctor refer me to Dr Randal. He was the same person who had tried to use aversion therapy to cure transsexualism and who was now the leading advocate in Britain of surgery to cure it.

That must have been a monumental change in Randal's thinking. I believe that it was to save my life, for without the promise of a female future, I could not have gone on living. Up till then it had been my family and their need of me which made living necessary, almost bearable. Without that need and without hope there was nothing.

It was at this time that a secret report on me by my doctor came into my possession. It was not friendly. He referred to me as being 'like a marine, neither soldier nor sailor', that I was 'some damned hermaphrodite'. He spoke of surgery as being 'against God' and that 'the bible spoke specifically against self-mutilation'. That would be a wide subject for discussion indeed, which could be carried to things like appendicitis, plastic surgery, any other corrective techniques, orthodontics for example. Any one who quotes the bible at me is automatically suspect. Quote moral ethics by all means, but not the views of man from more than two thousand years ago. Surely we have moved far enough forward not to believe all that, chapter and verse, otherwise myths like Jonah and the six day construction of this sadly used and glorious planet, would also be true! There is a joke I heard the other day that God being God and modest, told us that he took six days, but in fact he only took four and a half.

However, Dr Curl set me on the path at last, agreeing to send me to Dr Randall at Charing Cross and a few months later, I chose a new doctor who was sympathetic. My quest for a female role had taken off. I was thirty-six. Half my life had gone by painfully, shrouded by a mental anguish which troubled me nearly every minute of each day and which was a barrier to interacting fully with other people, because I was terrified of displaying the real me. Perhaps the rest of my life would be happier.

As I reflect on this 30 years later, I am reminded of what Dr Randal said of my feelings of guilt. 'You are no worse, no less or more guilty than any partner who leaves a marriage for another.' It was no consolation. I like the Prince of Wales, married in the knowledge that I had a problem. Yet I unlike Charles, did marry for love at least. And if Margaret and those in the medical and social services had had more understanding, the long-term outcome could have been better.

CHAPTER 11.

I revisited Dr Randal in the mid summer 1976. I was apprehensive for we had met before. My previous meeting with him some seven years ago had not gone well and I did not want a repetition. The new Charing Cross hospital was a far cry from the old. This was a custom built nineteen seventies building, with different wards on each wing of the fifteen or so stories. It was already starting to fray round the edges and wear and tear was unrepaired. It was also a bit of a prefab and time, six years since its commissioning, had not been kind to it. But it is one of London's and the UK's centres of excellence and learning. The decision to close it and several other first class hospitals in the capital at the beginning of the 90's, by Mrs Bottomley, Thatcher's Health Minister, made no sense to me. But of course, I may be biased. That decision was rethought. Bottomley also said that she would not pay for unnecessary sex change operations, as though people went through the process on a whim. Another absurd opinion from a woman one would have thought would have some sense.

Virginia Hilda Brunette Maxwell Garnett was born in Dunoon to W. John Garnett, former director of what was then called The Industrial Society, and Barbara Rutherford-Smith, former pupil of the School of St Helen and St Katharine, teacher and elected Conservative member of the Inner London Education Authority. Her aunt on her father's side was Labour Greater London Council Member Peggy Jay. She first met Peter, now Sir Peter Bottomley her husband, when she was 12 and they married in 1967.

Bottomley was educated at Putney High School, an independent school for girls in Putney in south-west London, before going up to the University of Essex (BA). She later graduated from the London School of Economics with the degree of Master of Arts (MA). She began her working life as a social scientist, researcher for Child Poverty Action Group, social worker, Justice of the Peace, and Chairman of the Inner London Juvenile Court.

I have given here part of Virginia's entry in Wikipedia, to show that qualifications and even experience can count for nothing. As a scholar and as a responsible Minister, she should have made some attempt to understand transsexualism before making such a pronouncement. She was a woman of the World and frankly I would expect more. If she could be so fundamentally wrong about a subject I know about, how many more crass decisions are made by such people before they have done any research. Twelve years later, she appeared to be sympathetic to Transsexualism and is of course, now in the House of Lords. No wonder the nation is in a mess.

My new visit to Randal came at last. I found my way to reception on the third floor and a harassed woman directed me to some chairs around the corner in the corridor that surrounds the central lift system. There was one person waiting before me, for what treatment I knew not. She entered and I could only hear muffled voices, not that I wanted to know her business, but I was looking for reassurance, wanting to know what sort of interviews went on in there. I walked by the office door, to see what I could through the frosted glass of the panels that ran each side of the door. All I saw was the blurred image of a white coat. 'They're coming to take you away, ha ha,' to quote a song of several years ago, the men in white coats. Would they take me away?

At last and it was only fifteen minutes after the appointed time, he appeared to summon me into the office. He still had the same lugubrious air, a soft voice, the voice of an undertaker in church perhaps, and a dark suit to go with it. The similarity to Wally my old English master, still struck me, in his features, his bulk and above all the gloomy soft, plaintiff, reproachful, yet bullying voice. There were about four students there, crowded into that tiny eight feet square office. I wondered what went through their minds as we patients performed our tricks.

This time I was determined to speak up and stick up for myself, but the first question threw me completely.

'You saw me a little over seven years ago, why has it taken you so long to come back?'

I thought about it. 'I had things to do, and the treatment you prescribed last time wasn't what I wanted.'

'Why not? Did you not want to be....normal, to lead a...normal life.'

'No. It wasn't what I felt to be right. You wanted to change my mind, I wanted to change my body.'

'But if it had made you well, you would have been happy, would you not?'

'It would not have made me well. The treatment didn't work, did it.' I was making a statement.

'What makes you say that?'

'I know it. That's why it is no longer used.' I could see the students were interested. Perhaps this was different for them.

'That's not strictly true. However.' He looked at the notes. I felt that I had won the first round. He was changing the subject. It was a great victory, but at the same time I was afraid of offending him. I needed him much more than he needed me and I had to convince him of certain things, as he was to make clear. It was like playing a game but being uncertain of the rules.

He gave a short history of me to the students. The girl looked sympathetic, one of the men let a smile flicker across his face.

'There is nothing funny here,' said the great man, 'I am sure that he is quite serious about this.' The student removed the smile.

'If I take you as a patient, then you have to abide by the rules. Broadly they are these. You have to convince me that you are of a sane and sound mind and that you are stable enough to handle this change, which can be stressful. Before I supply you with any hormones, which by the way, only have a cosmetic effect, you have to demonstrate your ability to pass as a female. That means that you have to appear here before me, in the female role. If at any time I suspect that you are breaking the rules, then I will withdraw my support. In addition and as a condition of prolonged treatment and eventual surgery, you have to work and support yourself as a woman. After the appropriate time, depending on your ability to abide by these rules, I will recommend surgery. Do you understand?'

'How long?'

'It is up to you. Not less than four years, I have many patients.'

'I have wasted so much time already. Can't it be sooner?'

'Those are the conditions laid down by the DHSS. Do you want to be a patient?'

'Yes.'

'Will you be coming as a female next time?'

'I don't know.' Suddenly the thought of that impersonation in front of all these faces, seemed a cliff to climb.

'I can give you a card that will explain your position, should the police pick you up. It should keep you out of trouble, as long as you are not importuning.' He smiled his fat cat smile and I believed he was joking. 'Make an appointment for three months time. It is up to you, you know.' He looked at me over the top of his glasses. I was dismissed.

As I sat in the train on my journey back to Norfolk, many thoughts and emotions ran through my mind. Firstly, after all the doubts, the traumas, the despair, the awful sense of failure as a human being that I had carried for thirty-six years, I experienced elation. At last something had gone right. A lifeline had been thrown to me and whatever happened I would hang on to it. My belief in myself had at last been supported by the DHSS. An involuntary gurgle of excitement left my lips and I looked round at the other occupants of the carriage to see whether they had noticed. One man looked quizzically at me. I had the awful feeling that he would see what path I was beginning. I should have to keep my feelings hidden still.

My memory went back to that first meeting with Randall, seven years ago. Having met a blank wall in the shape of Dr. 'C' and the Norfolk psychiatrist, I had tried to be the person the world seemed to want me to be. I began to think I was touched, that all these jumbled feelings and desires, were some sort of aberration. I succeeded in staying almost normal for two or three years, almost believing that I had conquered the demon. Then it came back, more strongly than before, more desperate, my future more clouded. When my efforts to be 'normal' failed once more and my wife knew something of my problem, I agreed to Dr. 'C's biblical diagnosis that, it had to be, 'rooted out'.

He had referred me to Dr. Randall, who was then prescribing aversion therapy. This treatment was developed after the Korean war, using techniques supposed to have been used to brainwash prisoners of the Chinese/North Korean alliance. It had been shown that animals could be taught behaviour too. A dog or ape would perform a task for a reward, usually food. Animals had also learned not to do things by receiving a shock when they attempted a particular task. Great science! That is exactly the theory of the electric fence in farming. As children, we had learned either to wear rubber boots when we touched the wire or not to touch it at all. A trick we developed, was to wear rubber boots, hold the wire and touch a companion who would feel the jolt. Pigs, sheep, cattle and sheep dogs, soon learn never to touch the fence. When animals have learned, one can switch off the current and they will still stay clear.

This same theory was applied to humans. It was alleged by psychiatrists that habits like alcohol, smoking, cross dressing, homosexuality and, transsexualism, could be eradicated by aversion therapy. It was believed, due to research by Dr. Money's team at John Hopkins University, that much of sexuality was nurture rather than nature. In other words it was learned behaviour rather than any basic physical sexual difference of the brain. In aversion therapy, the patient would be allowed a smoke or shown an image, and accordingly receive a reward or an electric shock of varying intensity. Of course, the difference between animals and mankind is one of intelligence. If a criminal knows that when he holds up a bank, ten thickset policemen are going to jump on him, he won't go in. If he believes that the bank is a soft touch with no security and the local constabulary are all sitting down to their annual staff lunch, he will go in. A human not only has memory, but intelligence. That is why the therapy didn't work. It must have provided practitioners with some good fun though.

Such had been my despair that I had agreed to try this obnoxious treatment. I saw Randal at the old Charing Cross Hospital. The building was antiquated, white tiles, people sitting in corridors, mounds of paper. It was a dispiriting place. My heart sank as I picked my way amongst the waiting patients and found the hole in the wall they called reception. I felt like running away.

The room I was shown into seemed to be a wash room. It was. I wondered if they were going to beat the demon out of me, then wash my blood down the drain in the centre of the room. In this frightening and incongruous setting, was the Great Man and 10 or so students sat in a semicircle. I could imagine that students went along to this session as a little light relief, a good wheeze. I was asked to sit in the chair facing this semicircle. Randal apologised for the setting, which he said was a temporary arrangement. As Randal gave a summary of my syndrome as supplied by my GP, there were a few sniggers. They weren't corrected. I felt that I was in Bedlam, and the local populace was peering through the bars at the cavorting inmate. I could hardly reply to the questions, I just wanted to escape. After fifteen minutes of nonsense, when Randal imposed his will to carry out his chosen treatment, I managed to escape. I reached the steps of St. Martins, Trafalgar Square where I sank to the ground and just sat watching the traffic and the people. The pigeons circled, the cabs rushed by, buses lumbered and lurched. It was a beautiful late spring day. It all seemed monotone. I wandered aimlessly towards Leicester Square, then to Berkeley Square. I turned into a kosher restaurant, but didn't stay. I back tracked towards Soho and China town. None of it excited me. I had no appetite for food or life. I had reached another dead end, I knew that already, yet I would try to take Randall's treatment further.

I was instructed by Dr. Randall's assistant that I should supply photos of myself both as a female and as a male, in various degrees of dress and undress. Margaret said I should try the treatment. Wow, what a show they must have had in his clinic! I wonder what happened to all the photos afterwards. Let's hope they were not sold on to some porn magazine. I took one set of slides as directed, turning the living room into a studio when I had time alone. Margaret gave me the space by visiting her sister. It was a long business, setting up, setting the self-exposure on the camera, dressing, undressing, posing, exposing. I sent the film direct to the clinic where they processed it, as I might have been arrested for pornography. I never saw the results, but was told they were very nice photos. I didn't want to see them. They were a sign of my dysfunction in society.

I never went to the clinic. I read an article in the Times casting doubt on the treatment. I had also formed my own conclusion, that having had these feelings for as long as I could remember, and as I hadn't been able to end them for my own sake or for the sake of those I loved, it would not work. I had tried, I really had tried.

That wasn't my only doubt. The idea that the psyche should be changed, when in my opinion, the self, the soul, is more important than the flesh, seemed fundamentally wrong. I was proved right. The treatment proved to be a failure and was dropped. I will explain later the new theories on transsexualism.

On the train, my mind turned to other matters arising from my second meeting with Randall. I now knew what I had to do. Doing it was the difficult part. To any 'normal' heterosexual male, these conditions would be not only absurd but impossible. I ask any heterosexual satisfied in their own sex to consider whether they would want to or could fulfil Randall's conditions. To me they were difficulties. There were two important conditions I had to fulfil. The first was living as a woman, the next working as a woman.

I was still living in the family home, alone. Margaret and the children had gone to her mother's two miles away. There was nothing to stop my dressing as a woman immediately, except that Norfolk is a very small world and word would go round like wildfire. This might cause my family and almost certainly my children, difficulties that they ought not to have. My work then was as a representative for a wholesale food company, Booker of the literature prize fame. I spoke to my manager, explaining what was happening. 'When do you want to leave?' he asked.

'I'll let you know. Early next year.'

'It will be a pity to see you go, but well, you wouldn't want to stay on here, would you? Wouldn't work.'

'No, I guess not.'

I continued to work hard. My sales figures were looking good, the best in the branch. It was going to be a wrench finding another job. It seemed a very greasy pole to climb, to escape my masculinity.

I had to have clothes. I bought a few women's clothes as a male, making out that they were presents. There was also the problem of looking like a woman, not only dressing like a woman, but acting like a woman, in a convincing enough manner that I did not cause interest. A disturbance, even a road traffic incident could result in arrest, even with Dr Randal's little card in my bag. I wish I had kept that card, I never needed it and I don't know where it went. It is only as I write this on a fine summer's day in the comfort of my living room, that I remember having it.

I saw Randal again in late summer, 'Why are you not dressed as a female? I have offered what you profess to want. Why haven't you made a decision?' He was cold and hectoring.

I announced my plans. He wasn't satisfied. I should have come in the female role. 'There is no need to do everything at once. I expect to see you as a woman next time or I shall not continue treatment. Meanwhile, here is another prescription.' He handed me another three months prescription for stilboestrol, the synthetic oestrogen later discovered to be a carcinogenic. I swallowed the tablets gladly. Almost immediately, my breasts began to swell. They became quite sore and tender. I began to put on weight, only a few pounds, but I saw it as a sign that I was thriving.

One grim grey Saturday, I dressed carefully, made myself up and went to Norwich as a female. As I drove out of my drive, I could hardly breathe, so tense was I. I spent all day in and out of shops, finding what suited, what didn't, carefully spending my budget and mapping out a wardrobe. I bought clothes that were classic rather than showy, smart but unassuming. In spite of the dull September day, with a chill in the air, I was alight inside with the adrenalin and joy this activity produced. I came home laden. I had never had so many parcels. Yet, underneath my joy, there was a gnawing sorrow, that I couldn't be a normal father of a perfect family.

My first visit to the hospital as a female was in the autumn, before assuming the female role full time. I took great care with my appearance. I had innate good dress sense. I have never understood why some women find dressing so difficult and the frightful mess we as a sex get into is quite amazing. One only has to walk the high street to see fashion victims and those with either no idea or no inclination to be smart, whether dressy or casual. Anything goes in these times and that is good, but one should still try to cut a figure. If one is really clueless, regarding shape, form, colour, then there are helpful hints in the shops, dressed dummies, clothes put together as ensembles, etc. There are any amount of magazines and TV programmes. I used these hints, but did not really need them. I was frequently complimented on my dress at work and I still am to this day. However, as has been pointed out to me, some people do have a real problem getting dress right and it seems just as much a difficulty for them, as colour blindness is for some.

I arrived at the reception desk on the third floor of Charing Cross Hospital with a new persona. They only knew me by my male name, but the woman receptionist without a flicker, just altered the records. She asked me to sit near the counter so she could let me know when to go in. An especially nice thing then happened. She brought me a cup of tea. As she put it down she said, 'You look very nice, the best looking woman we've had here today.' She was Irish, and the words lilted off her tongue lifting my spirits and my confidence.

Dr Randal expressed no surprise. He asked for a photo for his wall, which was plastered with other conversion jobs. At that time I believe the hospital was doing between forty and sixty operations per year, so he had a good many to see, probably three hundred or so on his list. I checked on the surgery list. There was my name, the woman clerk showed me, number 186. I was on the way.

I needed somewhere to live. A customer, Don and his second wife Marion, volunteered a room in their house. This seemed to be the best option. I needed some company, I liked them a lot and I was grateful for the offer. My plan was to leave work at the end of January, change my identity and move in with them as a woman. Then I would attempt to find work in my new persona. This would free the house for Margaret and the children to move back to.

I was moonlighting as a waiter at a local three star hotel to accrue the extra cash I was going to need. This was something that I had done before, whenever money was tight. The hotel trade in Britain is staffed by moonlighters, the desperate, and the no hopers. Practically no training is given either to dining room staff or to kitchen staff. That is why our standards are so low. There are more exceptions to this than there used to be and particularly in some restaurants and good hotels, training has become top class. I was a top class silver service waiter, but the standards amongst some of my colleagues and kitchen staff was frankly, embarrassing. Many hotels employ illegal immigrants as cleaners, the homeless as kitchen porters. It is an antisocial trade. The names on the wages book ranged from John Smith to Michael Mouse.

Steve was a nice enough young lad. He was a fellow waiter, not very good at it, and couldn't care less about the customers. He delighted in tweaking nipples, an amusing habit, but not when one is taking stilboestrol. I had to get annoyed before he would stop. As I was on my own, I volunteered to work through Christmas with all the other 'sad gits'. I was glad I did. The customers were in party mood and so were we. The artificial snowballs whistled through the air in the dining room and found their way into the kitchen. Steve and I versus the sous chefs, who had the brain wave of throwing them back after they had dropped in the soup. They hit the tiled wall soggily, then slid to the floor. Steve and I managed to duck the volleys of snowballs and stay clean. We left them to clean up. The customers thought the soup very good.

Having seen what goes on behind the scenes, one might think twice about eating out. I have seen a waiter turn quickly carrying eggs and bacon, and the breakfast has slid off the plate onto the floor, the eggs still whole. One quick scoop and the breakfast is back on the plate. There have been thumbs in soup, dripping noses stirring sauces, drunken chefs, no chefs. One waiter called Speedy, worked hard but had little experience. His ambition in life was to be a local Tory Party agent. He believed that unless you tried, you would attain nothing. A commendable spirit. But there are limits to what is sensible. He *would* try to carry four soups through the swing door before he had learned to carry three. As he passed through the door, it was already returning. It caught his arm putting him off balance. He staggered into the dining room, getting lower all the time as he fought to control the rocking plates. He hit a stand containing ice and a bottle of wine, which he sent skittering across the floor, the soups followed in a tidal wave of minestrone and crockery. Poor Speedy was sacked on the spot.

I worked with a Chinese couple who were most professional. It was amusing to see them reading the Times at staff breakfast while the others read the Sun or Mirror. They would eventually have their own restaurant and time working in a hotel was merely a means of achieving a goal.

Meanwhile, in my day job, we had the National Sales dinner at Heathrow. In the afternoon four of us went to Highbury to see Arsenal. I always enjoyed our football forays which seemed to be a tradition before a firm's function. John was my best mate among the lads and a football buff. He had the misfortune to be a Wolverhampton supporter. We always seemed to end up at Highbury where the fans were friendly. They would ask where we were from, and just laugh with pity when we replied Norwich.

In the evening, we assembled in the Hotel banquet room, all done up in dickey bows. There was not one woman on the sales staff, but today probably 50% would be female. Imagine my surprise when my name was announced for the prize for the most increase in turnover out of 130 sales reps. It was a pity that in six weeks I would be leaving, with absolutely no idea if I would ever work again. It was always interesting to meet guys from other areas and to hear of their problems. In Norfolk, we had too many green fields in between calls. In London, one guy had so many Patels, that he gave them numbers, one to twenty-three, that they used to identify themselves when phoning in.

Christmas came. It was a bad time. This would I suspected, be the last Christmas I would be with the children. The odds were stacked against me, and while I had not come to terms with it, I realised that it was more than likely. It was also the first Christmas in ten years that I was not with Margaret. My brother too, had separated and his new girl friend was giving him grief. We were a most unhappy family. I remember best, playing with my son, then nearly five. I had bought him a helicopter that flew around in a circle. The art was to get it to land in the right place. I was thrilled to find that he could do it. That was really the only good moment.

At the branch dinner in January, the sales director paid me public compliment. In his short speech, he said he was sorry to see me go and wished me well. Two weeks later, I said goodbye to the lads and that was that, a chapter closed. The company car had gone, replaced with a dirty old van. It certainly felt like hard times.

Back home, in my lonely cottage, I packed up my personal belongings and departed with my cat for Don and Marion's, twenty five miles away. I cried as I drove. The future seemed suddenly so full of difficulties, the past so full of pain. I cried for the loss of Margaret, the loss of my children and of my home upon which I had worked so hard. I had lost everything for the sake of this inner self that would not be silenced. I was setting out on the route to Mrs. Bottomley's unnecessary sex change operation. If I was prepared to give all that I had, it could hardly have been unnecessary.

I walked into Don's to find a roaring open fire, peace and harmony. They revived my flagging spirits. From now on, I was female. They were both very supportive. It was January 30th 1977. I was born again at 37 years old.

The next week I signed on for the dole. I explained to the clerk what was happening and she immediately handed me on to a very considerate woman manager of the Fakenham Job Centre. It was a much better reception than I expected. Later, as my unemployment stretched into months, she asked tentatively, if I would find work. By then, I had heard that I would have a job and was waiting for the start date. She was as glad for me as I was. Following that first visit, I received a call from the DHSS office in Kings Lynn, asking if they could visit me. I agreed of course, with dread of what they wanted.

A man accordingly turned up, chubby, his hair awry, holding a battered briefcase. He seemed dour and I suspected the worst. He took all my details, past work, family, doctor, prospects. Once more, I found him if not charming, considerate and kindly. He reassured me, and told me that he would give all the assistance he could. The civil servant is much maligned, the butt of so many jokes. I found the more senior officers, intelligent, hardworking and sympathetic.

About two months later, I received a call from the police, passed on to me by Marion who had answered the phone. They confirmed my identity then expressed a wish to see me. They would come to me, they said. The two days wait before their visit was hard to bear. Three large men eventually trooped into the living room. Marion made an excuse to go, but I asked her to remain. They were CID from Norfolk Police investigating the murder of a young boy which had taken place in the Fakenham area and a possible connection with the disappearance of April Fabb from the Cromer area. They asked a few questions, then said one to another, 'we know where this is coming from'. Someone, a 'friend' or an acquaintance had told the police that I could be the murderer. After all, I had been mobile and I was of course, a sexual deviant. They apologised for their intrusion and told me I had no need to worry, they weren't interested in me. They inferred that it had been a malicious call. I hid my feelings, from them, from Don and Marion and from my family, but within I was devastated that anyone could think that of me or want to harm me. That is one of the problems, particularly for male 'deviants', that they have every kind of accusation heaped upon them. Thus homosexuals are also child molesters and cross dressers etc., but it is seldom so. Luckily, as a more open society emerges, this kind of prejudice recedes. But the strife within the Church of England over homosexual clergy and the antagonism to female priests let alone bishops, is horrifying, unchristian and uncharitable.

Shortly after that, I saw an advert for clerical officers and assistants in the civil service. I spoke to Marion. She said, 'Go for it, you're certain to get in.' I sent off for the application form. I completed it, honestly stating my position. The law is that a false statement on an application, for example, of qualifications, can result in instant dismissal. I didn't want to gain a job and lose it through misrepresentation.

I drove into Norwich, found a parking spot and reported. I was shown to a waiting room and eventually summoned before the board. There were three on the board, the usual Civil Service format. Their questions were reasonable and easy. I felt quite comfortable sitting before them as a woman. All went well. Towards the end, they started on my sexual status. If they gave me a job, they wanted to know, how would I get on with the other staff? I replied that I would behave as any other female, and that no offence would be committed on my side. I joked that I was hardly likely to get my pipe out and put my feet on the desks. They agreed, that by my appearance they didn't think I would. One chap volunteered that he wouldn't have known, had I not stated my transsexuality. It had gone remarkably well.

Four weeks later, I received a letter offering me a post but with no start date. They would call for me when a vacancy arose. I was elated, as was Marion, no doubt breathing a sigh of relief that I wasn't going to be hanging around them forever.

I knew nothing of the civil service then, and little more about HMSO, who had conducted the interview. I never expected to be given a job. Four weeks later, I received a letter offering me work. It was as the lowest form of clerical worker, a clerical assistant, unestablished, health risk. The letter apologised for the low standard of work offered but urged me to take the job. I needed no bidding. The unestablishment meant that I was on probation and could be dismissed if my behaviour or health record suffered because of my condition. I remained healthy, never lost a day in four years and had the best record in the department. Eventually, after my employers pleaded with the civil service commission, I was pronounced established.

All the time this was going on, so was the divorce, the untying of a marriage, each step causing me pain, each step diminishing me, relieving me of possessions, taking away my rights. I dreaded the solicitor's letters. I felt oppressed, hunted, uncertain of myself and of my place in the world. I didn't fight. It was an extremely difficult period.

In addition Don and I were getting on each other's nerves. There was a certain amount of jealousy I'm sure, for Marion and I were very close for a time. It was Don's second marriage, and he was still embittered against the first wife, to whom unusually he had to pay maintenance. It did not seem justice to me and he had my sympathy. But there was in him a certain inferiority that was provoked also by my sometimes blunt remarks and I have to admit, sharp tongue. We disagreed about drugs. He was for legalising them all, I wasn't. He was exceedingly antagonistic towards the church, while I believe that for most it does no harm and may be a positive force, though I am an atheist. He could also be racist.

As a couple, they were having some problems. As is usual, the third party becomes the whipping person. I left there rather bitterly. What had started out as a really friendly act had all gone sour. Don was particularly vindictive, while Marion was sympathetic to my face, but absolutely neutral in his presence. I understood her position. Having sold me a duff car and extracted the last of my cash, doing me a 'favour', Don refused to annul the transaction.

I went to stay with my parents. They were very supportive, had accepted me when many others would not have known how to handle it. Some would have cut me off. I decided after three weeks, that I was better off with them. I phoned Don to get my stuff, hardly what one would call belongings, the few things that I had taken from my family home. It was not convenient, whatever time I suggested. In the end, using my key, my brother and I just entered while they were out and packed it all in the car and a trailer. I found that he had been using my tools, they were all over 'my bedroom', where the floors were up, as Don was apparently repairing joists. In addition, he had thrown my cat out. I rescued her from their half-ruined barn, covered in fleas. She welcomed me pathetically, clung to me and I could see just how distressed she was. They had fed her very little. It was a harsh act to a lovely, friendly, dumb animal and an unforgivable attack upon me. I never want to see Don again.

Three years later, Marion phoned me to say that Don was away, and would I like to come over for the evening. Like a fool I went, thinking that for old time's sake and with fond memories of the support she had given me, she really wanted to make amends. What I really found was that she wanted as many people as possible for a clothing party she was holding next day. I didn't go to the wretched party. How can people be so mercenary and cruel?

I started work. It was pretty mundane stuff, but that was all I had required, as I believed that I had enough to contend with, without pressure in work. As a survey in a magazine dealing with stress stated, I was charting up all the most stressful experiences at once. A divorce, a bereavement in the terms of lost contact, not only with Margaret and the dear children, but also with all my old friends from whom I had cut myself off; a change of job; moving house; starting a new job; changing or at least amending my sex. The latter seemed pretty easy compared with all the rest. I settled down into a hermaphroditic existence very easily, intensely pleased with my blossoming breasts arriving twenty years too late, and trying to ignore the bits, I wished hence. It all seemed to come quite naturally.

Whether I really needed to cut myself adrift from my past, I do not know. It seemed the least stressful thing to do at the time and I could not cope with snide remarks, the back biting there inevitably would have been had I not. However, had I been a different person and faced them all, given as good as they might have given me, it could have proved a better way. There were not many I would have missed anyway. John and Lillian, their true names, from my old work, and that would have probably been the sum.

It was time to go to Charing Cross Hospital again. Dr Randall was difficult to like. He continually played devil's advocate and put one under pressure to conform, to obey, to accept the rules and adapt. It was a tough regime and he was a tough master. I sat outside his small office, when there emerged a nice looking woman in a trouser suit. There had been raised voices inside and I had wondered what was going on.

'You next?' She asked.

'I would seem to be,' I replied. 'What was that all about?'

'Trousers. I'll wait for you, then we can swap notes.'

'I'd like that.'

Randall poked his frog face out. 'Next.'

My interview took about ten minutes. And it went something like this.

'I last saw you three months ago. How have you been?'

'Fine.'

'You are still working?'

'Yes.'

'What at?'

'The Civil Service.'

'They are treating you all right?'

'Yes.'

'No difficulties.'

'No.'

'You still haven't let me have a photograph of yourself for my gallery. Will you do so? I like to keep a record of my patients.'

He had a wall covered in photos. I never gave him one.

'Yes, I'll try to arrange it.'

'You dress well. It is good that you are not way out or wear sleazy frocks. You may have heard raised voices with the previous patient. She will wear trousers, when I have expressly forbidden it. I do not understand why someone should want to change their sex but not their dress. It is beyond me.'

'And your family. Your divorce is ongoing? You know that I cannot do anything for you unless you are divorced. The law will not allow marriage between a female nor a man and a transsexual woman, or vice versa.'

'It's going through.'

'What about boy friends?'

'I don't have one.'

'Why not? You want to be female. Females usually have boy friends. Is that not how it goes?'

'Yes, usually. If the circumstances are right. Not every woman has a man, nor wants to change into a man because they don't have a boyfriend.'

'I await developments then, with baited breath. We shall see what the future holds. You may go. Come and see me in three months!'

He was the bizarre one not me.

Adelle was waiting for me outside. We introduced ourselves. 'How was he?

'His usual lugubrious self. I find him most difficult. He was upset with you and your trousers.' I have to say, she had on a very good feminine trouser suit.

'Its a battle we often have. He tells me not to wear them, I say, trousers do not make a man, nor a skirt a woman. In any case, what's the matter with this? It's an expensive trouser suit.'

'You look great.' She did. She had the greenest eyes and her makeup was perfect, enough, not overdone. Her shortish dark red hair was feminine. She was about five feet nine. 'You have the most wonderful eyes,' I said.

'Tinted contacts. You look very pretty, and so petite.' It was the first time anyone had spoken to me like that apart from Marion.

We went to Harrods. She regaled me with stories about other transsexuals she knew from her days in Manchester, some who were decidedly unbalanced and struggling. Adelle had no Manchester accent and I believe came from a well off family. She had had a rib removed to give her a better figure. She worked for the civil service as an Executive officer but her passion was singing. I would see her later on television as a singer in a group, looking very glamorous. I wonder where she is now.

(She is still singing in the group very successfully 2012.)

The transsexual trail is a long road. Many books have now been written, most do not like to dwell on the aspect of the mechanics. It is after all, a rather painful rebirth, and life really starts from the time of that rebirth. For all these years since I first set off down the path, I have shut out the past. It has been too painful, too embarrassing, and my life as a male was not something I wished to remember. Dannie, who will enter this story again later, has changed that. She has given me a new perspective and the strength to tell the tale. It is a journey both emotionally draining and cathartic.

If any one of you reading this is a transsexual as yet unfulfilled, I would say, 'have courage'. It is now easier, the phenomenon understood to some extent, the value of surgery recognised. The law has been changed to give protection. Unnecessary sex-change operations. Whoever heard of such a thing? Who would want their bits altered unless they were in the most dire straits? To most people, such a course would be the utmost horror; therefore anyone wanting it must indeed need therapy of some sort. However, Bottomley's decree made in 1993, was twenty-one years ago as I write, and knowledge is improving all the time. Attitudes have changed and are changing. Whereas in my time successful reassignments occurred in those over thirty, the age is now much lower. In Holland they consider that the sooner therapy begins, the better, even before puberty and the effects that has on altering the body is positive. Oh how I wish that had been for me.

What every transsexual will say, so that it has almost become a cliché, is that they are a man or woman, trapped in a woman's or man's body. It is that feeling, a fundamental haemorrhage between psyche and body that people have found so difficult to understand. It has therefore become a joke, the usual way the human deals with difficult questions. Sexuality is not a matter for internal debate. The human knows instinctively, what sex they are, whether hetero or homosexual, male or female. Where transsexuals differ is that they know whether they are female or male regardless of their physical appearance.

There have been two schools of thought about the reasons for this phenomenon. The first claimed that conditioning is responsible, that over close mothers, or dominant over protective mothers, or weak or absent fathers, create or nurture rather fey, gentle and shy children, who then want to be like the mother. The belief was that sexuality was as much nurture as nature. Dr Randall held that opinion, believing that it was a purely psychological syndrome. This I believe is a complete myth. Why is it then that siblings are not also affected, they have the same mother? It was because of this believe in conditioning that children born with indeterminate genitalia, so called intersex children, were reassigned to a sex according to the surgeon's opinion of whether the genitalia looked more male or female. In an infamous case in Winnepeg, Canada, in the 1960's, twin boys were sent for circumcision. A tragic error occurred, and the penis of one was burnt off. A prominent, world renowned psychologist, Dr. John Money, propounded a theory that 'gender identity' was not fully formed at birth. He defined 'gender identity' as being what makes us feel, think and behave as girls or boys. His view was that this identity was not fully fixed until the age of two and that brains are malleable, nurture overcoming nature. He recommended that the child should be reassigned as female by surgeons at John Hopkins University. The surgery was carried out. The child grew up unhappy. *She* always played with *her* brother's toys, never *her* own dolls etc. At the age of fourteen, *she* rebelled, took on the appearance of a male, later underwent hormone therapy and now lives as a man with a wife and step children and has had surgery to reverse the castration that took place on Money's advice. The tragedy was compounded by the fact that for thirty years, the process whereby the child, Bruce, was changed to Brenda, was claimed as a victory and evidenced as proof of Money's theory. Over the years this theory had been questioned by several practitioners, and particularly by Dr. Milton Diamond who theorised that sexual orientation was already formed in the brain before birth. Money's 'proof' stood in the way. The revelation of the real Bruce/Brenda outcome has demolished the theory that sex is merely a matter of physical appearance and is not fixed until the age of two.

Another appalling fact is that children born with indeterminate genitalia, who as babies have been assigned to one sex or another more or less at the whim of a surgeon according to physical attributes, were never allowed time to develop as cognitive beings to assess their true 'gender identity' as defined by their behaviour. Not only that, there has been no study and no follow up to see whether assignment had proved correct.

There is a growing corpus of evidence that these unfortunate intersex cases are caused by events in the womb during pregnancy. They are not to do with the genetics of the foetus but are accidents of the pregnancy process. The hypothesis is that during pregnancy, there is an imbalance of hormones in the womb and that this affects the brain and/or the physical attributes of the unborn child. Dr Milton Diamond has experimented with effects of testosterone on animals, and has found that injecting it into the mother, the hormone will find its way via the umbilical cord into the foetus, which when born may have internal female organs but externally may appear male.

While Money believed in sexual neutrality at birth, others were looking for differences that could explain why boys are boys and girls are girls not only physically, but in attitudes. To many it would seem obvious that there is a difference, and naive that one could believe that it is due to nurture. It was the fashion in the 70s to deny sexual difference. Everything was put down to nurture. It was considered wrong to allow girls to be too girly or for boys to have aggressive toys. Dr Roger Gorski, (University of California), chose a species that are well known to man, and has been experimented on extensively, rats. He set about dissecting their brains, slice by slice, looking for a difference between the male and female. They found nothing at first, then one of his students came upon a small area which was consistently different comparing one sex to the other. In comparing slides of the brains, slice by slice, there was an obvious difference in an area in the centre of the brain called the hypothalamus. On average this area was twice the size in the male as in the female. Gorski applied the earlier findings of Diamond to the problem. He injected pregnant rats with testosterone with the result that females were born with male brains.

In Holland at the Netherlands Institute of Brain Research, Professor Dick Swaab was interested in applying this knowledge to humans. Disease free brains are difficult to obtain, but he managed to acquire 100 brains to work on. Employing the same techniques as Gorski, he found the same differences in what they now knew to be the SDN (sexually dimorphic nucleus). They suspected that they had found the answer to gender identity. To test this they turned to a unique set of individuals, transsexuals.

The Dutch team managed to obtain the brains of twelve transsexuals, women who had been born male and had been reassigned because they thought of themselves as women. In each case, they found that the Sexual Dimorphic Nuclei were indeed female. This shows that far from sex change being a whim as Mrs. Bottomley believed, transsexuals are indeed right when they believe they are born into the wrong body, and that as Dr Randall had finally concluded, the best but not entirely satisfactory treatment, is to match the sexual appearance of the body to the brain. Randall was right but for all the wrong reasons.

In her book, 'Sexing the Body', Anne Fausto-Sterling discusses the futility of the nature/nurture debate. She is very critical of assigning gender simply as male and female, stressing that these are two extremes of a continuum. The attitude of the House of Lords, who consider that 'straight' men can be turned to homosexuality before the age of 18 by proselytising gays, would seem to be absurd. I maintain that sexual preference is set in people from a very early age, and probably as discussed above, pre-birth, although they may not always discover it themselves or allow themselves to indulge in this preference for reasons of family, peer or social pressure. In most there is no choice. They will be typically male or female. Others have indeterminate preference what we label as bisexual. Others will be homosexual. Like many transsexuals whose syndrome is evidenced at an early age, many gays make no 'choice' and their preference and inclination is known to them and often to the parents from an early age.

There are degrees of 'compulsion'. In each and every human being there are a whole range of emotions and needs of varying intensity. In my case the compulsion was such that my existence as a male was anathema. Everyday, a longing to be female was paramount. I have discussed this with a potential female to male TS, who ultimately decided to remain female but has adopted a lesbian way of life and taken a woman as partner. She finds that fulfilling and, when I said that I had no choice, she doubted that my feelings could be so strong. Unfortunately, talking of these matters aroused such great passions within her, bringing back all the old desires with which she thought she had come to terms, our friendship has had to be suspended because she cannot deal with her real psyche.

Meanwhile the divorce dragged on. The nisi and the absolute; the judgement by someone I never saw; the making over of the house to Margaret; her new boy friend moving into the house that largely I had built; the final decision that I would not be able to see the children again until they were sixteen. It was all bad news. Asked to pay the mortgage, I would not nor could I afford to. I was being asked to pay for a house that would never be of benefit in any way to me. I considered the request to be punitive. I was already paying maintenance for the children I was not able to see and on my paltry salary, it was all I could afford. I led a very quiet life. I shut myself away from people; had no social life except for my immediate family and one or two others. It was eight years before I would start to emerge from the carapace with which I protected myself and really start to interact socially again.

It is a lonely road. Most transsexuals will say that. Before re-assignment the loneliness is one of the spirit. There may be friends and there may be family, but so often, the hurt, this maiming of the spirit because the psyche does not fit with the body, prevents full and meaningful interaction with the rest of the world.

.

ACKNOWLEDGEMENTS.

The above, taken from a transcript of 'The Boy Who Was Turned Into A Girl' broadcast on BBC 2 @ 9.00pm Thursday 7th December 2000.

http://www.bbc.co.uk/science/horizon/boyturned girl_info.shtml

Further Reading.

'Sexing the Body' Anne Faustao Sterling, Basic Books, 2000. A critical appraisal of the nature/nurture debate and of assigning gender merely into male and female, instead stressing that these are two extremes of a continuum.

'Sex on the Brain' Deborah Blum, Penguin Books, 1997. Blum retails the scientific quest to prove that male and female characteristics are not social constructs but that there is strong bias for our gender-typical behaviour. She recounts the experiments and observations made to disprove the behaviourists attitude of gender being purely environmentally determined.

Web-links:

www.bbc.co.uk/health/body_chemistry

The BBC's body chemistry pages unravel the mysterious ways our hormones work.

www.med.jhu.edu/pedendo/intersex/

www.jhu.edu/~jhumag/0900web/babes.html

The John Hopkins University website has pages devoted to abnormal sex differentiation as well as more about David Reimer's story.

CHAPTER 12.

It was not long before I was recognised at work for what I was at that time, a male in drag. True, I did have burgeoning breasts augmented by cunningly designed and home made foam rubber, my hair was nice, my legs passable and my make up average for the time, but that was all. Admitting this even now, after twenty years, is quite difficult. As time went on, the hormones had a profound effect on the penis and testes. That organ has a will of its own, stubbornly uncontrollable, causing embarrassment by its habit of becoming excited at the most inappropriate times and remaining passive when its master would have it perform, much like a family pet. It also has the power to rule the senses. There are legions of politicians who have lost their jobs and respect through allowing sexual attraction to rule them. I have observed it at work, where men frequently make fools of themselves over a pretty girl all due to the unruly behaviour of that protuberance. Mine was now inert and I was glad.

My discovery though, was not due to appearance, nor to my actions. Norfolk was a then a county of around one million people. That is a reasonably small number and one could not escape contact with some acquaintance or someone who is someone's brother, mother, or neighbour. So it was, that I was recognised by a person my mother had once complained about, a postman who had been rude and was now working in the same office. Soon I was summoned to Personnel to explain. I told them that, yes it was true, but my personal life was my affair and that I had applied quite openly for a post there and had been invited to work for them. There was nothing they could do, either to remove me, which would be sexual discrimination or to protect me, except to speak to the person who had recognised me. It was a bad moment and one for which I would suffer for a long time to come.

The fellow apologised, but later, face to face with me, denied that it was he. I did not and do not believe him. I saw his animation and his pointing. I made no mistake.

I progressed, first to clerical officer, working almost alone, reconciling accounts that seemed a problem for the other staff who had done this work before me. The clerical officer, studying accountancy but who was destined to fail, had made a mess of the whole thing. His boss, a higher executive Officer, a peculiar woman named Glenys, married, no children but two cats, had taken it on but also failed and had a few days sick. Poor Glenys, took me as her pet and used me to bully other staff who were much higher in rank. They described her as 'the harridan'. She divided the world into two classes, cat people nice, non cat people evil. A harridan and women's libber in the office, she was a doormat at home.

The accountant selected me because of my banking experience. Together, we designed a reconciliation form, so that each balance would go to the appropriate side. It was then merely a matter of figures. Long hot evenings alone, sweating over the books in Port Loko, had taught me how to arrive at a trial balance and how to assess the difference. It was just a laborious matter then of tracking it down. Mostly, I arrived at a balance without help. Occasionally, Jackson the accountant would come up with something only known to him. There were several mysteries in Government accounting. Working mostly on my own, my main contacts were sections responsible for certain items. I was busy and reasonably happy. There were hard moments, for example, overhearing a colleague talking to the union representative who was saying, 'he she better not try to kiss me'. I put it down to ignorance, but it was hurtful. I should have confronted it, said, 'What makes you think I would find you attractive, even if you weren't such an ugly old bastard', there being at least 25 years difference in our ages.

After the year end reconciliations, the chief accountant called me into the office. One of the other accountants was there too and I recognised some of my figures on the blackboard. The Chief, a handsome six foot four inch rugby player, pointed at the figures. 'We can't get this to agree. Can you tell us how you did it?'

My first reaction was to assume that I had made a mistake. I blushed.

'Well, it balanced when I did it. What's the difference?'

Keith pointed to a figure scribbled at the bottom. Even at a glance I could see that it was twice the amount of a single entry in my figures.

'Either I got it wrong, or that figure should be a debit not a credit.'

It was their turn to blush. He turned to the junior accountant. 'You nit. Just turn your back while I kick you.' Next time they had a difference, Keith said, 'We may call on you. We better try to do it ourselves. We must try harder.' He later became managing director of a printing and publishing company, where I am told, he was hated.

They printed Harry Potter among other popular books. I found him great to work for. Like me, he didn't tolerate fools.

It was 1979. One of the Thatcher government's first actions was to make HMSO pay its own way. This was ten years before the conception of Government Agencies. We were a sort of guinea pig for what would later become the norm, when half of government became a business rather than a service.

The Government asked us what we needed to become a business? The concept turned government accounting on its head. Previously, we were given a budget by the Treasury to cover all central government's spending on stationery, machinery and printing. We then told each department what they could spend and what on, down to the last £10 of paper-clips. In addition, councils, quangos and other public bodies and institutions could purchase from us on a payment basis. Now, we would depend upon all our customers paying for what they bought out of their own budgets. Our top management did a few calculations, I suspect on the back of an envelope over a nice lunch. We needed, they said, a facility of £15,000,000, as a float, to pay the staff and the bills until Departments started paying us. Of course it was too little, but that might have been a blessing, for the Government had pulled a fast one. They offered us the money at 3.5%. Everyone considered this a good deal, as the Bank rate was 15%. After four months our management had a fit. The actual interest charged was 3.5% above Bank rate of 15%. Somehow we managed to make enough profit to pay off the debt but it was touch and go. It must have held us back considerably, particularly when computerisation was revolutionising business practice.

My accounting success brought me to the attention of Personnel. They pleaded my case to the Civil Service who eventually made me an established officer. Soon afterwards I moved to a section in contact with the public. This was very good for me. Shy and still blushing at forty, I had to overcome these disabilities and face the world. Gradually I became much more outgoing. Now, I care very little about people's opinion of me, as long as I am happy and don't offend other people unduly.

My new boss, Viv, was a gruff Londoner with little charm. He had been in trouble for bullying and had been sent for training in staff management. My first job was to purchase 60 and 70 gram paper, the bread and butter of our government Printing which included Hansard and most of the other parliamentary papers. It was a large tonnage, several thousand per year, and had to be on tap ready for the whims of parliament. Viv had a favourite paper mill, one that treated him to the odd dinner, but I thought them arrogant and inflexible. They did what they wanted, pallets too large, stacks too high, minimum orders too large, next day delivery, too difficult. This Kent mill liked to boast about the size of their paper making machine, six metres wide and some eighty metres long, it churned out paper at that time, faster than any other mill in the UK. On my numerous visits to the mill, much to my amusement and their chagrin, it never worked in my presence. They considered me something of a Jonah.

While at lunch one day, Viv took it upon himself to meddle in my purchasing. When I returned I found that he had placed an order with them for several hundred tonnes of paper. I took him to task, told him not to meddle without speaking to me first, and said that if it happened again, I would report it up. He apologised and took me for a coffee. A year later, he took early retirement.

The same month, January 1981, that I started this job and three and a half years after my second visit to Dr Randall, I received my summons to hospital. We had both kept our sides of the bargain. I entered hospital in March and sat in the day room until a bed was ready. The day room, a mere 8 years old, was in a sad state of repair, the carpet stained and worn, the whole place stinking of cigarettes, the paint stained and grimy. Worst of all were the cigarette burns upon the table, the chair arms, and etched into the carpet. This depressing and slum like condition shocked me and instilled in me even more apprehension at what would follow. I found it difficult to come to terms with the awfulness of that room and of the human race that could besmirch it so.

A nurse came through looking for me, but went away again without speaking. Eventually she returned and told me she had not been able to believe that I was a transsexual, complimented me on the dress I wore, which I had made myself, and then took my details. It was a nice compliment, that somewhat soothed my anxiety and dismay at my surroundings.

I was soon shown into a separate room, with my own bathroom. This at least was clean. The radio worked. There was hot water and a view of Hammersmith Flyover.

It was Thursday. First there was a talk with a junior doctor, a nice girl of around twenty-six, who asked me whether I still wished to have surgery, that of course I knew it was radical and irreversible? I should think so. Then poor darling, she had to carry out an intimate examination, which was not so good for me either. It was all very embarrassing but it would get worse.

Tonight would be my last meal, although the operation would not be until Monday morning. After Thursday night, I was only allowed water. It was a fearsome regime, the idea being to clear out the bowel so that there would be no complications with fouled bandages. Actually, I felt no great hunger, up to and after the operation. It meant too, that I was spared the awful bland hospital food that one suspected had been ill prepared and left lying around too long. The fast would last eight days.

There was another transsexual too, a person in her fifties, destined only to have partial surgery. She seemed to want to cheat the system, firstly by infiltrating the staff restaurant and having an extra meal before the fast. That seemed a ridiculous idea to me. We had waited a long time for this surgery; to start cheating now was absurd. She was of a fairly low mentality and we had nothing in common. The surgery I believed would actually be a disaster for her.

There were the usual tests, and then there was a rather horrible washing out of the anus, just to make sure of no contamination. Today, fashionable people pay to have colonic irrigation, I received the service, compliments of the NHS. The poor student nurse hated the task as much as I did. Sunday night was also shaving night, officiated over by a big black nurse, who told me to remember to say goodbye to my bits tomorrow morning. She thought that highly amusing, but she was good-natured, so I allowed her jest to raise a smile.

It was a time for real self-examination, a time to ask myself whether this really was what I wanted. A young nurse actually put this to me. Was I having second thoughts? You may think that by now I should have been sure and I was, but my other fellow traveller down the corridor, awoke from the operation to think she had made a mistake! There was a scene, as one of the nurses told me. It is a potentially traumatic step as I am sure most readers will recognise, unable to comprehend such a desire.

There was another TS there, a giantess who had just had her operation. She had the most enormous black, beehive hairdo, although the style had gone out several years previously. Her hair was jet, her legs were long and slender and her skin milk white and smooth. In spite of her size and her style, that was at least fifteen years out of date, she looked very good as a woman. Her ambition was to go into one of Manchester's best clubs, pick men up and take them home, 'To screw the life out of them, look you', she lilted in her Welsh accent. She was a revelation to me, huge and feminine, a fearsome man eating woman, who, I am quite positive, has fulfilled her ambition. I hope she has eaten her fill. I was invited to make her acquaintance, but left it till she felt like visiting me. I did not need the company of any other TS, did not want to belong to a club for a third sex, and did not want as some do, to go to the Beaumont Society, which caters for transvestites. I was not one. I just wanted to be a woman and to lead a woman's life. I merely wished my body to fit my mind. I had no real ambitions regarding men. My outlook was entirely asexual at that time, and my purpose was to resolve the continuous quarrel between my psyche and body.

Before the operation, one needed to be very sure. Positive as I was, little devils of doubt skipped into my mind prodding and stabbing at me. The rules that I'd had to play by were: observation by Dr. Randall; the four year probation period; to live as a woman for that time while making one's way in the world, working and supporting oneself. This was to make sure that the surgeon's knife did not create more turmoil than it was curing. I played the game straight, did not cheat at all as some did, with one object; to make myself whole, one body with one soul, fitting, dovetailing one into the other.

The eve of the operation, however, I slept well and for a poor sleeper to say that, meant I could not have been very troubled.

I had to sign the usual forms authorising surgery and informing next of kin. A pretty little nurse with a mop of the most beautiful curling red hair, who was especially friendly, also asked if I had any second thoughts. My answer was no and I have never regretted it. Of course, if I had a wish, it would be to have been born female. The variety I have experienced in my life that 'normal people' never know, cannot make up for a natural existence. I would not wish my defect on anyone. Far better to be happy in your own skin of whatever sex.

The next day began early. At seven I had a premed, and at half past eight I was on my way up in the lift to the operating theatre on the top floor. My favourite nurse was with me, a little courtesy which was most appreciated. I held her hand as I was wheeled out of the lift and into the theatre. I was scared, but it was only the fear of the surgeon's knife. My impression was of green, walls and gowns and masks, some bright lights, some white surfaces, cupboards I think, and then I was passed on, my nurse saying good luck. That was the last I remembered.

I awoke, back in my room, three nurses round me, rubbing my hands and talking to me. There were questions, to find out whether I had all my marbles, I presume, what was my name, what colour was my hairbrush. I was asked to keep an eye on my drip, not to let it run out or there would be a problem. They left me alone and I drifted off to sleep. I awoke to find the drip nearly empty and rang the bell for the nurses who came running. Self-service nursing. The drip was down to the last few drops of saline and was replaced, for I had lost a lot of blood and I was anaemic.

They told me that my mother had rung while I was in recovery. I went to sleep again. Next morning they gave me a blanket bath, but after that, I'm pleased to say, I was allowed to get out to wash, carrying my litre bottle of urine wherever I went.

I had a room full of flowers, from several people at work, some friends and my family. It was lovely. There were a dozen or so cards, all nice to have, and an aid to recovery. It was much more than I expected.

I was bound up, my whole crotch, bottom and hips swathed in bandages, a catheter issued from this strapped to my thigh, so that I could pass urine into the bottle, which was measured, examined and emptied by the nurses, who commented on the good colour or not. One can manage without food, but water is a necessity. I had to drink half a litre every two hours, just plain water, no squash, tea, or any other beverage that would create excreta of however small an amount. I would not have any food until lunch on Saturday, so there was a long week ahead.

The team, surgeon, registrar, junior doctor, ward sister and nurse, sometimes another doctor as well, came in every day. I was sitting up in bed, the radio playing Beethoven, when they trooped in on the Thursday. The sister switched the music off, much to my annoyance and the surgeon, Professor Philips saw my look and ordered it turned back on, saying, 'I like that too.'

I awoke in the night, my skin itching like mad from the bandages, to find that I had been pulling and scratching at them in my sleep. When the nurses saw the state of them, they thought I had been taking a peek at my new anatomy, and I believed, thought that there was some psycho rejection. On the contrary, it was merely the cotton wool irritating my skin. On Saturday, the black nurse announced that she had the privilege of taking out some of the stitches and the drains. It would hurt a little she said and then as a sweetener, that I would then have a light meal.

She entered with a trolley, shut the door behind her and then removed the bandages. She snipped away at the stitches, then started to pull the drains out. The pain was excruciating, and I called her several names, mostly of Anglo-Saxon origin and some about her parents, while swinging from the bar above the bed. I think she was upset, but I was more so. As soon as she had pulled the last one, the pain was over. I felt really sorry and apologised to her later. There had been long stitches, running down each side of the labia, each one running a half inch through the flesh, but it was the drains running there that really hurt. It was like the horror torture we used to imagine at school, of sliding down a razor blade. More stitches were to come out tomorrow, when the Prof. himself would do the honours, removing the packing from the vagina. I dreaded it.

It proved to be painless, uncomfortable, undignified but really painless, and he did it with such gentleness, care and good manners, talking to me all the time, that it seemed over very quickly. He was a wonderful gentleman and a great surgeon.

To construct the vagina, they use the skin of the penis and the scrotum, then cut and thrust up inside and use the skin as a lining. Sounds painful. My only pain the whole time until the final removal of the stitches was when the first stitches were being pulled. I still had the catheter. That was taken out next. I was then supposed to pee normally, but I could not. It was replaced, to await the recovery of the traumatised flesh. When he next took it out, there was still no pee. He ordered it replaced and left for at least the next forty-eight hours, writing it up in the notes.

Eight hours later the male junior doctor ordered it removed. It was ten in the morning and I had as usual, been drinking the prescribed amount of water since waking at six. I could not pass a drop. At eleven, he ordered me into the bath, with all the taps switched on, to encourage things. I was still drinking because if I didn't, the nurses said, my kidneys would pack up. The trouble was that of course the problem wasn't in my head, but in my flesh. I wanted to pee, desperately, my bladder swollen, my stomach distended. All the lower abdomen pain was present, which is associated with enforced bladder control. After quarter of an hour, a young black male nurse came in, a nice kind and rather handsome boy. I asked him to tell sister what was going on, but he didn't. He stood uncertainly, then went away to come back a few moments later. I told him that I could not stand the pain much longer, please tell sister what the doctor is doing. He departed. It was a difficult situation for a young probationer, but potentially life threatening for me.

Within a minute, sister appeared, a staff nurse in tow and another young student following behind. They pulled me from the bath, dried me down and put me to bed. They inserted the catheter immediately, not a painful process, but not what one would wish to experience. I peed a litre straight off. They changed the bottle, put a clamp on the catheter so that I would not empty too quickly or I would go into spasm. I filled another bottle over the next hour. I felt a lot better for that. At the same time, the doctor was sent for. Sister, who I would guess was of Indian descent, gave him the dressing down of his life. 'Read the notes next time, I am reporting this' she said, but I knew that he had read the notes, a nurse had also told him and he had known better than the surgeon, the arrogant young man. It gives you confidence in doctors and the health service.

Not waiting for the waterworks to recover, they discharged me. They needed the bed and I made my way home, by taxi and train and a lift from the station to home. It was a journey of one hundred and thirty miles, but it seemed like a thousand. I was really tired and felt and looked very ill.

Ten days later, still with the catheter, I had to return. The journey was on a Sunday, when trains are likely to go backwards as much as forwards and take forever. It was the day of the first London Marathon. One or two runners climbed aboard the tube as I made my way from Liverpool Street station to Hammersmith. Then I had a walk of half a mile on a dull grey Sunday morning in Southwest London, hoping for a taxi, but not finding one. The distance had seemed nothing when I was fit, but on that Sunday, it seemed as though I too had run the marathon. I found my way up to the ward, found the room I had vacated ten days before, and collapsed upon the bed. The nurse, who came to settle me down, could not understand why I was so exhausted. She was the coldest one there and wore the same Christian badge that my friend at school had worn, Christian Fellowship, just to prove what a good person she was deep down, if one could dig that far. If only she could have been in my place, I would gladly have been in hers, but without the badge.

In spite of the breakdown in caring at times, I shall be forever grateful to most of the nurses, the surgeons and of course, the enigmatic and difficult Dr Randall, now deceased of a heart attack. Professor Philips handy work has been described by my doctor as a work of art, and 'one would never know unless you got up close.' I have to say that men have got very close indeed and still haven't known. This rather destroys my theory about where men keep their brains, but as another friend says vulgarly, with a man, any hole will do. I'm sure that does not apply to you dear reader.

I left there feeling pretty. The Pakistani registrar travelling in the lift with me quite accidentally, touched my arm as we left it, saying, 'You are a very pretty lady, have fun.' I was complete at last, more able than at any time in my life, to take on the world and to enjoy myself.

CHAPTER 13.

For three years after the operation, I remained hermit like with few young friends, shunning company, refusing invitations. I was still very shy, very unsure of myself in company. I was aware of others fear of me, particularly men who knew my history, who seemed to think that I would 'leap on their bones'. They should have been so lucky. Had their fear not made them shun me, they would have discovered a person far more diverse than any born female partner, more full of fun, with wider interests and a challenge to them, that few naturally born women could match. It was their weakness; the almost universal fear men have regarding loss of masculine repute that made them difficult. In South America, this machismo excludes women from all but traditional male/female interaction. Here in good old 'enlightened' United Kingdom, our world is full of prejudice, ageist, sexist, racist, homophobic, and any departure from the norm is looked on with one fear or another.

This nation that I love in spite of its destruction by successive governments, has an infinite ability to delude itself. We reject ideas from abroad, scoff at the European Court of Justice, deride EU regulations. The Establishment would have us believe that we have the freest press; the Mother of Parliaments', i.e. the best democracy in the world, adversarial parliament being superior to collective opinion. We have that magic quality that enhances our Island by being a Constitutional Monarchy. We are supposedly blest with the most freedom; the best judicial system; the most honest police force; the best army; the best health service; the best education; the most effective banking system; the cheapest food; the best farming methods; the greatest love of animals; etc.,etc. All the above, and many more, are mere propaganda put about by the ruling classes to maintain credibility with the people and to perpetuate the status quo. It all goes back to Victorian times when fear of the new industrial classes drove our rulers to create these myths to protect themselves and the monarchy. Further back still, the French revolution had a profound effect, for the aristocracy in Britain feared for their heads and Parliament and the Lords built this constitutional monarchy to prevent any such revolt of the working classes. Every one of the superiority myths will not stand comparison with other European countries, but belief in them blocks the way to reformation. As our people travel more, they begin to shed their prejudice and acknowledge the qualities that exist elsewhere. For example, there is greater freedom of information in America or Sweden; more sexual equality in Holland; a better health service in France; better education in Germany and France and many other countries. A more pragmatic and effective foreign policy in Germany, France and many other countries where the gung-ho send a gunboat attitudes no longer exist. BSE and foot and mouth show how far our efficient farming practice has gone wrong. And yet over the last 13 years we have been the envy of Europe economically. Now it has all come crashing down, because that too was a myth, prosperity built on plastic and a financial system completely out of control, run by people who did not understand what they were doing. It was a magnified form of Port Lokian finance.

There is also the fact that most men want to dominate women to some extent. It maybe driving, or picking the annual holiday or always taking possession of the TV remote. Occasionally it can be complete domination. For this reason, they often find it difficult to deal with a strong minded female, both in the home and at work. Some men like a challenge, but on their terms.

I eventually met one man who accepted the challenge. He was a stranger and, being ignorant of my past, he accepted me for what I appeared to be, a very feminine woman with 'tomboyish traits'. It wasn't long however, before he was giving me unwanted advice and wanting me to wear a housecoat. Ugh!

That of course is the secret to others' perception of me. My history, the fact that I had been male, changes the way they react and their knowledge of that history changes the way I react to them. All this in the subconscious and conscious made me wary of disclosing my history. I only admit it to my closest friends and I have been proved right to be discreet about myself, for I would have a long-term relationship with a man who was and is, not only heterosexual and virile, but also intelligent and experienced. He was never to know my history over a period of nine years and to this day.

It is also unfortunately a facet of human nature that secrets are difficult to keep. While going through an emotional trauma, seventeen years after my rebirth, I told my closest friend my complete history in confidence. She then told her husband, children, parents and her friends, so that the whole story came back to me via another mutual friend who lives close by. I will say no more.

For me the alternative to a quiet life in the heterosexual world was a move into the gay world, where most sorts of deviation live side by side like outlaws in Nottingham forest. I would not have known where to start in that world. It frightened me even more than the world I lived in, and when later I would enter the gay world for a short period, I found it alien and with just as much prejudice. I did not belong there either.

The aftermath of the divorce was still rumbling on and, still hurting. This together with the difficulties at work that kept me in my shell, made me retiring and diffident.

It is only now, when my confidence is greater, that I believe it would have been better and made things easier for myself, if I had been more outgoing, more up front, joking about sex as I do now, but defending myself vehemently instead of allowing the whispering and slights, life could have been more exciting. Getting the balance is difficult and I have just about found it at last.

And then there was Linda. She came to work for me and for whatever reason, set out to be my friend, although there was a distance of seventeen years between us. I was suddenly subjected to the kind of female companionship, I had read of in slushy schoolgirl books and it turned my head, making me quite dependent on her. I was extremely vulnerable, starved of companionship, shy, timid in social gatherings and without anyone to love me except for my mother.

Linda was a girl who liked a wild life. She had gone on the meat wagon, the weekly bus that picked up girls to take to one of the American bases, where they were expected to dance and talk to the sex starved troops. She made the trip only twice, enough to win the heart of Clyde who phoned her frequently afterwards and to whom she was always politely discouraging. Linda would replace the receiver with a slight grimace. She'd also had several other boy friends and was known to be a modern girl who could accept or reject a man, with a grin.

At her suggestion we booked to go to Greece together. Neither of us had ever been there before, indeed over the last few years, I had not been abroad at all. We decided, on recommendation, to go to Corfu, made sure that we would avoid the worst parts of that once lovely island, selected the hotel and paid the deposit. Thereafter, there seemed to be a cooling towards me, a lack of trust and I was into yet another, for me, painful relationship. I did not know what others, had said about our friendship, but I imagined much.

The first problem for me was getting my passport as a woman. I followed the advice given to me at Charing Cross, asked my GP to endorse the photos in a particular way and write a note explaining my position. In fact it was quite simple, all she had to say was that she knew me to be living and working permanently as a woman. In the event, the letter was not what I asked for and the Passport office came back wanting more information. I remonstrated first with them, then with the doctor, but she was too arrogant, or too thick or just too plain bloody stubborn to change the wording. It was a trivial difference of emphasis, and she had really written the endorsement one would write for a 'normal person', saying, 'I can't see why that won't do'. Should I have more trouble, she would do something about it. I could not understand her attitude. When faced with some red tape, it is best to just follow the form, and make it easy on oneself, yet here was she, mistakenly defending me, but making problems where there need not have been any. I seemed to be in a stalemate.

In desperation, I went to my old boss Maurice and told him the whole story. He phoned a friend who was a solicitor, who advised him. Then he phoned the Passport office, spoke to the officer responsible and all was fixed. My passport arrived a few weeks later.

I shall be forever grateful to Maurice for that and for other times of support. He is a true friend. Provocative when trying to assess my real feelings, he will sometimes push me to the limit, so that even I know what I really feel, but I know that he will always do his utmost for me. One of natures true gentlemen, I am indeed fortunate that he took me on to work for him, saw my potential and later became both friend and confident.

My doctor, a lovely and good-looking lady, I have now ditched. That affair with the passport and idiot diagnoses of my mother and me, her habit of starting to write a prescription for pills almost as soon as one sat in the surgery, showed me that she had lost her brains somewhere, probably on the golf course she loved so much.

It was June when Linda and I set off for Corfu, a cool evening in the UK, and we spent all night in that tourist hell of Gatwick, where from the hour of around midnight until eight in the morning, there is hardly a shop open. There should be a rest room, where one can actually sleep, with an attendant to keep out undesirables and there ought to be a cinema or video room too. Instead, one just sleeps or tries to, on a bench and guards one's baggage eyeing warily the odd beggar who loiters and importunes. I believe air passengers to be the most ill-used customers in the world. There is no evidence that this is about to change. Most airports treat their customers with all the manners of sheepherders on market day, while attempting to fleece them at the same time. The new cut price fares offer even less service.

Greece in the early 80s came as a shock. The heat, the impression of its being an abandoned building site and the general air of neglect and dustiness were not what we had expected. It was much more third world than we had thought. The ride from the airport made us wonder what we had come to, but on reaching the hotel we were not disappointed. The room could have been better decorated and furnished, but it was clean and the swimming pool was full of cool fresh clear spring water, that was also chlorine free. We had a good view of the bay and mountains from our top story room where the mosquitoes did not reach. The downside of this top floor was however, the heat generated by the flat concrete roof.

We set out to enjoy ourselves with the first week flashing by, a blur of sunlight, bars, dust, extreme heat and pink bodies smothered in cooling coconut scented, after sun lotion. I learned to water-ski, so did Linda, but her fear of water held her back. We got on well enough, and then I began to get on her nerves. Somehow jealousy crept in and it was all to do with men, whose attention I feared and wished to avoid, yet somehow attracted.

It started when we rented mopeds and set off on a tour of the northern part of the island. We made for poor Paleokastritsa, once one of the most beautiful places in the world, almost completely spoiled and obliterated by hotels, discos, bars, cafes and stalls selling all sorts of cheap and not so cheap, tourist trash. From there we made our way over the mountains, to see the real Greece. Her bike kept giving up the ghost, wanting a rest before continuing again. I found later that she kept pulling the choke on, which caused it to stop until the flood of petrol evaporated. It was in one of these enforced stops that we heard bikes coming up behind us. She suggested that we wait, make friends and then go on with them. If she had seen who they were, I didn't know, I certainly hadn't caught sight of them. I was in a state of some trepidation by the time they caught up and stopped by us.

They turned out to be three Greek boys on two bikes. On a trail bike was an older boy, in his thirties, not handsome, but looking smart in jeans and a white shirt. As pillion passenger, he had another lad of about twenty-two. On the moped there was a handsome young fellow of around twenty-four. Of course, we had discovered in the first twelve hours in Greece, that the locals considered English women bed fodder. Their own women were locked away or chaperoned so the sex starved Greeks positively salivated over the free and easy ways of the British women. I was worried and upset by this attitude towards us, which was far from respectful, whereas Linda laughed and shrugged it off, awaiting the right offer. Her idea of joining forces therefore alarmed me, but I went along with it. Instead of making for Agios Georgios as we had intended, they convinced Linda we should go directly north, where they said, it was very beautiful. I concurred.

We arrived at the coast, saw the sandy small cliffs and inlets of Sidari, and stopped for a snack, a salad and souvlaki, beers and coke. The elder boy Costas, suggested that I go on the back of the motorbike with him. It would be better they said, I did not know why, and urged by Linda, too shy to argue, I agreed. Costas and I set off down the road at a brisk pace, sixty or so I would suppose, no helmet, hanging on to the muscular back of someone I didn't know. After the first ten miles, I began to enjoy it. He could handle the bike, even though some of the way was on what was no more than a sandy track. We two would roar ahead, path finding, then return to the slower mopeds. The sun shone, my hair blew out in classic style behind me and I began to love the sensation.

Linda on the other hand was not having a good time. Her bike was either slow, or she would not ride so quickly and the younger boys left her behind constantly. Costas told them off, ordered them to look after her, then we were off again. I began to be worried about this separation and wondered whether I would be raped in an olive grove or what. Linda told me later that the same thought had gone through her mind and at one point when we were gone some time, she feared for my safety, but that in her imagination, it would not have been rape. She visualised Costas and I writhing ecstatically beneath the lovely olive leaves. That should have told me something about the way she thought of me, but it didn't.

We arrived at length at Kalami, a delightful small bay where Larry Durrell had once lived. Larry was the brother of Gerald Durrell, the naturalist and author. Larry was the older brother, a serious literati who wrote among other works, the Alexandria Quartet.

We had another drink, swam in the cool aquamarine water, then we were on our way again. It was from here on, that the road followed the shore, zigzagging round hairpins, with a sharp drop down to the sea, the mountains rising on our right hand, a spectacular and classic Mediterranean setting. It was like a film set. I felt as if I was playing the lead for once, posing nonchalantly on the back of the bike as we sped by slower cars. By now I was thoroughly enjoying myself, the closeness to Costas, the feel of his muscular body, the sun, the spectacular scenery, the tricky road, posing on the back, no helmet to restrict my hair, for me the whole journey was a thrill. I drank it in.

At length, an excited Adrienne and a disgruntled Linda arrived back at the hotel. There we parted company with the boys, the hotel staff watching, apparently quite amused that we had arrived with these young Greeks. Linda had agreed to meet them in a disco later. Once more, I was nervous of doing so, but Linda seemed to think nothing of it.

We dressed, ate dinner and made for the disco by taxi, Linda speaking French to the driver that impressed him and me, but afterwards, I found out that she only had one sentence and not a modicum more, even pronouncing vin to rhyme with dustbin. After the disco, where we all bought our own drinks, it was time for bed. Costas asked and I agreed. He would be my second male lover. I was fairly drunk, which helped make the decision and the two of us set off for our hotel, while Linda went to theirs.

My hotel would not let him in, much to my embarrassment, so we adopted plan B, kicked the younger boy out of his room and made love. It was not too good for me, I don't know how good it was for him, but the drink had worn off, I was now aware and scared, just longing not to be there at all. It is easy to see how a girl can change her mind too late, then shout rape and the man, unprepared to be disappointed, his passion raised, is not prepared to listen when she says no and he is then accused of rape. That does not mean that I am defending men in their passion. It should be possible in any situation for one party to refuse another at any point, but date rape is an extremely tricky subject and there are degrees of guilt born out of situations. A conviction for rape is a very serious matter, I would imagine difficult to live down for either party. Both sexes are vulnerable, men from false accusation, women from rape itself. The permissive society has made life very complicated. However, I decided to go with the flow, got it over with quickly enough, then lay beside this stranger, waiting for the dawn, listening to the noise of Greece, the distant and ever present whine of mopeds, raised voices, lorries grinding along. I resolved not to get into this situation again, even though Costas appeared to be a nice and considerate young man.

The experience taught me a valuable lesson; that casual sex was just not worth the bother. It also taught me that date rape is a non crime. If one has voluntarily put oneself in the position where sex is possible and the expected outcome, then a woman should just lay back and take the experience. It is not the end of the world, and no worse than giving ones conjugal rights unwillingly. Too much has been made of this. Woman have it in their power to avoid such situations.

A knock at the door and Linda's voice were welcome. I dressed in the bathroom, said ciao and we caught a taxi and went home, walking into the hotel at seven, observed and remarked by the staff with much merriment. After a quick shower which in no way made me feel clean, we went to breakfast. I felt very conspicuous.

We lay all day by the pool, reading. I listened to Dire Straits, fretting about the night before. It troubled me greatly for some reason. I felt degraded, ashamed of myself, although this joining of two human bodies is a meaningless enough act if looked at without emotion as Linda could do. Emotionally driven it affected me deeply. The dividing line was indeed indistinct and for several years afterwards, the live version of 'Tunnel of Love' which I played that day, would reduce me to tears. Strange the emotive power of music. It has so many associations for me.

One continuing fear from that night of passion was AIDS, then little known but becoming a big talking point. Right from the start, I never considered it to be a 'gay problem'. I saw the potential threat to the whole human race, particularly knowing that there are a large number of bisexuals, or people who swing between the two sexes for one reason or another, or change as I have done recently. My Greek lover had been a junior officer on a container ship. Their last voyage had been up the West Coast of the USA, where AIDS was just beginning to be recognised as an epidemic amongst the sexually active, particularly gay and heterosexual prostitutes. We all know sailors' reputations and I was frightened. I resolved to be much more careful in future.

Linda grumbled later, that she always got the selfish two-minute wonder, and seemed resentful of me. She would have been welcome to my share. I spent the day in bitter regret, Linda in resentment of me that I had taken her lover, when I knew that she had chosen the handsome boy, not the experienced one. I had taken the leavings and had really struck lucky; I was just not able to react to him.

The next day we went water skiing. When she was in the water, I was in the boat with Spiro. She, hating the water, had to wait while he flirted with me, then cunningly and dextrously flipped off my bikini top. She shouted and never forgave me. The rest of the holiday was difficult and she moaned on about her boy friend and what she would do with her love life when she got home. Once home, we still had to work together, and that proved difficult.

Shortly after however, we did go out on the town, with her express purpose of finding some men with money as well as charm and libido, because her boy friend had let her down. We had tears in the office for three days. We took a birthday card to Maurice, ate some cake and had a gin and tonic, then moved on. Our fourth stop of the night was a large four star hotel. As we entered the bar, I observed a handsome fellow with grey hair sitting at the bar with a male friend. We exchanged glances. In that split second, there was a flash of attraction between us, that 'chemistry' that is so inexplicable. He looked like Jeff Chandler the film star of the fifties and sixties. After another Pernod, my tipple of the moment that I had mixed with earlier gins, I started on the olives that by chance were in front of the handsome fellow. He talked to me as he passed me the olives and after the bar closed, they invited us to have a drink with them as they were staying there. I refused but Linda was all for it, so we stayed. I had gin, because the hall porter had no Pernod in his pantry, a daft thing to do, and a daft way to run a hotel, so typically British.

Then we were invited for coffee. Ian, the handsome one with the grey hair asked me to go to his room to collect the cups, while his boss took Linda to his suite where we were to join them. I never went further than Ian's room. Having washed the cups, I then asked to use the toilet, throwing up all the cake, gin and Pernod, and about half a jar of olives. I felt very ill and, drunk. Ian rattled the door, asking if I was all right. I explained. I could hardly stay there all night, and emerged, weak and pathetic to find him in his underpants. It was to be a night of love, when I did things I had never dreamed of and nor had he, even though I was in a weak state. That is the male animal for you, never miss an opportunity. There were several sessions, as one of us awoke in the night, we would initiate another 'bash'. My inhibitions had all vanished, seemingly flushed down the loo with the olives, or perhaps the mixture I had consumed was the elusive formula for an aphrodisiac that really works. Really it was the danger and excitement of it that made it bearable. He was completely overwhelmed.

Next morning after showering, I dressed, stood looking out of the window, a view of uninspiring small factories, not wanting to look at him, once more wishing it all had never happened. Then he took me to Linda's. She, tired of waiting for us, had eventually gone home in my car. She was not a happy Linda. From there on our relationship was difficult, and caused me much heartache. She had been my first bosom pal girl friend and when her friendship was withdrawn, I felt it badly.

Having lost her, I had gained Ian, and we were to remain lovers on and off for the next five years, until I realised that sex was not something I particularly liked with men. As time went on, I dreaded it, dreaded his embrace, the male smell, his thick body and coarse skin. Unable to express this to him, I made his life very difficult. I needed love too, to be in love with the person I had recurrent sex with and if there was no love, then I really had no need of sex. After the first flush, when I had been infatuated, I had realised that I did not love him, the first electric thrill had gone and had not been replaced with a deeper emotion. There were one or two other lovers during this time, none serious, just as uncomfortable. Yet I did have a deep regard for dear Ian, such that I am always pleased to hear from him and to see him.

For five years, apart from one or two periods when I finished with him, we did mean a lot to each other. No matter what I did, how mean and ungiving I was, he still came back and still comes back to get more heartache. I tell him that there is no chance, and he agrees to be a good friend, but he does not mean that. There is always that little chink of hope, that the dinner date will turn into a rerun of that first all nighter. And he is a good man, physically attractive, over six feet tall, not run to fat, does not drink to excess, nor smoke, will listen to a point of view, if only to reply, 'Bollocks' if he totally disagrees. He has a brain that is quick to assess and make a sound judgement, highly intelligent. I could have done far worse. Instead I played along, keeping him dangling, supplying what his wife wouldn't or couldn't, or had grown tired of, until I also grew tired of the excitement of this sort of illicit relationship and the abhorrence of contact with a male had grown to be an insurmountable obstacle.

We romped from hotel to hotel and, eventually into my bungalow. This was his idea. He had always wanted that, whether because he could then settle his expenses sheet satisfactorily or because he wanted his feet under our table, I don't know. It did nothing for me, being in bed with him in one room and mother next door. It was restrictive and with my hang-ups proved too much. I could not cope with it, coming to the conclusion that having slept our way round the UK to come back to my home, I had had enough. I subjected him then to the same sort of slow death that I have suffered since with others.

Of course, there are reasons why I did not want to cut him off. I had great affection for him, wanted to keep him as a friend and had not discovered at first hand how difficult it can be to remain friends with a lover. He also gave me respectability, a certain legitimacy. A male lover was proof of who I was, a female, attractive enough to pull a man both virile and handsome, a support to my battered ego. There were things that I didn't like about him too, he could be quite mean, and occasionally, very hard on me. He was sexually demanding, wanting that first night repeated ad infinitum. I began to feel like a sex toy and resented it. There was too, considerable guilt, that he had a wife and we were cheating on her and that I was not who he thought me to be. He called me a closed book, because I would never disclose my past, not even my age. That, he eventually found out by looking at my driving licence when taking me to face a prosecution for speeding. I was three years older than he was, but he thought me five years younger.

What this had done for me, was to show me that the monastic life I had subjected myself to, was unnecessary. I had more confidence and had cast off much of my shyness. I found that I now had a reputation for straight talking, a no nonsense approach and a dare devil attitude. I played up to it.

Windsurfing became my sport, learned in Corfu the year after Linda, and where I had a magical week on my own. I had booked apprehensively, but considered that an action holiday would attract singles. I left Stansted on an overcast September afternoon. I had driven down in a dull and dismal mood, but at the airport suddenly made a positive decision, that no matter what, I would have a good time. I remembered what one of the brochures had said, it is Greece, not England, and it is your holiday, you can hate it or love it. I arrived just as dusk was falling, tired and with a migraine. My room was downstairs, at the back and next to the kitchen. It was quite cool, that was appreciated, but when I tried the shower, the water was cold and the shower head would not stay on the hose. Having hosed down, I went to bed without dinner. In the night I had to put another blanket on the bed and swat two mosquitoes. I was already badly bitten. So far, my sense of humour was not finding an outlet.

The morning broke, sunny and warm. There was a slight clatter from the kitchen, a soft murmur of voices, and some weaverbirds twittered brightly. The water was still cold, but then I was British and brought up on cold or tepid water. Breakfast was pretty diabolical, but who likes breakfast anyway? I complained to the rep and to the hotel owner about the shower. They assured me that it would be put right today. After the rep's welcome speech, I made my way through the olive groves, a beautiful walk under those widespread and gnarled branches, covered in the misty green leaves which I have learned to love so much, to the beech this outfit used. It was a walk of absolute beauty, beneath the olives, but looking across the water to cliffs covered in brush and with cypress trees standing straight like so many fingers pointing to heaven. The water was intense blue, the sky cloudless, the sunlight sparkling on the rippled water, lighting the colours to show at their best. I had my first introduction to windsurfing, then showed my water-skiing off to everyone and to my surprise found how shy most people are at having a go, particularly men, so frightened of not living up to their self assured and competent image. When unable to start and follow me around the bay, they gave up quickly and ran from it.

It was a beautiful spot, the opposite side of a long inlet to Paleokastritsa. The olive groves and the cypress trees covered the hillsides and on our beech, we had no interlopers, nor any sewage, no one selling anything. I tried windsurfing, then gave up. I tried diving and hated it, finding that I could not clear my mask of water and feeling claustrophobic in all that equipment, an awful feeling of panic that made me shoot to the surface. A hand full of painful quills from an anemone confirmed that diving was not for me.

It was not until the last two days, that the windsurfing came together, and I sailed right across the bay and back. I was hooked. That week taught me how to love Greece, to separate the necessary from the desirable and to appreciate what Greece has to offer. The showerhead never was repaired, but it didn't really matter. I knew that by rights it should have been in proper order if I was to have full value for money, but it was a better and a happier way to go with the flow. My room at the back was at least cool, whereas some guests complained of the heat. A mosquito killer rid me of their bites. Greece offered, sun, water, plenty of fruit, not the best looking but full of flavour, lovely salads. Best of all, away from the tourist traps, there are some of the nicest, most hospitable and friendly people anywhere and there were many good moments with them.

On the beach one morning, I spent quite a long time with the rep, a nice girl who wore contact lenses that made her eyes the brightest blue. She was everything I would have liked to be, slim, blonde, attractive, self-assured, her skin tanned beautifully. The fisherman, the only one who used that small bay, arrived with his wife and produced a salad. The rep was invited to join them, then since I was alone, I too was asked to partake. With the salad was red mullet, retsina, beautiful bread soaked in good raw olive oil, and olives. It was a lovely feast, a biblical meal below a clear blue sky and the old fisherman and his wife were very sweet to me. I was greatly touched by this generosity.

I used a moped. Every day, after showering in the evening I would go off exploring. The hotel owner expressed the theory that I was a travel company rep, looking for new sites and he was afraid that he was going to lose his representation. I did my best to reassure him that I was not. He was very good at embarrassing the guests with Greek dancing. I, for revenge tried to get him to disco dance. He would not. When I lifted him from his chair there were hoots of laughter and even more when I dropped all fourteen or so stone of him accidentally.

Another day, on my travels, a man stepped into the road and flagged me down. He fed me with fresh figs, straight from the tree, unbelievably sweet and succulent, kissed me on the cheek and invited me to go fishing with him in his boat. Greeks and gifts came into my mind and I politely declined. On the same trip, an old man gave me almonds in return for a kiss. He must have been at least seventy-five the old devil.

They looked after me marvellously, and we had great fun. It was a great holiday, and taught me that I could enjoy myself on my own. I was lucky, the hotel had five honeymoon couples who all shared one large table and I and a single boy were invited to join them, thus the worst aspect for single travellers, eating alone, was eradicated. One of the new husbands phoned me several times afterwards. Naughty boy!

As a result of that success, I had several holidays in Greece, in company and alone. I love the country and the people. The 'Gods' found a wonderful place to live. A hard country, where one marvels at the years of toil involved in terracing a hillside, but also one with beautiful sunshine, fruit growing in abundance, the wonderful olive and in former times, an abundance of fish, now mostly imported because the fashionable Mediterranean has been fished out.

There are evocative scents, smoke from the burning olive prunings, donkey dung, wild thyme, oregano, mint, rosemary and honeysuckle. Groves of pine and cedar cloud your mind with the strength of their scent, while providing delicious shade for a picnic.

There are sounds, bees, crickets, frogs at night and the near and distant buzz of the moped. There are sights, a peasant way of life still, donkeys loaded with produce, an old and wizened woman riding or driving it, goats with bells ringing, wonderful scenery. In spring at night one can see hoards of fireflies and lightning in the night sky. There are foods, honey, Greek yoghurt, and salads with fetta cheese, green beans with tomato sauce, taramasalata, tsatsiki, humous, and drinks, ouzo and Greek brandy. Forget the wine!

Most of all, one should get off the beach and explore the hinterland. Here, you will find the best people, the unspoiled and natural way of life. Travel by moped or motor bike, carefully! Savour the scents along the way. Record the scenery as you go. Meet the Greeks with humility and in tranquillity and they will return fourfold.

I came home, purchased windsurfing gear and made a friend of Janet, whom I met beside the water, emerging like a mermaid from the deep on a stormy October day. She sold me a board, because at that time she worked for a water sports shop. She would later betray my confidences. I sailed all through that winter, hands aching with the cold and progressed rapidly. It proved an absorbing sport, and has given me much pleasure, the friendship of Janet and her husband Paul, with many fine holidays and memories.

CHAPTER 14.

The late 1980s were a time of great change in the civil service and particularly in HMSO. Suddenly we were all specialists. Some would be on 'customer service'; some buyers; some poor things, on the order processing sections. It was also the time when a new pay structure was introduced and future increments would be made against performance of 'key targets'. This was an excellent opportunity to promote those one liked and some managers seized the opportunity with relish. There were some notable over promotions and some inexplicable down grading. I did not benefit but neither did I gain.

At the same time, because of government restrictions on recruitment, we started to take on temporary and agency staff. These poor folk did the same work as those sometimes earning twice as much. Many were overqualified. We had numerous graduates, in law and in sciences working as clerks or typists. A biologist and a geologist were order processors. This was all part of the great Thatcher plan. We only needed a little 'Blue Book' and the turmoil would have rivalled the Chinese cultural revolution.

I am against agency staff unless used in exceptional circumstances. We saw them used instead of normal recruitment practice. It meant that they had restricted rights and no job security. Job security was another of Thatcher's pet hates, although of course, she was well protected as a Prime Minister. These educated young people, would often waste two years working for us in the hope that eventually we would offer full employment, only to find that they would only be re-employed on a temporary basis. They had emerged from university full of hope to find that their lives were on hold. It is a cruel way to treat employees, and a poor reward for good students. They were not good risks as borrowers, so they lived in poor property. They could not afford many of the small luxuries, like a car. There was the stench of cheating employers getting away with poor terms of employment. Thatcherism was doing its best to turn the clock back to the 19th Century. We were remodelling ourselves on that epitome of social perfection, the USA. Luckily the European social contract has done away with that exploitation.

This doctrine was compounded by encouraging experienced staff to retire early or to take generous redundancy. It wasn't however, as generous as for some other sectors, the miners or the fat cats Thatcher had crawled to. As a result, we had a workforce without experience or responsibility. Good as they were, without company ethos and with no product knowledge, these agency people were a liability. Customers complained bitterly that they never spoke to the same person and those they spoke to never knew anything nor wanted to. The changes in activities within the organisation meant that HMSO became uncontactable by its customers who no longer knew who to speak to. They were also frustrated at being held in a telephone queue of some minutes.

The sales force that I had advocated for the last 10 years found favour under a new director. This vindication of my ideas was of no benefit to me. I had become a specialist. I had ten years experience in the paper trade. I was known to almost every paper mill and merchant of any size throughout the UK and to some from abroad. In HMSO I had a reputation for being commercial with a vengeance. As a buyer, I was held back by the HMSO ethos from being tough. We were fair. We were firm. We believed in partnership with suppliers and consistency in product. We felt wrongly that we should give everyone a chance to supply us, a relic of the days when we were true civil servants. Consequently, we talked to every importuning supplier who felt the need to walk through our doors. We were safe. The old civil service motto, 'Follow last year's lead and you cannot make a mistake', meant that innovation was stifled. I was now involved in the purchase of copier paper.

This everyday commodity was of a very high specification. Paper is innately unstable. Leave it in a damp atmosphere and it takes in moisture. Put it next to a radiator and it dries out. Even opening a window or closing one can alter its nature. Having nursed it by keeping it in waterproof wrapping until needed and storing in equitable conditions, one then puts it into a machine that heats it from room temperature to 160 degrees centigrade in a flash. This temperature is needed to 'cook' the powdered toner on the sheet so that a permanent image is created. Therefore copier paper, that lowly animal which is of no concern at all to most people, has to be high quality, consistent, perfectly cut and with the exact moisture content required. Most complaints about machine jamming were attributed to the paper, but paper storage and room conditions were more often the cause.

By playing one supplier off against another, I managed to purchase paper at competitive prices for resale to the public sector. I was also responsible for marketing the commodity. In my time on copier, the annual volume rose from 13,000 tonnes per year to 20,000. It was then that the paper trade began to see us as a threat and started to attack what they saw as an easy market. Some did manage penetration, many others found the going much harder than they had thought and pulled out. My boss and her chosen favourite then moved with paper purchasing to another division and I was left with marketing.

The next fad in civil service life was business consultants. I have never seen the value of these generalists that come in and meddle in a business about which they know nothing. Most are supremely under-qualified to advise anyone. There are occasions of course, when people of sufficient stature and experience can look at a business with fresh eyes and point one in a new direction, or they can point up issues that should be attended to. Generally, the old adage, those who can, do, those who can't, teach, comes to mind. If most of these consultants were any good, they would be making a fortune themselves, rather than living like fleas on the back of other businesses. Our consultant, John had no experience of a business as large as ours, no knowledge of the stationery trade, or of the paper trade and within that sector, the specialist area of copier paper. He was though, a friend of one of the 'gods'.

There are two distinct markets in the world of copier paper. Informed, usually large users with high volume machines and experience in buying who are courted by several suppliers, and uninformed, small users, who probably send a clerk down to their local shop for a box or even as little as a ream at a time. I had customers who purchased 2000 reams plus at one time, some who bought in ten tonne loads, and one or two who bought by the 44 tonne lorry load.

At the age of 53, I was ordered out onto the road. As we were now being attacked by the competition we had to protect our market. I told them that they had left it too long for me personally to go out on a selling mission. They should find someone younger, I said. It was to no avail. They were convinced that I was the one for the job when I should have been better employed as sales manager. Their conception of my new role was that I should travel the length and breadth of the UK picking up new customers. None of them had the slightest inkling of sales or marketing. Their expectations were a totally impossible task. They wanted a 10% increase at a time when prices were under attack and so was our customer base. In the event, by nursing existing customers rather than cold canvassing new ones, I achieved 5% increase in sales.

It was a hectic life. I could be in Scotland or Wales, Newcastle or Canterbury. Inevitably, I had to spend much time in

London. That at least was good. I found London to be a vibrant and exciting place to be. I could park at various ministries, and made several acquaintances. I drove through the imposing gates of Somerset House, the Foreign Office, the Bank of England. It was at this time that I started working closely with Dannie, developing a joint sales strategy with her company, while also helping other suppliers to maximise sales on our behalf. I tried to eliminate poaching customers between our suppliers, and asked them to concentrate on new business.

I rediscovered London. Much is said about the capital by those in the provinces who seem to have a pathological fear of the place. 'I wouldn't drive up there!' They say. 'How do you find your way around?' 'Too busy!' 'Too hot!' 'Too dirty!'

London is magnificent. Thus it was that I had been with Dannie, driving down Victoria Street, when she asked, 'What do you do for sex?'

'So where are you going tonight?' The accent was on the where.

I was staying with my best friend and her husband as I often did when in the city. Tonight I had told them, I would be out to dinner. Janet was very protective, indeed it was almost like having an elder sister or a mother, though she is seven years younger. I appreciated the love shown to me but I had to tell her not to interfere. I hid little from Janet, nor her from me, except my past. I had never trusted her with it, but then I trusted no one, not her especially. The trouble is, that a secret shared is no longer a secret.

'You know the couple of girls I told you about? Well, they have invited me to dinner.'

'Ah, Danielle and her friend. Can you cope with that?'

'Cope with what?' I was defensive of my new friend and was being deliberately obtuse. I said the words with a smile on my face though, not wanting to hurt Janet either. What had she in her mind, I wondered, that I would have to 'cope' with. I saw no threat to me, saw nothing that would offend me. Danielle was a friend, how could anything she did, upset me.

'Just I wouldn't like anything to happen to you. Have a good evening.' She kissed me and held onto my hand, as if an event of some moment was to take place. I couldn't understand her over protective attitude.

'I'm going to dinner, not an orgy. I'll tell you all about it tomorrow,' I said lightly.

I was however quite excited at the evening before me. Driving away from Janet, I realised that this date was one of the more exciting ones I'd had. Danielle I liked a lot. Her strange mixture of toughness and gentleness, her beauty deliberately played down, made her an intriguing character. To put this together with a gay lifestyle, in itself a mystery to me, made the prospect even more enticing. There was in me a degree of the voyeur that I despised so in others when I was the object of their inquisitiveness. Dannie called it tourism, when the world's straight wanted to look into the gay life. Tourists went to gay bars, breathlessly expectant that they might have to fight for their virtue, Dannie maintained. I hoped that our friendship was more important than my curiosity.

Most of all, there was the tenderness and understanding shown to me, and after that first exchange, she had acted like a man towards me, very gentlemanly, protective and considerate. I was amused by this change in her, but also flattered. The whole relationship had changed, yet still I hardly realised it.

I picked her up from work on a bright sunny spring afternoon. The air was warm, the promise of a hot summer could be believed. To her direction, we drove through South London through streets unfamiliar to me, turning here, waiting for lights to change, talking to her and trying to remember the route for my return home. After a certain distance of meanness, the character of the streets changed to more opulent suburbia. We climbed above Peckam Rye, turned right and left once more and slewed into a private car park behind an attractive block of flats.

'Huh, here you are,' Dannie said as she opened the door, 'do come in and meet Leslie.'

Leslie was in the kitchen. She put her head on one side so that her hair fell away and did not restrict her vision of me. She smiled, shook my hand limply and moistly, then asked which wine I would like to drink of the three she had brought home. Dannie had explained that Leslie was the cook.

'I'm not much good in the apron,' Dannie had said with a smile, all part of her butch act. I was getting used to the pattern, the remarks which had deeper meanings of sexual orientation.

Leslie gave me a glass of wine, thanked me with obvious anticipation, for the bottle of bubbly which I had brought, and then launched into a dissertation on the relative merits and flavours of the three bottles of claret type wine from around the globe. Dannie reappeared, changed into her lounging gear, a sweat shirt and leggings.

'Come into the living room, you'll stink of cooking. Do you like kd. lang?'

'Yes, fine.' I had in fact seen the girl singer in concert on the box five nights before. Her appearance, she could have been a good looking young man, belied the exquisite and controlled voice. The disc was not a disappointment, sensuous, plaintiff, beguiling. The evening was fine and warm, the windows open, and being a top flat, one looked straight into the branches of the large maples of a small copse, that reached within a few feet of the sills. Two squirrels played in the branches. I was entranced.

I sat upon the sofa, while Dannie sat in an armchair, legs apart like a man. They were strong legs, her thighs hard and muscular. I knew she worked out, she had told me so. She got up, wandered into the kitchen and came back with the wine to refill my glass and her own, then she sat beside me.

'Tell me about yourself,' then she added, 'no you don't have to, but if you would like. I mean I'm interested.'

'What would you like to know?'

'Well, you've taken a big step. I would like to have been male, because I feel that men have it made. I won't attempt to change my sex, because I don't want to lose the sexual pleasure I have.' I realised that she was not telling me the whole truth about her orientation. 'You must have wanted something rather badly.'

'From my earliest memory, all I ever wanted was to be female. This compromise has at least allowed me to live with myself, made my body outwardly female so that my mind can live and expand within it.'

'Tell me of those early memories.'

'My first memory of having difficulty with my sexuality was at the hairdressers.' Suddenly embarrassed, I wondered whether to go on. I paused, distracted, all the old memories upwelling. For some unknown reason, difficult though it is, I wanted to tell her. She divined my distress.

'It's OK. Take your time. You're safe here.'

'I think I am. I don't know my age then, but I remember plainly being in the pushchair, so I couldn't have been more than three or four. As a child, I had a mass of golden curls. In the hairdressers I demanded a ribbon for my hair, created a fuss and threw such a tantrum that they had to find me one. Of course, as soon as my childish mind had recognised that I had done something abnormal, I then wanted it removed. Mother was beside herself poor thing. That memory is as vivid now as if it was last year. Other things have disappeared from my brain, but that, the first awareness of a dissatisfaction with myself, remains. It's quite a painful memory and if I think about it now, relive it, I feel quite lost and panicky.'

Dannie sipped her wine, her marvellous eyes looking down the fine skin of her nose at me, her expression inscrutable. She could have been a psychiatrist, except that she showed more interest. 'Lots of kids must do that. Like that kid you told me of in the cafe, the little girl in the dress who told every one she was a boy.' She referred to an incident a few days earlier, when a child in a motorway cafe with her mother and grandparents, had swung on the bench of the next table before confiding in me that she was 'a boy'.

I told her of other matters from my childhood. All the time she listened intently. When I stopped she would throw in another question. I carried on revealing myself.

'It was shortly after that, that I would find old clothes of my mothers to dress in. I particularly remember a silky striped dress, which I loved the feel of, and the colours, navy and green. I was heartbroken when she gave the dress to the rag and bone man.' I stopped, suddenly self-conscious, embarrassment flooding in to halt my flow.

Dannie smiled. 'I can understand, I had the same feelings reversed. Tell some more.' She placed a hand on mine. Her touch did not disturb me, there was no thrill, no shock. It was a friendly contact, no more than that. What was Janet so afraid of for me I wondered? What could befall me, here where it was so tranquil and safe?

I was saved from further revelations by a call from the kitchen. The food was ready, chilli which I had told Dannie I liked, among other things, and she had asked Leslie to make it. It wasn't good, not enough tomato as Dannie pointed out. She was plainly disappointed, especially after telling me what a good cook Leslie was. She showed her disapproval, rather unfeelingly.

I said, 'It's fine,' just so that I did not drive a wedge between them. I managed a small second helping too, to reassure them both that I was not merely being polite.

After dinner, we sat and chatted, they drank the wine while I had mineral water as I had to drive back to Janet's, ten miles north. The evening was beautiful, incredibly warm for spring and the sun died lazily. They played music as the dusk gathered, a suburban dusk of blue light and street lights shining through leafy boughs of almost translucent spring green leaves.

'So,' I said, 'are you gay or lesbian or dykes. Which word do you like to use?' I felt at home, mellow, familiar. I said it with a smile and a genuine wish to learn and understand the culture of friends.

'Gay, lesbian is OK too. Dyke is really a bit derogatory.'

'The girls I met in Greece, the ones I told you about, called each other dykes.'

'Yeah, well it's OK, but more of an American term.'

The girls I had met in Greece were certainly dykes, boyish in spite of their enormous breasts which had all the young men talking. They were also from south London, appearing to be on a recruiting drive. One had made me a proposal while clinging to my waist on the back of my motor bike at seventy kph, on a pitch dark road. I had declined politely, without offence. When I had recounted this adventure to Danielle some two years ago, she had made no comment.

'Dyke has connotations of the masculine side. Bull dyke is a term for a tough, rough very masculine woman, so it isn't a term we really like,' Dannie said, 'besides, it's a term men tend to use about us.'

'And the opposite of that?'

'Would be fem.'

'And you would call me what?'

'Definitely a fem. The make-up, the nail varnish, skirts and heels, the coquettish ways.' She giggled throatily, laughing at my expense.

'Thanks. First time I've been called a coquette.'

'I've seen you in the office, making eyes at Cass, looking at him from beneath your hair. What a tart.' She gave her little giggle again, throaty, low pitched for a woman, infectious, intriguing, mysterious. Androgeny seemed to be the in thing. This cross over from woman to male gripped me in suspense. I was never quite sure what would come next, which side of Danielle would show itself. Leslie was much more straight forward. For the most part she said little. She was obviously educated, tended to look down on Danielle, I thought, yet was obviously very fond of her. I looked for the same fondness for her from Dannie. I didn't see it.

'Adrienne could come on holiday with us, couldn't she?' Dannie said.

'Yes, if she wanted to.'

I noticed a strange reluctance in Leslie. She didn't seem keen at all. In any case, my company would not like me to holiday in another company's villa. I said so.

'Why? Where's the harm? We are only friends.' Dannie couldn't see how compromising this was. She seemed upset that I would not be able to go.

Soon it was eleven and with work the next day it was time to take my leave. I got up and collected my things. Dannie had already gone ahead to open the doors and to see me to the car, leaving me to follow after having said goodbye to Leslie. I thanked her, and pecked her cheek. She seemed to tower over me in the doorway and there was an expression of pure hate in her face beneath the flesh which spoke of too much alcohol.

'No snogging on the stairs,' she yelled after us as we descended. I was more than surprised. I hadn't displayed any more than friendship for Dannie, and I couldn't understand the remark. Anyway, I hadn't expressed any lesbian feelings or intentions.

I told Dannie what she had said.

'Huh, said that did she, oh.' she shrugged. 'So you're on holiday next week. I'll miss working with you. What are you doing, going somewhere?'

'No. Things to do at home, garden, chores. Might windsurf if the winds are strong enough.'

'Why not come down here, say Thursday night, stay a couple of nights. You could do the shops in the day while I'm working.'

I thought quickly. It was an attractive idea. Of course, I could have stayed with Janet, but Dannie had made the invitation and I had enjoyed a pleasant and funny evening with the two of them, which I looked forward to repeating. I considered their partnership rather sweet, love and caring are after all, admirable qualities, however expressed. I had felt no threat except for Leslie's parting shot which I thought was the drink speaking.

'OK, you're on, thank you, that would be nice,' I accepted.

We parted without touching. No kiss or embrace as Janet and I always did. I realised I was disappointed.

'Drive carefully, and keep the doors locked,' she said. It was good advice in South London.

CHAPTER 15.

When I awoke the next day I realised it was late. Janet and her husband were on their way to bed when I'd arrived home the night before and I had not seen them long enough to say anymore than good night. I had noted their inquisitive looks though. It was surprising, this great interest in my friendship with a gay woman. This morning as I roused myself from an unusually deep sleep, I could hear them already downstairs. I showered, washed my hair and dressed. Janet had amused me with her homophobia and I decided to play up to it. With my damp hair slicked back like a man, and just a touch of lipstick, I went down just in time to see her husband Paul off.

'Well, just one night, you can see the change in me,' I said.

They responded with a laugh, then as he departed in the car, Janet turned, gripped my arm and asked, 'How did it go?'

'Fine. They were very sweet. It was quite touching to see them caring for each other, and they made me very welcome. They didn't leap on my bones. I'm still the same person, unchanged, not converted, but they have my sympathy if that is not too patronising. It is not an easy life, you know.'

'So what are they like, these two?'

I described the way things were, the sexual orientation, their appearance. My impression of Leslie was, 'large', especially when she seemed to tower over me as I said goodbye. In a disagreement, one would have trouble dealing with her. Dannie had said as much. She was overweight, could have probably lost a couple of stone, and her height of about five feet ten inches did not take away the bulky look. Apart from that, it had seemed to me as though inside that bulk there had been a nice young woman once. She worked as manager of a bar off Kingsway. The alcohol was taking its toll though, her face had that drink induced pudginess already, not a nice sight in a woman under thirty.

'So the little one is the butch one?' Janet was plainly fascinated by the thought that a manly woman would have a partner taller than her. This should have told me something about Janet. I was to find out that she was like Pooh, 'a bear of little brain'.

'We all come in all shapes and sizes. Size does not denote sexuality, does it?'

'No, but usually the man is taller. It's strange, I can't take it in really, it just seems wrong. Poor things.' Janet's view of large is not the same as mine. For example, I am five and a half feet tall size 12 and most people call me slightly built, but to Janet, I am large. Then she is five feet two and under eight stone!

'Oh Janet, usually the man is taller than a woman, that is a biological fact, but only usually. There are men smaller than women aren't there. And really, I think your pity is misplaced. We all have to live as we can don't we. How our minds are, affects our behaviour. There is nothing wrong in loving someone as long as it is reciprocated.'

'I just feel that they are like that because they are frightened of the real thing, that something went wrong in their puberty to put them off normal sex. They should have therapy to make them normal.'

'Your views are so out of date. Will you be taking them into an asylum for retraining. No, you can't change people from the way they are or want to be, and the way they feel natural. Otherwise as an atheist and, if I was to be prime minister, I might order all believers of every creed to be brain washed. It wouldn't be right and it wouldn't work. In any case, I believe that gays are born, not bred. Some may be latent, ambivalent about sex or bisexual, and are swayed by reaction to certain partners, but generally I do not believe that the gay life is a rash, contagious and dangerous. You can see, particularly in the faces of many gay men, that they are gay. That can't result from experience or contagion, it has to be in their make-up as individuals, implanted before birth. It is in their DNA.'

Janet changed the subject, but I could see it troubled her. Her fear was mystifying. When I drove away that day reflecting on our conversation I was slightly irritated by it.

'I don't think your attitude to religion is right either, but never mind.' Janet said.

I smiled.

Danielle and I were together again, working around the city, calling on mutual customers. She could not leave my experience alone, wanting to know how I had come to this point. Bit by bit, I gave her my story, increasingly confident that here at last was another understanding human being.

The rest of the day we only made small talk, getting to know each other's likes and hates. Dannie didn't like to discuss politics or religion. She could get quite steamed up about it, saying it was wrong to argue about people's beliefs, while I was prepared to debate the subjects quite openly. It doesn't matter to me what people think of my atheistic beliefs, I am strong enough in them not to mind other's opinions and I like to debate such things. The human race would never progress would it, without thought provoking debate? Here was another taboo. I was beginning to see that she had several. At least she and Janet had something in common. That made me smile quite a lot.

I didn't argue the point, it just didn't matter to me what she believed in. I was so disillusioned with politics, that I could see little good in any of the parties. I was cynical in the extreme and annoyed by party cant. Janet was sometimes horrified by my remarks about religion, and my conversations with a god I did not believe in, who I could therefore berate without fear of a thunder bolt or eternal damnation. I am considered to be outspoken, but much of it is a pose, and many of my remarks are made tongue in cheek, attention seeking perhaps, said to get a reaction. I am loved for it by those that know me, feared by those that don't, I am told. Strange how others see one. I believe I am a pussycat, they see a snarling lioness.

Dannie was I found, a lot less straightforward than I had thought. Added to her manner of making some things in life absolutely taboo, was the mixture of masculine and feminine. I was forever on my toes, wondering which way the pendulum would swing. For example, she could describe a fight, draw herself up, make a fist and describe and demonstrate the way a blow was made, fist, arm and body moving like a prize fighter's, not limp like a girl. I might have been talking to a young man of nineteen or twenty. Then on more feminine subjects, treatment of women or children, even the treatment of men, back would come the caring feminine side of her, and she would again be Danielle rather than Dannie. Try as I might, I could not work it out. Added to this was her care for me, the normal gentlemanly things like carrying heavy parcels, walking on the outside of the pavement, opening doors and being generally protective. All these actions went by unspoken, I politely thanked her for them, and that was that. There was also the 'I'll drive syndrome', asserting herself just like a man. Curiously, even that didn't offend me. It was confusing, but enjoyable. She was good company, different, exciting, confusing. I had never known anyone like her.

That afternoon, as I stood in her office, I heard her phoning her best friend, another butch dyke called Barbara. She was saying, 'I've got a new girl friend, Adrienne.' I was surprised. It was embarrassing too, for if I could hear that, then so could others. It was patently a lie too, in the context of her definition. Later I challenged her, told her what I had heard.

'I meant you to,' she said.

'But it's not true, and in any case, if I could hear, then so could others. You are compromising me and my friendship.'

'Sorreee. I was just joking with a friend, and wanted to tease you. Won't happen again.'

The subject was closed. Even that didn't really sink in to my naive brain. I thought it another one of her jokes, a harmless tease. I should have challenged her, but I saw only friendship. I am a sucker for that.

'Anyway, they don't all know I'm gay.' She meant her colleagues.

'If one knows, they all know.'

'No, you're wrong.'

'Don't fool yourself. There are no secrets, people have to talk, have to display their knowledge, either to prove how well they know you, or to get at you, particularly when the information is sexual.'

'Don't think so.' I was surprised at this naiveté in someone so streetwise. Another contradiction.

'Well Cass knows and I know you have slept with at least two of the women in this office.'

'I still think you are wrong.'

Before I said goodbye at the end of the working week, she said, 'Send me your photo, a nice topless one from your holidays.' She laughed infectiously.

I laughed in reply., 'Whatever for?'

'We like to have photos of all our friends.' Her face became troubled. 'Have I upset you?'

'No, I think it's funny, you're funny.'

She giggled again, throatily, seductively and looked me in the eyes with her strange piercing gaze.

As the week at home progressed, I became ever more excited about the two days stay with them ahead of me. I had not realised how fond I was of Dannie until now. I found a photo in one of the holiday albums, a shot of me sitting topless in Greece, tanned and happy, taken by Ellen seven years ago. It had been at the back, protected from public view by a piece of plain card. I am quite proud of my female form. I never questioned the ethics, the meaning of her asking for this, nor of my giving it. I toyed with sending it, then put it away. The evening still lingered in my mind, the utter openness and ease I had felt, more relaxed than I had ever been, amongst people who did not condemn me for my sexuality. It had been a rare experience, to share my secret and yet to have our friendship grow stronger. Playing with the word processor, I wrote two poems, one about my state and one of their effect on me. On impulse I posted poems and photo to her, then instantly regretted it.

She phoned to say she had received my letter. I was unsure how to behave.

'Ah well, I thought I would play up to you, give you a laugh. I hope you've torn it up.'

'Cause not. It's on our notice board in the kitchen, so our visitors can see it. Nice boobs.'

'You rat. You're kidding me.' I was in a confusion of emotions, not wanting to be so displayed, yet enjoying being teased by her and having her attention.

'Yeah, it's safe, don't worry.'

'What about the poems?'

'They're good, we liked them.'

'You showed Leslie?'

'Of course.'

'And the photo?'

'Yes. We'll talk about it when you come down. You are still coming?'

'Mm...yes, but I don't know how I'm going to look you in the face.'

'Nothing to worry about. You're safe with us.'

'I'll see you next week. Pick you up at work then?'

'That will be nice.'

I was suddenly apprehensive. My impetuous nature had taken me further than I now thought prudent, and I had already given too much of myself. Janet, more wise than me in relationships, had warned me before about giving too much too early. But that is my nature, once won, I give completely with a fawnlike attentiveness. Still, I had no fear of them, I knew who I was and who Dannie was. I was certain of my sexuality. Why then was I so excited about seeing her again? It was I suppose the opportunity to be quite open with someone after 50 years of hiding my true self.

Thursday the following week. At half past five I was waiting outside her office. All her colleagues knew me well. It was a hot London evening, 28C the papers said, the sky a clear pale blue as I sat outside in the staff car park waiting for her. Even with all the windows and the sunroof open, the car seemed airless and my heart seemed to be at maximum output. I was apprehensive, feeling conspicuous, marked.

'Hello, nice to see you,' she said, opening the door having deserted the office to welcome me, even though it was not time to finish work.

'You too.'

She had hardly settled in the passenger seat, before there was a knock on her window which she had wound up on entering. Simon the purchasing director was peering in. There was a smirk on his face, as he asked, 'What are you two up to.'

'I was just asking Adrienne if she was coming in,' Dannie said. It was a defensive remark, perhaps also a possessive remark, making sure that Simon knew that she was one of the company's main contacts with me.

I knew they did not like each other. Dannie also believed that Simon had no knowledge of her gay life style, which I thought highly unlikely. I was embarrassed by their attention to me. The look on his face meant that he thought much more than he would say. I knew him, knew his looks when digging the dirt. He had an affair with a friend in my office, a girl living with someone from the local Norwich Mafia. It had ended because he was in fear of finding himself beaten up.

'Oh good, only we have one or two points.' He said. 'Perhaps we could go up in the boardroom. It'll be quieter there. I'll tell Cass where we're going.'

This was an unusual invitation. Good customer I might be, with free and easy access, but invitations to the boardroom to talk had only occurred twice in ten years. Mostly we would talk in my office or over a drink in a pub. Apprehension intensified. Was this going to be business, or was it to do with my friendship with Dannie? She had a fear, probably groundless, but one which I respected, that her company frowned on close relationships with customers. Could this be what it was all about?

I followed Simon up the open staircase to the boardroom. We made small talk, until Cass arrived. They wanted to talk strategy, that was all. We had a short chat, then Dannie entered. For some reason, I lost complete concentration, dithered and faltered, then just looked at her. It was the strangest feeling, as though I was completely out of control, as though all my emotions were displayed in neon for them to see. I was helpless, in bondage, a possession without a will of my own. I struggled for some control. When I turned back, Cass was watching me with a strange smile on his face, what I call his avuncular look, the loving and indulgent uncle. My mind was floating, out of my body and I appeared to be watching myself. I stretched my legs against the table support and thrust back in my chair. That at least brought my mind back to my body. It was all highly confusing and I was glad when we were able to get away, but I was not to relax.

As Dannie and I left, Jane one of her colleagues, followed us down the road on her way home, one car between us. I felt that I was under surveillance. Paranoia, but it was backed up by Dannie saying, 'She'll be asking where we were going, tomorrow.'

Why should I feel like this? I was only a friend, why should Dannie's reputation be an embarrassment to me? I suddenly felt a terrible confusion over this friendship, wondering where it was going, why it was happening. We sat in silence while I tried to concentrate on the traffic, turning onto the Old Kent Road. As often happened with Dannie, her next remark came like a bolt.

'So what happened in there, where was the confident person I usually know?'

'I suddenly went to pieces. Couldn't help it.'

She was looking at me, quite seriously.

'You shouldn't react like that, they'll think something's going on, and there isn't is there?' She was being quite severe with me. 'Look, if they thought we were having an affair, they would give me the sack. You can't behave in that way.'

'Instinctive. Why did you come into the meeting? I didn't hear them ask you to come. I was surprised and it won't happen again, but don't you take liberties.' I had always received deference from her in the past.

'What was all that looking at me when you should have been listening to Cass? You really have to be careful.'

'Yes I know. But there is something going on, and they will have seen it. I arrive, you come out to the car. We have a meeting, you invite yourself. We leave together. Knowing your sexuality, they are bound to speculate. To heterosexual men and probably women also, we are all their fantasies.'

'But there is nothing going on, is there? I mean I'm with Leslie, and I love her. You are just visiting us as a friend.'

'No, there's nothing going on. I don't know why I went to pieces.'

I wasn't sure then, why I had behaved so strangely. Afterwards I wondered if it was apprehension at a longer stay with them. Was some of Janet's fear and suspicion transferring to me? Now, as I write, I wonder whether my body language was saying what my inner self already knew and my conscious mind had not yet recognised.

Suddenly she changed tack. I had never felt as dominated by anyone before. She could be aggressive one moment, and gentle the next. It was disconcerting. No one I had ever known had varied so much towards me. To define my feelings then would have been impossible. I had never been with anyone who could make me feel so feminine, nor so vulnerable. Her damned androgyny confused me completely. I enjoyed it. But I could not define her sex. I knew her to be female, but everything she did and the way she spoke, her phraseology, even her husky voice made me react as if she were male. It was living in a house of mirrors where the eyes cannot tell what is real and what is mere reflection. I seemed to be free falling into a world of androgyny and I was enjoying the sensations too much to pull the ripcord. I only hoped that I would not come back to earth with too much of a bump.

After the telling off, now she was all lightness again.

'Do you know where you'll sleep tonight?'

'Where?'

'There's a choice, you can have our bed, or share it with Leslie, or on the cushions, or the blow up bed or in between Leslie and me.' She giggled and as I took my eyes from the road and looked at her, she added, 'I favour the last solution.' Scared?'

'If there is nothing going on, then what is all this rubbish you are spouting?'

'Scared?'

'No.' I wasn't. Petrified might have described what I felt. I was suddenly beginning to think Janet was right. Was I in danger after all? What was happening to me? And the emotions which I now felt, what did they mean? It was like having a flirtation, which I had not done for seven years, hurt then and determined not to be so again, in love with someone who at first drew the love out of me, then shut the door in my face. Since then I'd had a boy friend, who loved me more than I did him. At least I was not the one getting hurt for a change, but it was never satisfactory. But Dannie was a woman, there was no doubt about that. Was I so vulnerable that I could let a woman's friendship get to me like this? I thought about it momentarily, but the heavy traffic forbade any deep thought.

She was quiet for a time, which allowed my mind to collect its reason, but I found no solution, no understanding of what was happening to me.

South London. Claustrophobic, the traffic thronging narrow streets, the air heavy and hot, full of fumes. We stop at traffic lights at the bottom of Peckham Rye. We both watch a beautiful black couple in a BMW convertible. The girl is stunning, her skin has a sheen not seen on whites, just as black horses outshine greys. Her slim arm drapes over the side of the door, ending in a hand which is a work of art in itself fingers tapering to dark red nails. Limbs I could kill for.

When we arrived at the flat, Leslie watched from the window as we unpacked my luggage. Dannie carried my bag in, while I brought the wine and flowers. Inside I felt relaxed again. They were just as friendly as before, there was no sexual advance, I was merely a guest. Tonight Dannie had been told to cook for her friend, Leslie had insisted, Dannie told me. A picture of this partnership began to emerge which puzzled me. Dannie was dominant yet dominated. Leslie had ways of subjugating her, and it puzzled me how this could be. Then the same was true of many a heterosexual relationship. Certainly Dannie had begun to dominate me. I rather liked it but at the same time resented her impertinence. In this partnership it was not quite like that. Dannie was the landlord, Leslie her tenant. There was a rift, things were not as happy as either of them made out. There were currents running counter to the stream, and the waters were as dull and opaque as the Thames.

Dannie struggled in the kitchen. I wanted to help but wasn't allowed to. The wine flowed. Leslie said she has to do it. It took a long time and I sat with Leslie as she displayed her knowledge of wine and pop music. Leslie kept opening the bottles and drank most of it. It appeared to have little effect on her. At last the dinner was ready, Dannie having she said, created her masterpiece, the dish she was successful at. Leslie let her down, saying that she had chosen the recipe as being one Danielle could manage. It was a small betrayal and one which pointed to an insidious continual demoralisation, that Dannie would later tell me of. I could not read the signs then. It is only now, that I can see how Leslie attempted to subjugate Danielle and Dannie's answer was to run away, just as she had for a week back in January. I was to find they were destroying each other.

She had made a good meal, sole fillets with a lime sauce, baked potatoes and greens. It was very pleasant, but my appetite had deserted me, caught as I was in a fit of anxiety over I knew not what. I was too nervous to eat.

As the evening wore on I began to relax again. Dannie and I sat on the sofa talking, while Leslie played disc after disc, just selecting a track here and there, sitting on the floor, singing and rocking herself and emptying her glass. We hardly drank, but the three bottles of champagne I had brought from a trip to France had disappeared.

It was after midnight and no one made any move to go to bed. Dannie had metamorphosed. Now I looked at her and she was a young man, sitting close beside me. It was like some fantasy, like seeing a transformation on film. I felt completely powerless, without will, without care.

Over the next weeks we knocked about together whenever I was in London. I could be in Southampton one day and Newcastle the next. I was working ridiculous hours, a full day and then driving three hundred miles. Life was exciting though and I guess I lived on adrenalin. This romance with Dannie formed a large part of the adrenalin rush. I was starved of love and now I had it or so it seemed.

I found though that Danni had her own rules. She was the flirt, not I. Any woman was game and she would play up to any little chick that crossed her path. She played a game with me of push me pull you. Unavailable for all sorts of weird excuses, then ringing me up when I was in Leeds, Hull, Glasgow or Taunton, asking how long before I was in London again. In the end I would become really tired of the continued play with my emotions, but it would take time.

CHAPTER 16.

Working in London, we ended up in Regents Park at lunch time, sitting on a seat with cans of coke, not talking much. I am suddenly excited and aroused by her. Is it this fine, late spring day in the season of love? Is it that I have denied myself too long and am ripe for an adventure? Or is this it, the love that I haven't ever felt so violently before? I want to touch, to feel the warmth of her body, the throbbing life of her, but already, that has been made a taboo. We do not touch in public, she has said that.

'We had so much to talk about, yet today we find it difficult,' she said.

'It's all got rather serious, hasn't it,' I replied nervously. 'When we were just friends, even colleagues, we could say almost anything, now it all seems to matter too much.'

'Why does it? We are still the same, I'm with Leslie, nothing has really happened.'

I had played rugby in this same park thirty five years ago. Was I that same person? Oh yes, but it was almost incomprehensible, even to me, that I had been that person and this woman, besotted with another woman.

Life had to go on. Throughout my life that has been my maxim, accompanied by the animal instinct to fight and survive. Some people just give up, throw themselves under a train or off a bridge but that is not in my DNA. There would be better times, or at least bearable times. That knowledge has driven me on down the flood of life's course, sometimes as ineffectual as a pooh stick in determining my future, but determined to stay afloat.

Away all week, at home there were the usual chores to do on the weekend. With a heart very much elsewhere, I set about them. I made out the shopping list, loaded the washing machine and set it going, then in desperation phoned Janet who had come home to see her parents. She had also brought my landspeed, a set of wheels like a six foot long skate board used to sail on the beach in the mode of a wind surfer, which they had borrowed three months before. I needed a shoulder to cry on and my best friend was to hand.

Her mother answered the phone. I made a few pleasantries, but she sensed there was a desperation about me and soon passed me over to Janet.

'Hi,' the word, short as it caught in my throat.

'Hello, are you all right? What's the matter?'

'Where are we going to meet so that I can collect the wheels?'

'I thought that we could meet up at the show tonight, if that's all right?'

I was silent, inwardly sobbing over a love affair that had never started.

'There's something wrong isn't there. Can you tell me?'

I managed a negative, before emotion screwed all the control from my voice.

'Poor darling. I have a few things to do, but if I put them off, we could meet this morning, at the usual place.' That was a pub on the riverside, about halfway between us.

I managed to say that I would see her at ten thirty, knowing that she would be late as was her habit. As it happened, mother did not want to go into the town, so there was one complication out of the way. I ate no breakfast. I had now been a day without sustenance.

I had known Janet for eight years. In that time she had once or twice fished into my background, but I had never told her any of it. She had respected this, but I know that it hurt her, this lack of confidence I displayed. Of course, it was not her personally I distrusted, just the whole human race. Tell a secret, and you tell the world is the norm. There seems to be no honour. Lately our government has displayed a great aptitude for the calculated leak, the off the record, in confidence release of information, which is used to break the news of another more serious matter. It is not honourable. Ex Prime Ministers, Ministers, spies, dish the dirt. Spin, the newer phenomenon, is only another word for propaganda, or truth twisted for advantage.

I have experienced plenty of discrimination, usually behind the back, seldom to my face, difficult to prove, even harder to combat. Working for my company, I have therefore had a double handicap, that of being a woman and of being transsexual, which depending on the person's point of view can be a matter of all sorts of emotions from, disgust through fear to horror.

If people don't know my past, they react to me in an entirely different way. They will treat me as female. Those that know but do not know me well, treat me in an entirely different manner. I suppose that is understandable, but surely it is the person inside the shell of a body that matters. The flesh, the souls clothing, is of no more import than a cloak or the cover of a book. I cannot understand the preoccupation at Alderhey and elsewhere, over missing body parts. When one is dead and the spirit has left the body, the carcass is as nothing.

Now was the time, I felt to confide in Janet. I needed her as I had never needed a friend before. I trusted her to be sensible and to judge me on the good times we had had together. As I sat in the car by the river, I tried to think of any way I could not tell her, but decided to trust to the love she had often expressed for me and reveal all. It took quite a time, an agonising hour and a half in which I spoke of things I did not wish to speak of ever, tears rolling down my cheeks, her arms about me. Above all, I had to tell her of falling for another woman and feared that this would be the most difficult subject of all, given her attitude to the gay world.

She was great in that moment. However, from that moment on, our friendship had changed.

That night we met up, saw the cabaret her daughter's boy friend had organised and starred in, then had a short bop. Life looked a little rosier, but I was still pretty miserable company for my mother. (Much later, I would find that even Janet had betrayed my confidence, telling her family and her friends in London, my history coming back to me via mutual friends living near me. (She justified it by magnanimously saying that her family was also my family.) I still saw it as betrayal.

I was in London again. On the first day, Wednesday, I met her from work. This was our first meeting since that appallingly emotional Friday, twelve days ago. We had spoken on the phone everyday as I drove around the north. As I was staying at a hotel in Hampstead, we drove out there in the early evening of a fine London spring day, when the temperatures had reached the mid-seventies.

There is no city I know, like London on a good day. It is a fine city, easily rivalling the best in Europe, with a buzz like no other. Just drive from Westminster, round Trafalgar Square where traffic comes from all sides and strikes terror into country drivers, then up Charing Cross Road, leaving the hubbub of Soho on your left, and Covent

Garden down dark streets on your right, passing theatres and book shops, see the teeming street, let the excitement of it enter your soul, observe the people, don't just look at the crowd, but pick them out, note their races, looks, dress and style and I defy you to be bored. Or if you will, stroll upon an early morning, crossing St. James' Park, thence past the Palace, across Green Park and Piccadilly, through Berkeley Square and New Bond St, to Oxford St. There is beauty and there is excitement. I love the place. Paris in comparison is very beautiful, a classic city, but feels quite empty, almost provincial.

This evening, we pass by Soho and Leicester Square, as we move northwards along Charing Cross Road. That half-mile square of central London is an area where gay people feel safer, the place where Dannie feels secure.

And yet fear lurks too as in other great cities, below ground, where hurtling screeching Tube trains, pump gales of wind round endless empty passageways and where the next corner might be your last, or indeed, on the train itself especially in the loneliness of the late evening. There were at that time several cases of mobbing, when a group of yobs would terrorise a carriage and rob people.

Fellow travellers in the Tube are as diverse as can be. Chic mixed with drab, clean and filthy, sweet and frightening, these are your fellows in the confines of this noisy and gusty labyrinth, which can occasionally be more frightening than any funfair ghost train. And above too, where a quiet suburban street can suddenly turn into a living nightmare. Creatures as evil as only man can be, exercise their greed and malevolence on their fellow man, an old woman knocked down for her pension, a young mother's baby threatened for a pitifully empty purse. Young males are stabbed to death for a chance remark or look. I will experience this violence in this year, one robbery and two break-ins and another attempted on my car. Above and below the city throbs with life as various as the village pond, from minnowed splendour to primeval slime. And there are strange people here.

Here are the dead eyes people. It is their land. In this place one learns the art of being blind yet seeing, for eye contact can be dangerous. An inquisitive stare can lead to death, especially for the young male, or a gay couple. They can be punched to the ground and kicked black and blue, or feel the heat of cold steel as a blade slices into them, just because their sexual preference is different or wear the wrong clothes.

For this, says Dannie to me, whom she regards as an innocent abroad, is the reason we do not look like a pair. She is overtly feminine, with a beguiling boyishness, rather than a butch-bull dyke appearance, and she uses make-up, just enough to enhance this illusion of tomboy innocence. It fooled me for a long time, but then one sees what one will. Later I will find that gay men and lesbians recognise her for what she is, while she passes in the straight world. That is not the only reason though for her appearance. She does not want to be the crew-cut or shaven bull-dyke with one earring and muscles bulging beneath an ample bosom. She knows who she is, a woman who loves women, female feminine women. She would have been a boy had choice been hers and likes boyish things. She will never carry a handbag, not even mine for a short time. She does not like dresses or skirts and to be truthful, they do not like her, somehow accentuating the male in her rather than emphasising the feminine.

Her hair is cut short at the sides but longer on top, the sort of cut a fashionable public schoolboy with a hint of the homosexual might have chosen thirty years ago, but it is a modern style. Her hair is soft and fine and she blow dries it, so that it falls in feathers. I love to touch it, and she loves it to be stroked. I have found out that caressing the back of her shock can evince a moan of pleasure and catlike, she will writhe sensuously. She is strong, with the upper thigh development of a footballer, as she had been, but her arms, though strong too, are fine and without definition unless under tension. She is five feet four, sixty-four inches, and eight and a half stone. She is proud of her physique, loves sport and physical prowess as a coltish schoolboy does, talks football, boxing and motor sport with the men. Plays golf, tennis and used to race her 250 Yamaha production racer.

All this I know already. Much more I need to know. I look at her, as a lepidopterist might admire and marvel at a butterfly, wanting to understand how she thinks, what motivates her. I cannot believe her presence. I cannot believe my being here with this beautiful person by my side. Why is she spending time with me? There must be many more fascinating people to be with. I would get inside her head and in time she will want to get in mine, I hope.

As we pass, Dannie points out the Silver Moon Feminist Book shop, now closed. There are other sights to see, other gay and lesbian meeting places that she speaks of, in this other world, the alternative way of life that she will no doubt introduce me to. I am a naive student, nervously excited at the prospect. Leaving Charing Cross Road and crossing Oxford Street, we traversed the Tottenham

Court Road, full of electronics shops and crossed the Euston Road, the famous station off to our right. Into Hampstead Road and straight on through St. Pancras. Already we are in the suburbs and there is a subtle change, petrol stations have reappeared, many small cafes, the traffic seems more certain of its destination. There is more space, the air lighter as we rise up Haverstock Hill. My spirit is high, but anxiety at what she will say to me has made me cold so that I sit on my hands, even on this warm late afternoon.

At the hotel, I check in and she waits to help me carry my bags up. My heart is gladdened by this small supportive act. She carries my case as if it is feather light. Already, her magic is working upon me, her androgynous attraction holds a fascination that I have never felt before so intensely for any other person. The room is small and full of furniture. She stands at the window, one arm bent at the elbow upon the sill, the pose of an arrogant young man. She watches silently as I unpack. I clean my teeth as I always do upon arrival anywhere, but this time in the hope too, that her mouth will find mine. There is an embarrassed silence. I touch her and momentarily she puts her arms around me.

We find Hampstead Heath and park on a peripheral road by large and desirable residences built over sixty years ago in an age when beauty was still valued. We wander a hundred yards or so into natural park land, and find a seat within a wooded glade. We are not alone. There are numerous single men, some with dogs, mostly without, wandering with some purpose by paths which to me are not clearly marked. I assume that they are making their way from one side of the park to the other on short cuts, but then I am untutored.

'We keep our eyes open,' Dannie says, beginning my education again, 'you never know. These guys are probably all on the search, gay. They call it camping.'

I'm so innocent. I'm amazed, not that it should take place, but that there should be so many of them out. It does not shock. It is a pitiable thing, a dangerous pursuit I would suppose and my heart feels for them. The loneliness I felt in the depths of my desires has taught me how painful is the want of another soul to share one's inner self with, to love, to hold, to cherish.

'What am I going to do about you?' She looks into me, holding one hand in hers.

She took me to Soho to her favourite gay bar. She had stood at the bar nearly every night for weeks, talking to no one, she tells me, after her long term lover had left her and she had moved to London. I visualised as she wished me to. It was a sad thought that a person should have to do that. It brought home to me how hard it is to come to terms with being gay and just what agonies are involved, the worst of all, the utter loneliness of it. That was an aspect that I could fully appreciate, from my own experience. Yet I was a nice person too, as nice as the average in every other aspect of character. So it is for gay people. Does it really matter what they do in their personal lives? Does it matter which sex one is attracted to? Are not male and female both just animals anyway? What is bad about one human loving another, even of the same sex? Why do gays raise such fear and hatred in some people? Why do the Abrahamic religions so interdict homosexuals? What would Jesus have said about that?

I was not comfortable in that noisy gay bar. It was nothing to do with the customers, nor what they were or were not doing, which was actually very little. It was a sad dive. I have been in several gay bars and none have impressed. They are largely sad places, full of self-deceit. There was unrest in my mind too that they could see through me, a failure of my self-confidence and the effect that might have on Dannie. Looking feminine, in skirt heels and makeup, I was really out of place. For the first time, I wondered that I was here in this separate strata of society, when all I had ever wanted was to be 'normal'. The bar was dingy and dirty, decorated in the style of a sixties milk bar, and I was not ready for it. She, sensing my unease, said, 'Come on let's go.'

We left and wandered into China town. She invited me to slip my arm through hers in a most boyish fashion. It was so disconcerting. Here, I could see, was a place where she felt really at home, among the clubs and bars and the centre of the gay community in London. Here one could take little privileges, subtly display affection. Soho, Leicester Square and Covent Garden, this is her favourite playground, with I suspect, a feeling of familiarity and safety which she does not feel elsewhere. There is about her a constant feeling of danger, fear lurking in the form of gay bashers and the fear too of other dykes, butch and bull, who will fight over a femme and of course though butch, Dannie is not big and hardly bull. For that I love her, I do not want her to be that tough. It is this androgynous mixture of male and female which attracts me so. Her fear is an impediment, for I would hold her and caress her, kiss in public and hold her hand, for I am in love and that is my natural inclination, to touch and show affection. I miss this familiarity and have to restrain myself. If I forget for one moment, she will pull me up sharp with, 'Behave, what do you think you are doing?' It is a further enslavement, for I have to concede, she knows more of the dangers of this life than I.

We selected a Chinese restaurant, she was looking for a particular one, but failed to find it. I asked her to choose, which she did, conferring with me whether I needed a meat dish, as she only ate vegetarian or fish. She ordered crab with ginger, squid with garlic and Singapore noodles, without meat. It was good, but I ate little, delighted though, to see her joy at this feast.

It was not yet mid summer. Warm dry evenings. People from every nation strolled around the streets of China town, but there were so many Chinese that the photos I took of her leaning on the Chinese gates, appeared to be taken in Singapore or Hong Kong. Her pose is boyish, leaning bent armed, deliberately accentuating her male side. She was bashful, fidgetted boyishly and supported herself on her arms for a few seconds, one hand on each gate, her feet off the ground. It is not the action of a thirty year old woman, but that is her. She did not have to be like that to attract me. Yet she is so like a young man, as much so as, she told me, I am feminine in movement and expression and I am sure that she like me, does not consciously put on this act. We expressed ourselves as is our natural inclination and in that, we were very alike, but mirrored opposites.

I was more relaxed with Dannie than I had ever been with anyone. We did not always agree, but it did not matter. To see her devour food, most of my portion as well because love had snarled up my digestive tract, was a reward in itself and food for my soul. For the first time I was released from all inhibitions. I expressed my love for her in any way I wished, impulsively, without thinking should I or shouldn't I. It was liberating. I felt more feminine with this small butch woman, than I had ever felt in my life and that allowed me to express myself to her in ways that I had been afraid to do with others in the past. The one disappointment was, that I could not make public display of my love. This was hard for me, for I would have had her hold my hand, put an arm about my waist, kiss me in view of others, caress as I would her, for I would have liked the whole world to see the love between us. In my entranced mind, I thought that all would have understood and celebrated this tenderness. They would not.

The next day was hard. I left the hotel at eight, and drove north against the rush hour, to see buyers in the Northern boroughs. In the Afternoon, I had a three-thirty appointment with a southern University at the bottom of the M3. I was fighting my timetable from the start, the first buyer not appearing till after 9.30. Lunch was a

Mars bar, washed down with half a litre of water, parked in the University grounds and watching a scrappy hockey match. Reporting to the buyer, I was shown into the office half an hour before the appointed time. He proved to be a nice fellow, an old stager who liked to present a history of University purchasing to any new contact. They'd had a reorganisation, there was the hint of corruption and bodies having been dismissed.

At five I walked out of the door. Dannie was on the phone as soon as I switched it on, asking where I was, where I would be tomorrow and was I coming into their office. It left me with a warm glow. She cared more than I had believed.

I ate fish and chips in Camden, too tired to want anything more, and at eight was in my hotel room in Hampstead. The staff had left the window open, the room was cold on a bitter spring evening. I crept into bed fully clothed to find warmth and fell fast asleep.

I awoke to find darkness had fallen, and got down to work. I set up my fax machine to find that it would not work. I took the fax draught down to reception and asked them to send it. Sitting waiting for my copy, I looked at the clock. It was 2.30am. No wonder the receptionist had been puzzled by this request. Back in my room, I worked for another hour, then returned to bed, sleeping soundly.

There was an enormous change in me. As Janet said, 'You are not your normal self. You must come back to earth.'

What she means is that I *am* acting differently, which I have failed to recognise. I am far more feminine. Always a smart dresser for work, I am making myself more feminine, using more make-up, taking care of my nails, scrubbing myself squeaky clean, making sure my wild hair does not get out of hand. As someone at work said to me, 'Just stepped out of the bandbox again?'

I was far happier. It had been noticed in the office. As I left Janet one morning, I skipped and danced across the road to my car, pirouetting as she said something to my back, my brief case flying out at the end of my arm. If I had got outside myself and watched me, as I did some months later, I would have compared myself with a female cat I had once, which in its puberty, had gone berserk, skipped scattily, wound itself about my feet sensuously, came in from binges of love making almost exhausted, dirty, smelling of a tom, but was as soft and loving as any of the ten or so cats I have ever owned, was sweet of temper, contented and wanted little food. I was light, loving, gentle. I wanted to touch people, to leave a little of this enormous love upon them, to colour their lives just as I did as a child in my magic colouring book, when a touch of a watery brush would bring the line drawing to sparkling life.

I lost weight. Love and hard work were taking their toll, but as I had a desire to get back to the weight I was three or four years ago, I did not worry about it. I knew the cause, as my friend Sue said, imitating an American singer, 'it's lurve, baby'. Dannie suffered no such problem. She could drink and eat. Our favourite dishes were Singapore noodles, but with shrimps instead of pork, and crab with ginger. The latter is extremely tricky and messy. Extracting the meat from a half crushed crab that has been coated in a pungent brown ginger sauce is not something one wants to do in ones best clothes. We always ate with chop sticks and had become adept. The food was good, plentiful and cheap. We always used the same restaurant, and even in busy Soho, they recognised us. I drove there, parking in the underground park which stinks of urine and pipes drip liquid we were careful to avoid. We both made a mess on the linen tablecloth, Dannie always conscious that she seemed to make more mess than me. Her portion of the white cloth was bestrewn with sauce stains and noodles. It did not matter, the cloth would be changed anyway. I loved her for that, too.

I was still learning about her. There was much to understand, there being so many contradictions. I am told by someone else later, that I am five people, to which I replied, 'as few as that!' Those were, a little girl, an assertive woman, a seductive and attractive woman, a tomboy, and a daredevil. Their opinion, not mine. That is complex and confusing for others, just as Dannie's two people were confusing for me. Actually, I saw no reason why I should not have different personas.

CHAPTER 17.

I tried to make sense of the relationship that had taken over my life, questioning everything, examining Dannie's behaviour. That I had started to do so, should really have told me that something was amiss.

Does she love me, or does she not? There are things that puzzle me. The way on some nights she is available, then at the drop of a hat, will go home early, leaving me like a floundering fish.

There is too, her suspected endometriosis, a painful condition of bleeding outside the womb where the womb adheres to the lining often caused by disease or past surgery. I have seen her reduced to a pale shadow of her normal self within minutes of an attack, her face ashen, her hands clutched across her stomach. She has an appointment with the consultant, and has asked whether I will be able to go with her. I have agreed. But this complaint could also be a most useful excuse for non-appearance, and to my shame, I believe that it has been on occasion. And yet, when I am away on my travels, she is always on the phone, asking where I am, what I'm doing, when will I be down (in London she means), again.

The day before this hospital appointment, the two of us accompanied a customer to Birmingham to see a factory that makes carbonless paper. I picked up Dannie first and then we waited in Westminster for the customer. As we sat waiting in the car, she had little to say, except that she was excited about tonight when we shall be together.

The customer appeared and took a seat in the back. As a print manager, for one of the largest Government Ministries, he was important to us. In spite of Dannie's pleading, I drove. The journey was easy, straight up the M1/M6. The customer proved a nervous driver. He was apparently used to settling in one motorway lane and sticking there for ever. He finds my lane switching disconcerting. I explain that according to the Highway Code, our Company's best seller, there are no fast or slow lanes on a motorway and the code states that the outer lanes are for overtaking. I therefore use the inner lane when free of slow vehicles. Within three years from this visit, the customer will have been made redundant and will become a taxi driver. It will suit him, for although he will no doubt have done 'the knowledge', most taxi drivers do not appear to have studied the Highway Code. This was the new civil service. There is no job security anymore, in the civil service, in banks, insurance or any of the once considered, safe occupations.

The week after the hospital visit was the week before going to Portugal with Sue. Dannie was to go four weeks later with Leslie and Leslie's friends. She is not looking forward to that. She criticises her 'partner' all the time, her dirtiness and drunkenness in particular. I wanted to go with Sue, but would rather have been going with Dannie. Even Dannie's best friend, Bridget, said that we should have been going together. It was a mess.

I was seeing customers around the southern arc of suburban London and she was constantly on the phone, asking my location and when I would be coming in. So we were together again, but not every night. Sometimes without giving a reason she was not available

Too quickly, the week passed. On the Friday afternoon we said goodbye. We arranged that Dannie would take us to the airport in my car. I was already sad at the thought of parting for two weeks.

'I'm going to miss you. It would have been so wonderful if we could have gone together.' she says.

I spoke to Dannie from Portugal every day except at the weekends. I have not really enjoyed the holiday. Because I had been ill, it was not too soon, but also I loved Dannie dearly and I had missed her. I wanted to spend the rest of my life with her, but I knew that to be a dream.

I phoned to tell her what time the flight should arrive. Her voice was soft as usual, but I think, worried about this meeting. There was something else too. She had been to a club she said and been in a fight. I felt she was trying to tell me something else, perhaps that she had met someone. I worried then forgot it. She said she would check the arrival time her end before setting out.

Sue and I packed as much as we could. The coach was due mid afternoon, so we decided to lounge by the pool. Belatedly I tried to tan myself a little, but I was very conscious of the dangers of exposure to the harsh sunlight and of its ageing effect and that especially, had no appeal at all. The risks outweighed the desire for a short-lived cosmetic tan. My sunbathing was dilatory and ineffective, while Sue soaked the rays up like a power cell. My warnings of premature ageing and cancer had no effect. Her skin was a delightful shade of brown.

I lay thinking about Dannie and my need of her. What was it that made me want her so? The thrill of her. That is not in doubt. For the first time in my life, I had been aroused just by the thought of another being. I had orgasmed in my dreams. Her touch, shocked, sending shivers tingling through me, as if an opiate were coursing through my veins. Her attention, her need for me that flattered my soul and persuaded for the first time in years, that I am valued, loved as a whole being. Yes, there had been Greg, but because I did not reciprocate his need for me, the value he bestowed upon me was diminished. Because I did not disclose my true identity, I felt as if I was acting a part.

At the airport, Sue tanked up on gin and tonic before the flight. Her speech was slurred, her fear of flying real, her white knuckled hands clenched, one covered by my own as we parted company with the heat shimmering runway and the Algarve, tourist's Portugal.

Our descent to Gatwick was spectacular, the sun setting across a horizontal blanket of cloud that slowly enveloped this heavy, frail craft we were strapped in. As we broke through the cloud layer, I saw right across Portland where so many good hours have been spent with Janet windsurfing, and all the way to Torbay, where grey mistiness obscures longer sight, the unfamiliar view of the familiar filled me with awe and delight of present and past.

As we walked out of arrivals, Dannie was nowhere in sight, then suddenly appeared and as I turned the video onto her, she turned away shyly as I knew she would.

I ask after Leslie and she tells me that she is still her lodger. I say, 'I thought you were giving her notice. You know how she feels, are you being fair to her, to me?'

Even in the darkness of the car, I can see her eyes are like an angry cat.

'Nothing to do with you, it's between her and me. I do things in my time.'

When we arrive at her home, she is out and away, walking up the street. I call her back. 'We need to talk this out.'

'Not now. She's home waiting for me.' A quick peck on the lips and she goes into the darkness of the passageway leading to her flat.

I drive home full of doubts. I know that something has happened while I have been away. I am sad.

CHAPTER 18.

The doubts I had about her were not resolved. Suddenly she was too busy to see me. All the usual excuses came out, Leslie, or she was really tired, or not feeling well. There were some new ones too, an insurance man coming round; a man offering a job. Even when we were together, she had to get home early, having promised to tape something for bloody Leslie. This last was the most unlikely of all.

What does it all mean? I am of course aware that I harbour suspicions about people, often for imagined slights and lack of affection towards me. It is all part of my low self-esteem. I know it, but I can't control it. Yet I do not believe that I am so neurotic that all my doubts in this case were imagined. My ultra sensitivity has been proved right to some degree throughout my life.

The tale she told me on the phone just before we returned from Portugal revolves in my mind. She had gone out alone to a club and had got into a fight. I thought at the time that she was trying to tell me something, but hadn't the stomach for it, nor to challenge her. The thought had now entered my head that she had met someone. Perhaps she had been fighting over some girl she had flirted with. I know it had happened before when she had ended up with a black eye and lied that she had been mugged. Lesbians, like all women of a certain ilk, can be violent.

I had only three nights in London, but I was not with her that first night. She had suddenly found reason why she could not see me. Even worse disappointment followed. I was now not invited to her birthday party.

The next week was her last before she was to go to Portugal and I wondered what would happen then. Would it be any better? How should we part? Would she phone me from Portugal?

Because Janet was having a mid life crisis, for which she had my sympathy, but which was totally beyond my ken or my help, I found somewhere else to stay. Janet saw me as an addition to her own problems and could not cope with me. She had not said so, I just sensed it. She was also out of sorts with their best friends who had an on off relationship. It seemed that Janet and Paul had no room for anyone other than themselves. Janet was in the depths of despair, worrying that she is too old for her husband who is ten years her junior. She worried too, about all sorts of nonsense, things her mother had said to her as a child, her health, her diet. She had gone macrobiotic, stewed up Japanese twigs instead of tea, ate disgustingly brown rice, wouldn't touch milk, potatoes, meat, cheese and a whole list of other common foods. She has a fear too, of MS, caused by I believe, a misguided GP's casual analysis without scientific basis. At the time it had been made, mid eighties, the cause of MS had been unknown. All my words refuting this threat had been ignored. Unsurprisingly, she had lost weight. She suddenly looked frumpy. The fashionable hairdo had been replaced by a bad perm. She had gone to a ball in a frumpy gown that resembled the awful flouncey Austrian drapes she had put up in her Victorian terraced house.

She cried. I phone her, say 'how are you?' and she tells me, for the next forty minutes during which I could only grunt. At last, exasperated, I said, 'Well, that's all about you.' Then she said, 'How are you?' 'Oh I'm all right. I've got to go now. Love you.' I could not cope with her. I sent her a few weeks before this, twelve reasons to be happy, a husband who dotes on her, her looks, figure, money, lifestyle, health, children who love her, holidays, friends, sexual orientation, home and myself. Compared to me she is richly endowed with the good things of this world.

I could not find a hotel, so Dannie had arranged that I would stay with her best friend, her mate, Bridget. It was while sitting outside Bridget's flat, waiting for her to rise from sleep to go on another twelve hour night shift, that I had had the awful phone conversation with Dannie. Why should she suddenly have changed so towards me? Was there someone else? Was I not enough or too much? Was she really in love with the gay scene, the flirting and the drinking? Did she see me as a barrier to this, just as Leslie had been? Or had she her eye on someone else? I suspected so.

I had driven across London to the address in Dollis Hill. It had been a drive full of doubt, stark reality stealing in like the sea wrack which creeps upon the Norfolk coast in summer, that changes bright warm evening light to dull chill in a moment. So my love seemed to have chilled. The mists of doubt surrounded my heart, and froze out that ecstatic love of life she, her being, had set afire. Frozen, the title of a later Madonna song. I could have written it myself. Loves future was no more. I knew it, because Dannie was not a moody person, did not appear to suffer from stress, and therefore did not normally say things that the mood of the moment have evinced, but that would later be regretted. Yet I would not believe it. Hope carried me on, this human quality of never say die, hope, that is essential to the progress of the being, but which can bring such bitter disappointment.

The day did not help my mood, for what had begun with gay bright bobbing clouds floating in a sky of clear blue, had become dull grey oppression, heat with no sign of the sun, the air fouled and full. London had no magic for me. It was as full of menace as her words and as empty of joy as my heart. Stripped of romance, I see this city again as I saw it before Dannie, a sad old bag lady of a city, stockings holed, hair awry, coat threadbare and stained. I was driving away from one I had worshipped and seen as superhuman to see a woman I hardly knew.

Bridget came to the door and asked me in. She was petite, slim going to thin, her face bony and hard, boyish. Her dark hair was short and slicked back, but there was make-up on her face, just as with Dannie.

While she dressed, I pressed her work shirt for her, just a gesture for her hospitality. Then we talked a little, of course about Dannie. She was not reassuring. She said she did not know what Dannie was playing at. Too quickly, she was off to work. I watched her go from the lounge window, striding out in her Doc Martin's, a knapsack over one shoulder, a soldier of the lesbian army. A wave of empathy, almost affection for this woman I hardly know, filled my breast. She turned suddenly as if she had sensed my eyes following her, then she waived and I waived back, but I still stood rooted to the window, at a complete loss. After ten more strides she turned again, gave a broad grin, blew a kiss, which I returned, glad of this small act of affection from someone I knew more from Dannie's tales of her than from personal contact.

The evening was horrible, grey and depressing. I didn't think of the party going on without me. I could not go out, for I had no key and to leave a door open or unlocked in London, would be infinitely stupid. Eventually I went to bed, just diving into Bridget's king size. Mercifully I fell asleep. I had thought enough all day, I did not want to think all night too.

In the morning I woke at my usual time of six o'clock, got up, dressed, put on my make up. I ate some toast and had a cup of coffee. I made sure that everything was tidy for Bridget's return, my things all packed, the washing up done, the water hot so that she could bathe.

At last I heard her and she greeted me shyly. I found it strange how shy these reputedly flirtatious dykes are, but concluded that they are no different to young men. They exuded a confidence that they have not and making their conquests must be as much an effort as it is a thrill.

It was Dannie's birthday. I had a portable disc player for her. Bridget at least is appreciative of it. She decided to come with me to pick Dannie up. When we come back into the city to work, she had planned to have her hair cut before returning home.

It was an hour's journey from north to south London and that was pushing through the traffic, which included keeping pace with a police car with its flashing light for part of the journey, around Marble Arch, Mayfair and down to Westminster. I thrust though, filling gaps, selecting faster lanes, looking ahead for impediments. Bridget said that we fitted, the car and I, like a hand in a glove. Bridget was a comfort, sitting there beside me, quietly telling me some truths about her friend and endeavoured to put a wiser lover's head upon my shoulders.

The morning was a grey affair, baring down on my mood. Kilburn High Road seemed covered with grey railway bridges. People seemed remote and alien. Even Hyde Park, Green Park, Birdcage Walk, all seemed grey, dull, joyless.

As we travelled, I asked her advice. What should I do, where do I stand? She was helpful and sympathetic, told me to back off, let Dannie do the phoning, and not to count on her too much, for I may get hurt. All this was bad news. It was not what I liked to hear. I wanted to phone several times a day, as we used to before it all became too serious. And of course, I thought, if she loved me as much as I loved her, she would have wanted me to and would not be frightened by it as Bridget said she was. There was sound reason in her advice, for if I did not phone her and then she did not phone me, I would at least know where I stood. It would be a cowardly way for Dannie to tell me though, a brave way for me to find out. Where she is concerned, I do not have that courage. I had put Bridget on the spot, asking her about her best friend's motives, but she seemed willing to help, said that Dannie was not doing right by me. She had not done right by Leslie either, keeping her hanging on, dangling by a heart string, while she withdrew her affection bit by bit and cheated on her with me.

'I told her,' Bridget said, 'to stop mucking you about. I said, you're dealing with a lady, not some bit of a girl having a gay fling. You deserve better.'

I had come full circle, from dislike of Leslie's glowering personality, to sympathy for her, feeling that honesty would have proved less cruel, much less destructive, than slow torture Dannie style. How could I feel that for someone my love spoke so ill of? Every story Dannie told me of her, was a picture of someone I would reject. Her slovenliness, lack of personal hygiene, her alcohol induced overweight, temper and violence. I loved darling Dannie still, the magic of her had me yet in its grip and just as with heroin or coke, I could not escape. I was still hopelessly hooked, the barb of her charms, the energy rush of her kisses, the little kindnesses she had performed for me, the good times that had bonded us, had me landed and floundering, no longer free, my confidence shattered. Just as an addict knows that drug abuse leads to ruin, so I knew that she was bad for me, but I would not give her up.

There was one other thing that worried me greatly. With Leslie, Dannie had an attitude of wanting to have her freedom, to go to discos alone or with her mate, Bridget. There were other occasions too, when she liked to have this freedom. 'We don't get up to anything,' she said of the disco nights, 'we just have a dance and a flirt, it's good for our egos, there's no harm in it. You women always want to tie us down.' What about Leslie's ego? How did being uninvited on these clubbing nights affect her? I should not like it. I believed that if one is in a relationship then one should share a life, not all the time, but certainly things like discos. And flirting, should they have been doing that? It sounded like youths on a Saturday night out to pull. There is a modern song, popular all 2013, Get Lucky, terrible comment on modern sex obsessed society

'There seems to be a lot of promiscuity,' I said of the gay scene when first we confided in each other. Nothing since had changed my mind, indeed it was confirmed. Could I survive in the scene? If I thought about it unemotionally, it did not really matter if she had sex with another woman. A man would have upset me, but I saw no chance of that, her sexual orientation was set I believed. But her absence from me while she flirted, perhaps made love to another, could I handle that emotionally? I thought not.

I had pressures too. There were pressures of the job itself. My boss said that I had not fulfilled all my key targets. I argued that because of the financial situation, they were impossible to achieve. I was right about that. The key targets were set arbitrarily, without any knowledge of the trade, selling or marketing. The price of paper had fallen, competition was even more intense. My sales were over five per cent up, but short of the enormous 10 per cent asked for.

Together, we work to adjust them, but they are still unfair and not achievable. Nor by one person responsible for a £20 million market travelling the whole of the UK, when most of the sales are to small customers and I had no control over purchasing strategy nor pricing. I depended on my association with large users and their influence to remain loyal. Morgan, my boss, wanted results but had put me in a straight jacket by putting pricing in someone else's bag and by giving me no proper inside support. Pricing wanted for a same day delivery, sometimes took days to come through. Office staff seemed to have no comprehension of customer service in the modern commercial world. Cass and I short circuited the system, delivered the goods and did the pricing later just to keep the customers happy.

Then there was my mother, obviously worried about my whereabouts, asking Janet if she knew where I was and, asking if I was being good? For God's sake! How bloody old did she think I was? If I wanted to be a bloody fool or a prostitute or a mistress, drug addict, or just a little femme dyke as Dannie told me I was, I would be. My mother's interference was intolerable with all the other pressures upon me. I felt oppressed from all sides.

I gave mother a ticking off, told her to stop her possessiveness, and let me get on with my life in private. This is my only life, not the best in the world, nor the worst. Hell by some standards, not anything that any normal person would want, but, survivable as is someone's life who is born with a physical disability.

My body *is* my disability. Had I been born in the right form, I believe I could have done anything, been anything. As I have found out, transsexualism has made life bearable, but not perfect. I had to correct my beautician, who said that it was my choice. What choice? Could I have chosen, either to stay male or to take this path? I believe that there was no other way from the day I was born, not pre-ordination, just the result of the DNA, the genes, the abnormality that happened in my mother's womb that had made me the way I am. Even the great Dr Randall had said that the problem would not go away but become ever more intolerable.

Would anyone with normal sexual orientation, or even gay, wish to subject themselves to the painful process of reorientation and conversion to a near approximation of the opposite sex, just for the hell of it? I think not. Certainly Dannie with her desire to be male, and her love of women, would not change her body. She had said to me, 'You must have wanted it very badly,' and she was right. I say this, not in self pity, but to disillusion those readers who would believe that choice existed for me, just as some believe that gays make a conscious choice. There is no more choice than a hetero has to be hetero, or a dog to be born a dog, or a cat a cat. There are degrees of course, as of any malady, and only twenty per cent of those attending gender identity clinic go on to have surgery.

Sexuality is a continuum, from hetero through bisexualism to ardently gay. And within the sexes, some are very masculine or very feminine with all shades between. The natural instincts if strongly enough based, will come out eventually, overcoming any conditioning that has been imposed. Some may find solace in the gay world, able to come to terms with an inappropriate body. I have an acquaintance who having examined the possibility of reassignment to male, decided to remain female and gay, but she is not happy. She has an inner burning fury, almost a hate for much of the world around her, suspicious, alienated.

There is a compulsion that is given particularly to the human, to pursue sexual preference. This can be seen in the 'normal', their pursuit of the opposite sex. How many men and some women, have lost their careers, landed in the divorce courts, ruined themselves in pursuit of sex. It is seen in gays longing for their own sex. It can be seen in those who go beyond the law, as gay men once were, but also in paedophiles who transgress time after time, even knowing the consequences; in repetitive rapists, whose sexual satisfaction is only achieved by complete domination and degradation of the victim. Many talk of 'cures', from therapy to castration, chemical or physical, none of which have proved effective in altering the basic drive and preference of these deviants. Most often, sexual deviants who break the laws are imprisoned, given at best indifferent psychotherapy, then released into the community to re-offend. While by no means endorsing paedophilia or rapists or other such criminal deviations, the treatments so far devised, are totally inadequate and mostly inappropriate.

Then there are differences in the treatment men and women have received for sexual deviations. Lesbianism is largely without legislation, while male homosexuality was condemned and made criminal until 1967.

Women have long dressed as men, sometimes pretended a male life, even as soldiers. That same behaviour in a man could result in a prison sentence and ridicule! But there is a difference here which has to be considered, that men dressing as women often achieve sexual satisfaction, while women are only displaying their maleness.

Most understand the compulsion within women to procreate, the pain caused by a barren relationship, the need that drives them to seek any means, however demanding to reproduce. That is an acceptable compulsion, there are many like those mentioned above that are still not understood and are therefore treated as criminal rather than as having a disability. A Church of England rector recently told me that he is vehemently opposed to homosexual priests. He stated that he had been at boarding school where there was homosexuality in the entirely male population. As soon as they got among girls, he proclaimed, they all became normal again. Poor deluded soul! Sexuality is a continuum, from one extreme to another. Some cross and recross the boundary of hetero and homosexuality. Many cannot and would not cross.

As to transsexuality, it is difficult to explain the hell it is, to hate being of the sex you are born with. It ends in a kind of split personality, the mind hating the body. I was two people, a male body and a female mind. There was no time in my male life when I would look at my nude body and think, 'that is nice'. It was a thing of shame, the anguish of Bottom realising that he had an ass's head. What is worse, is the conventions imposed by society on the natural sex, conventions of appearance, dress, work, and attitudes. The reactions of the rest of the populace to one, the everlasting envy one has of those born naturally to one's desired sex. It is supremely destructive and I suspect impossible for most 'normal' people to imagine. For the gay world, freedom under the law is arriving, has liberated it from legal censure, though still not from the ridicule and everyday discrimination of the world at large. The police still lie in ambush outside public toilets and either warn or prosecute adult males for importuning, for the law only allows homosexuality in the privacy of their own homes! Even holding hands in public can be a crime. There are all those jokes about, 'he's one of them, a shirt lifter, keep your backs to the wall.'

At last, due to the rulings of the ECHR in 2002 rather than any philanthropic actions of our own Government, those who cannot conform to the sexual norm, are to have rights, rights of 'marriage' and of employment. The bill has at last been approved by Parliament in May 2004. I have really lived outside the law for twenty-eight years by the time the Gender Recognition Act comes into force, 5th April 2005. I had to change employers. In future transsexuals will have the right to remain in their employment through the change. They will have the full rights of their reassigned sex under the law. If criminal a transsexual woman will be sent to a female prison, or if ill, taken onto a female ward. It has taken a long time, some martyrdom and much state cruelty but soon we will have a more equitable world.

Just try though to imagine this. Think what it would be like to be a woman waking up with a penis and no breasts, or a man waking with no penis and breasts, transformed while in sleep just as Puck with magic transformed poor Bottom into an ass. Everyday the pain is there and one tries not to see, tries to ignore the body that is so hated. I would avoid mirrors, particularly when undressed. And then throughout the day, every action had a different slant from the one desired. I saw women treated differently, I heard them talking to each other, I wanted to understand, to be a part of their society, but I could not enter their world. I had clothes, which were courser and less comfortable. I could not use nail varnish or make-up. The image my instincts told me to project could not be shown and would have been ridiculed. It was an imprisonment and meant that I was denied the right of self-expression. The self was in conflict with its surroundings. It bore down upon me so that eventually I believe, suicide or insanity would have resulted. Yet I am sure, you still do not understand.

Dannie had that imagination. She had that understanding. She knew something of that pain, and had been able to empathise. We were so similar in that, she born female wanting to be male, but wisely in her case, not sacrificing her sexual pleasure, and me, coming from the other way, meeting her, colliding and amalgamating, succouring each other. And now there seemed a rift.

It may be this. I believe part of her initial attraction to me was that I flattered her. I had after all, been male, had become a heterosexual female, and she had conquered me. I was also an important and respected customer, a real scalp to take, a method possibly of furthering her career. That was a supreme ego trip for her. It was a great adventure for me, but to say that belittles the intensity of my feeling, my deep love for her.

But there is a fundamental difference between us. As a woman who loves women, she has found sexual satisfaction, once she had recognised that in herself and had the courage to 'come out' to indulge her natural orientation. Among lesbian women therefore, she has no handicap. For me, there is always the fact of my sex at birth, which when known, can alter perceptions of my present sex. I am therefore caught in a trap, trapped in the midst of this gender web.

It was the last Friday before Dannie went to Portugal. As a farewell present and to indulge her expressed liking for classical music, I had booked the Proms, a concert of Tchaikovsky piano concerto no 2, and Rachmaninov Symphonic dances. It would be her first visit to the Royal Albert Hall and I was excited by the prospect, just as she is. I park in Prince Consort Road, a wide street, with good solid buildings, colleges and offices, Imperial College, The Royal School of Music, a street worthy of its name, and we made our way with others, up the steps via Albert Court towards the red brick of the Albert Hall, then into the auditorium. Dannie was impressed with the size of the interior, the massive organ and the aura, and said how she will tell her father. That was a recurring desire, to impress her father, and I wondered why she had that need. I did not ask. She was disappointed in the music, liking the no 1 concerto which everyone knows.

In the interval, I remembered that I had left the phone in the car. I was minded to go and fetch it, but we are standing in the corridor drinking, warm beer served in cans or plastic glasses. That was no way to cater for concert-goers and, at rip-off prices too, three times the price of that same can from a supermarket. The Hall was a slum, the seats uncomfortable, the refreshments of an unbelievably low standard, the atmosphere close on that late July evening. Do concert-goers have to be masochists, I wondered?

As the beer was hardly stimulating, Dannie had a new game, being my pimp and picking out some choice customers, an old and completely bald man with a round red face among others. Why she had chosen this game, I was not sure, but it may have had something to do with the fact that she suspects that I am not really gay, because I had picked out a man as being singularly attractive. She had seized on this casual observation, and asked why I hadn't found an attractive woman to mention, a question that I don't bother to answer, but she would have known anyway, that I find boyish women attractive sexually. After all, I was with her. Was it a way of demeaning me? It was funny, but irritating and I would rather she had not thought of it. I was losing interest in her too with her silly games.

There was a woman in a black dress, who had walked by twice on a man's arm. The dress looked too small and too short, and Dannie said, 'Fancy letting your mother go out looking like that.' It was quite cruel, for the woman was not that old, nor too mutton as lamb, but I would have perhaps been more careful in the choice of dress.

The concert was over, she had enjoyed it anyway. Next time she said, we will promenade. But I could tell there was much on her mind. She had told me that there was a job offer, but would tell me no details. She joked that she would be able to keep me! I do not want her to, but it is a strangely attractive idea. What it said was that she loved me and wanted me, so why had she been so peculiar this week, cold and distant, as though withdrawing from me, when just over two weeks before she was telling me that she loved me when I phoned from Portugal? I knew in my heart that her love for me was over, done, run its course, the bottle empty of all but the dregs, yet still, she keeps up a pretence.

When we reached the car, we saw that the window was missing from the front passenger door. It lay all over the seat in shards and the phone was no longer there. I was distraught, and Dannie took command. I felt this theft was an assault on me and one of the fears we all share in this city, had happened. I had become a victim.

We went into the office of Imperial College, asking if we could phone the police, but that was not possible. I walked up the street to the phone box, and telephoned the local station, then called Mercury to cancel the number. There were other people wanting to phone for the same reason. As I finished, the police arrived. I am impressed at their speed in answering the call, and directed them to my car where Dannie was doing what she could to clear up the mess. The police took details, gave me a crime number, 7138 at that station for motor crime in the month. I was staggered by the statistics and that I was now part of it. I felt I had become an underclass, at the mercy of others. I am shocked. I would have liked to come back next week armed with a pickaxe handle and to have ambushed the bandits. I would have broken their bloody legs, so that they would remember for the rest of their lives. It seemed to me in the aftershock, that swift and overwhelming punishment was the only remedy. Maybe vigilante action is now needed in this lawless society we have created, especially for violent or threatening crime. Yet to some extent, all crime is violent. There is always a victim hurt by the act. I believe that fines are quite counter productive, for the thieves either don't pay and disappear into the underworld, or just go out and steal to pay the fine. Neither does prison appear to have the desired results. Most habitual criminals reoffend. There is not much crime in Saudi where justice is swift and extreme. Moslems argue that it is cost effective and only a few hands have to be cut off to discourage theft. These thoughts rage through my mind. They, the criminal class, have destroyed my last evening out with her before she goes on holiday, and I would destroy them in the shock of it. I know, in my heart, that education, work and reforming therapy are the real antidotes to crime.

'Thank you for looking after me.'

'I'll always look after you.' It was another dedication of herself to me, yet because of her withdrawn behaviour, I hardly believed her. The words that would once have brought euphoria now sent a shiver of sorrow through me.

I sat in the back, away from the glass and Dannie drove. I leant forward and kissed her and she leant her head into me as we drove like a cat's caress. The feel of her soft cheek on mine is incredibly comforting. We sat down the street from her flat, then she came into the back to kiss me. This was our last night out before her holiday, the one I should have gone on. We were nervous, the open window making the car insecure, and she would not tarry. We watched as an urban fox wandered down the street, circled the car, then made off at a lope. We were entranced by this quite common occurrence.

I had decided to go home, rather than stay the night with Sue's boyfriend James, and I said goodnight, sadly, still in shock from the theft. I watched her in the mirror as I pulled away, my heart heavy, and hoped that she would have a good time in Portugal in spite of Leslie's presence.

I had a hundred and forty miles to drive without a window. I phoned mother to say that I would be home, so that she would not chain the front door, and I drove through the early hours of the morning, the wind blasting through the gap. Luck was with me. It did not rain.

My being was silent, my thoughts dull. I was in a kind of suspension, devoid of hope for the future, without fear of the present. It was the feeling of quiet before an approaching storm. It was the seed pearl of hurt and anger. I sensed a change in me, yet I would not accept it was happening. Black clouds were forming about me, the birds had ceased to sing, the wind had dropped to a whisper and though no rain had fallen, no lightning was seen or thunder heard, I knew that this summer of love would end in fury.

CHAPTER 19.

This affair with my darling Dannie started on the 27th April. That was the night she seduced me on her sofa, in front of her partner, and later came into my bed, albeit momentarily. It has been a summer when I learned that I still need love, still react, that a woman's kisses can give me an orgasm, something I would not have believed six months ago. It has been a summer of emotion, unsurpassed joy, and the depths of despair.

There have been terrific pressures on me, the job, the fact that although I have been using it to see her, I have worked to the best of my ability. It has been hard, working away and trying to look after my mother and the home. There are also the pressures that my mother has put on me, knowing that I am with people she doesn't know and is afraid for me and, for herself. There is Janet, who has tried to comfort me in spite of her own troubles, which I in turn have tried to deal with but do not fully understand. My cat has died, died in my arms as the vet's needle brought oblivion to a beloved creature, in pain from cancer. She was still beautiful in death. I cried and railed against the world as I covered her wrapped body with earth in the garden. And the greatest stress of all is Dannie.

She has said, 'I don't play games. I always say what I mean.'

I don't believe her. There are reasons for this. There have been promises made but not kept, rides on the bike, visits to my home, to quote, 'Don't bother with the garden, I'll do it.' 'There'll be plenty more weekends.' There have been dedications, 'I love you Adrienne.' 'I'll always take care of you.' 'I think of you all the time.' All this does not mean that she loves me.

I say to her every day, 'I love you.' I want her to know just how I feel about her. She will only say that when she feels like it, she says. What does that mean? Does she only love me sometimes? Then that is not enough. Broken dates.

Then too, she says that I should meet her away from the office, she cannot stand the gossip. She is the known dyke, so who has the reputation to lose? That is something that I decided about from the first, that I would not compromise my friendship by disguising it, by parking down the road and having a hole in the corner relationship. I gave myself to her fully.

This is the greatest slight of all, trying now to hide our love. That she changes her mind later, is of little comfort.

All this tells me that it is over and if not, then it should be.

It is time for me to take stock of this relationship, to add up the debits and the credits, and she has cost me plenty. There is the deposit on the motorbike, which I may or may not get back, two bottles of cologne from top fashion houses, calls from Portugal which consumed pounds and pounds, meals out, drinks and the fuel to see her. All this is of no account. I liked to treat her when she had little money, or I thought she had no money, but when I hear of the drinking binges and visits to clubs, I am not so sure that what money she has, is spent wisely I enjoyed sharing what I had with her, and she showed her enjoyment of such little treats, even the night we stood at the base and looked up at the immensity of Canary Wharf.

The real account is in promises. A promise made should be a promise kept. Even allowing for the complication of Leslie, the broken words are unforgivable.

There is too, her treatment of Leslie. Instead of being truthful and telling the poor girl that it is over, she has allowed their relationship to drag on, I fear for monetary gain. It is not until Leslie has suffered a partial breakdown, resulting in the loss of her job and Dannie's income from her, that she is finally told to go. Leslie goes home to her parents, Dannie tells me, with a breakdown. She says this without attaching any blame to herself. Their whole relationship is as I had supposed it to be, a matter of rent. Dannie used her wiles to attract Leslie because she could not afford her mortgage and all her other debts. I have come to feel empathy with poor Leslie, but I do know that Leslie is not without fault. She has murderous eyes, and is violent when drunk.

It is the tenth of August. Tomorrow Dannie says, she will give in her notice. She has an offer from another company. They will pay her as much as me, with the same car, but a better model, she boasts. I am pleased for her. But this has come out of the blue, although she had told me she was speaking to someone. She had asked my advice, before her holiday. Should she look elsewhere for work? I told her to talk to her present employer first. Cass tells her he needs to see better results before giving her better terms. I think he was fair.

After a month's absence, she has asked if I will meet her at a pub where she will be talking to her new boss. Like a robot, I turn up as commanded, thinking that by this time, and I am deliberately late, her new boss will have gone. I am disappointed to find him still there.

She greets me with, 'Come and sit down darling.' It is said for her benefit not for mine and for his hearing. She is displaying her hold over me, because I am an important account. She has changed her image already, softened her hair, allowed it to grow and the effect is more feminine. Then she is dressed differently too. Gone is the tweed jacket and mannish trousers. She is in a bright summer jacket, open necked shirt and shorts. A sporty young woman. It makes not the least difference to me. She could have pigtails and a split skirt, I would love her just the same. What really annoys is that in using me, she has betrayed our relationship and my sexuality. It is dismaying. I take no part in the discussion. She is trying to use her association with me to offer her new employer a route to our purchasing. I offer nothing. I say, 'We buy very little from this company but always through their Norwich branch.' A look of annoyance crosses her face.

On the drive home she picks a fight.

'You're so negative.'

'What do you mean?'

'That letter, when you went on holiday.....'

'You said that you liked it. You read it every day!' I exclaim.

'I know, but...'

'I was trying to be fair to you, in view of the difference in our ages. I would not want you to feel trapped. In any case, relationships don't last.' Look at yours with Leslie, I could say, or look at ours.

She knows she is in the wrong, finding fault where there is none to find. She seeks an alternative target.

'Whatever happened to the old self assured Adrienne. I liked that. You changed.'

'It is easy to give when you love someone. In any case, you changed. That's what made me so unhappy. You were so loving and caring, now you find fault. I love you, and you don't respect me for it.'

'You noticed I changed.' She smiles, a sly self satisfied smile and I hate her for it. She is now so cocky, now that she has this new job and considers herself my equal or my better. She will never be that.

'You're wrong, I do respect you....'

I attack her now. 'I don't need this, I have been pissed on enough.' I have said this deliberately. It is not self-pity, I am paraphrasing her when she said, 'I'll never hurt you, Adrienne, you have suffered enough.'

'Let me out of here.' Her eyes are angry as a cat's again, just like the night we returned from Portugal. It is a familiar ploy, when confronted with the truth, she will run. I know that she doesn't want to get out and wait for a bus.

'Do you want to get out?' I slow. We are in the outskirts of Peckham and I know she is frightened to walk there. She can get out if she likes. That would save a ten mile drive through south London, the same journey that once I loved. I am suddenly very weary, tired of her company when once her presence was like a shot of adrenaline.

'I can't help it if others have hurt you.' She pauses, I await her next tack. 'Leslie says that I'm aggressive. I've got a good brain, I know I'm right, so I say things forcefully.' She has already said to me, 'I'm not good enough for you, you are far more intelligent,' a remark that I refuted. I think differently now as she says this, trying to justify herself.

'I can't be aggressive with you. Aggression stops conversation, stifles discussion. Couples have to talk.' I know this to be right, and I am fighting back for once.

She quietens. I have no idea what has provoked this onslaught, and I want to know.

'What have I done?' I ask.

'You haven't done anything.'

I reach her road, park in the same place where we have always parked, where she first drove me wild with her kisses, such kisses that I had never experienced before, never expect to find other than with her.

In this place holding hands we watched the slow urban fox patrol the street, holding our breaths and marvelling at our luck in being so close.

She has calmed. She kisses me on the lips, the ones she said were lovely, then leaves the car, walks around it having retrieved her briefcase from the back seat and coming to my driver's window, kisses me again.

'I know that I'm being unfair to you, asking you to wait for me, but I need space.' Is this a dedication, or her weak way of gradually cutting me adrift. I cannot trust her words, although I want to.

As I move off, I call her to me, saying that I do not want to shout. 'You are still the best dyke I know,' and she smiles as I say the words. I know it is over.

I drive away, pulling up the hill, and she waves. My heart is heavy, my eyes filling with tears, and I can hardly see, nor do I know where I am going. Before me there are times when I will be lonely, when I thought we would be together. There are plans spoken of, which now lie mouldering. I am hurt, wounded by her attitude, and by her use of me. I am glad not to be Leslie.

Yet I love her, love her, love her.

Next morning, I phone Cass. Business cannot be mixed with love and affection, especially when the balance has so changed. Now that she has told me she is giving in her notice, I have to tell Cass. With trembling heart, I phone him at home. He takes the news well, calmly. He asks me to meet him later, so that we can decide on a damage limitation exercise.

Cass asks her to reconsider, but she now believes that she is too good for them, that her fortune lies elsewhere. He gives her the terms common in the trade. Three months notice, but agrees to two. She will leave immediately, on full pay for those two months, and must not work in the trade during that time.

Later, Cass and I meet. We talk it over in the boardroom. He is reassuring. What she knows, and her influence on our customers, is very little. We agree to pay them special attention over the next four months. Cass is a rock. Somehow though, I feel absurdly as though I am stabbing her in the back.

It is the seventeenth of August. Three weeks have passed since she left the company. I have hardly spoken to her. I am out with Cass, her old boss, who sees my distress and has plumbed it. I am too wounded to resist his probes and his gentleness has me in tears. He tells me that she is far more able to deal with an emotional crisis than I, and I know that to be right, for she has little emotion. He talks of her drinking, and the fact that it was responsible for the break up of a previous long term relationship. There is another lie she has told me. I have told her of my concern over her seeming need for alcohol and she was immediately aggressive. There are other things too, I would not wish to hear about her.

I meet with her best friend Bridget, picking her up in Berkeley Square. We then drive from the West End to the City to pick up her partner, Deborah. We drink coffee in Covent Garden, and they both remark on Dannie's drinking. It is as I have been told, she can drink until she no longer remembers. There have been 'moonies' in Leicester Square. Is this the person I want to share a life with? Is this the sort of behaviour that made her say, 'I'm not good enough for you' All this is no compensation. I would have her complete, happy, able to give, for her own sake. I am worried for her. Suddenly I realise that what I loved was a facade, a beautiful shell that sheltered a hermit crab.

Nineteenth of August. She says that she needs to talk to me, and we set a date. Whether she intends this to be goodbye or a reconciliation, I do not know. She wants to tell me something face to face. I suspect the worst, yet it is no longer that. I will see her next Tuesday the twenty-fourth. I am already free of her, the spell broken. All that remains is to sweep away the debris and I shall return to normal.

Sunday, the twenty-second. She phones at six thirty in the evening. She has been to the party she asked me not to attend, Deborah's birthday, then out on the town. She has just got home after a twenty-four hour binge. It is not a social call, she would like to change our meeting to Wednesday, but I stand my ground. My arrangements have been made and I want to get it over. Besides which, I am working. I cannot just bunk off for a silly woman.

'What then?' I ask.

'What do you mean?' She is shocked by my tone.

'We meet on Tuesday. Is that it? Are we finished? Will we see each other again?'

'I've just had a really good time. I want to be on my own. I have to do what is right for me.'

'Yes of course,' I say. 'I'll see you Tuesday.'

And I still love her. Damn.

But I know now that she is in love with the scene, the excitement of it, the binges, the cruising, the pull and conquest and on to the next victim. It is a game to inflate battered egos and she has demonstrated by her often spoken belief of her worth, how much she needs to prove her value. She said, and I thought it sweet then, 'My dad will be so proud, when he sees me in the company car. I'll have a phone too,' (like me she means). It is a competition, and all I offered was sharing and equality. She has to prove something, to herself as much as to her family, as much to me, and as much to Cass.

She has missed the point. One proves worth by actions, by hard work, or kindness, by strength and gentleness, by truth and by loyalty. I see little of this in her, but words. I still love her.

There will be other loves. There will be good times without Dannie. I have to believe that.

My stomach has tightened up as I drive through north London. I have been with a supplier from early morning, having driven over a hundred miles to get there. It has been a day when I have had to be mentally alert, trading partners are always looking for an advantage to promote themselves, and one can't give away too much. This one in particular, the largest supplier to my company, is tricky in the extreme, indulging in commercial espionage and using every angle. (Seven years later, their empire is collapsing and I am not sorry.) There have been other things on my mind too. However, I consider it to have been a successful meeting. I am pleased with the progress made with a supplier known to be 'difficult'.

Now, business over, my thoughts have turned fully to Dannie and nerves are tying me up.

It had been a sparkling day, warm sun, but there is now a cool breeze, white clouds fleeing the skies towards the south east. It is a late summer day, a hint of autumn about it, a quiet sadness in the countryside, wheat fields shorn, a sure sign of autumnal imminence. Autumn affects me. I find it sad, there is a quietude, a churchyard aura, the slow closing of a cold and bony hand about my heart, which if I let it, makes me melancholy. The only redeeming facet of winter for me, is that the skiing season starts. This September afternoon is cold, the sky mostly cloud covered, the light dulled, as are my feelings. I am now on my way south, contemplating phoning Dannie as I know I must, when the car phone rings.

'It's me. I'd have thought I would have heard from you by now. What's happening?' Her voice has a hard edge. It is as gruff as I've ever heard it. My mind flies from this pitch, the tenor of it, back to that happy day when she had put her hand upon mine in the restaurant, softly and firmly, and said in a voice of sweetness and unmistakable love, 'I love you Adrienne, I'm going to do something about Leslie, but I don't want to go straight into another relationship.' How those few words had raised me. The heights my emotions had soared to, I had never visited before. She loved me. I could not wish for a greater compliment. It washed away forty years of pain and made me whole and her love lit my world then, just as a sunbeam transforms a dull landscape.

Yet what was that love? I cannot know what was in her mind then, just as I do not understand what thoughts she has now. She sought me out, developed first a telephone relationship, then a personal one. When I was away, she would be there, at the end of the phone. Aberdeen airport, the A1 at Doncaster, a lay-by in the depths of North Lancastrian countryside, Battersea. My Angel, sat upon my shoulder, there to comfort. A joke. A giggle. Innuendo, a coded message of love, that only we understood. A word. Her tone. Her voice from a distance, sometimes throatily full of sexual appeal, sometimes as light as a choir girl's. Heart race. Life pulsing warmly, as I answered the phone to hear my beloved. That warmth, that ecstasy which would linger hours after I had replaced the receiver. That infusion. That positive charge which would enable me to pass another day in joy of being. The electrical pulse which brought me to life, raised me from an automaton to being a real person.

All this was wrong. I should have loved myself. I had loved her loving me. I was the Moon to her Sun, rather than Jupiter to Venus. I have my own value and have disregarded it in comparison to that she gave me. Janet has said, 'We love you for you!', and I did not recognise that for the compliment it was.

'I've just come out of a meeting.' I am slightly indignant, she knows that I am working, yet still expects me to make the arrangements, even though she sits at home. She rushes on, ignoring my answer.

'I've been to the doctor, because I've had so much pain.' Her voice has transformed now to one of pain, screwed up, taught, the last word clipped off. I have not heard her like this before. 'I've had an internal, and the doctor has really hurt me.' She is crying, I can't bear to hear her pain. The worst has happened to her, a man has inserted his hand into her.

'Poor darling. Is there something I can do for you if I come over?'

'No. I was going to say, don't come. It really hurts. He was really rough with me. I told him he should be struck off. I just want to go to bed with some pain killers.'

'So. What about tomorrow then. Shall I ring you in the morning?

'Yes.'

'What time?'

'Anytime. I'm not going anywhere.'

'OK. I'll ring in the morning.'

'Bye.' She has gone. I am left high and dry once again. My stomach on the point of bursting with nervousness at seeing her, has quietened already, knowing that I am now not going to. The physical relief is tempered by concern for her, and frustration over another break in plans which have been carefully made. And a small voice is saying 'don't believe her.'

Once more I am completely lost. Where to go, what to do? How can I dismiss this longing for her from my mind? The denial of her is unbearable. My face is filled with blood, there is pressure in my temples, and an ache in my throat, and tears well into my eyes, as I force my way from King's Cross to Old Street. I pass a street that we had gone up twice to a gay cafe, when love was new and exciting, pure and full of hope, and the magic of her was untarnished with doubt and deception, greed and selfishness. She was an immaculate being then, and I had fallen for her. I am bereft of joy, driving in an aimless and dreadful vacuum.

What is more sad, is that a small voice within has started to question. Is she really in pain? Is this just an act to put me off, so that she does not have to see me? For tomorrow she believes, I have to go home. Is she counting on that, and then she will be away to hide at her mother's? I know her to be a moral coward. I am torn, sympathy fighting cynicism. And I hate myself for this doubt. I love her still. She has been my god, the peak of desire, the person I have thought of everyday for four months. I would lay down my life for her, spend my last penny on her. I ring a customer in a Ministry and arrange to meet at a pub, then spend the afternoon discussing what other papers we can provide.

Afterwards I phone Janet, but she isn't there.

I drive to James's flat which he has kindly put at my disposal. I enter, dial the burglar alarm to stop its burbling, the only welcome there is, and shut the door behind me. There is only silence here. I have not been five minutes behind the door before I realise that I cannot stand the awful quiet which even the radio cannot dispel. I wonder whether to go to Dannie's anyway, to catch her with my successor, to see her going out on the motorbike, the bike which I have contributed to, and for which she commanded that I should purchase a crash helmet, that has been used but once. My mind is becoming twisted with doubt of her.

I need to speak to Bridget. The only way to do that is to go to her work. She will finish at six, and I have plenty of time. I iron two of James's shirts as a way of saying thank you, then drive to the West End. My face screws into tears of loss as I exit the City Docklands tunnel. The sun has appeared again, and shines directly into my face. A driver pears intently at me as I wait at traffic lights, as though he can see my pain. I put my sunglasses on, partly against the glare, partly to shield me from prying eyes. I feel safer from behind my mask, more anonymous still, hidden, my emotions shrouded, but the intense pain remains, vivid, burning into my soul and will leave indelible marks, acid etched. She has damaged me already.

Two lanes of traffic rush around the Tower of London. The car is alive for me, and I am in love with it. It will not hurt me unless I want it to. I hurtle down Lower Thames Street, leader of the pack, invincible behind the wheel. Adrenaline flows again and I recover myself. There is a brave show of illuminated cloud behind St. Paul's dome, brilliant white and gold, as I drive west. Northumberland Avenue, Trafalgar Square, Pall Mall, St. James's Street, Piccadilly. None of it means anything to me today.

I wait in the lobby, lounged in a comfortable seat until I see her come swinging along with her jaunty walk. Bridget is small, maybe five feet two, very slim, her face bony and boyish, but there is makeup beneath her cropped and slicked back hair. We wave, then she is with me, and I explain my presence.

'She hasn't got the balls to see you.' Her West Country accent is warm, but her words pour out in a stream. I have to listen hard to catch them all.

I'm silent. This verdict from Dannie's best friend shocks me. It confirms my worst fears, she really is the coward that I suspect her to be.

'Adrienne, you know I'm her best friend, but forget her, she's bad news, believe me. Just leave her alone babe, don't even phone her, because I'm telling you, she will fuck you up, and it's not fair. You'm been good to her, too good, you spoiled her. It's a shame.' Her brogue is good and honest. I do not cry. For once I am in control.

'She went to the doctor this afternoon, and he gave her an internal. She was crying on the phone. I don't think she would be faking that.'

'Well I don't know I'm sure, she tells so many lies. But you should stay away. Just tell her to get lost, for your sake, she won't do you any good. I took her into the bedroom last Saturday when she came to ours, and I told her I'm sick of hearing about her, and she hasn't got any time to listen to my problems.'

'I'm sorry to involve you Bridget.'

'No, that's not what I'm saying. She's my best friend right, but I'm telling you, for your sake, keep away. You can talk to me all you like, it's her I don't want to hear. I had a flaming row with her, and told her to leave me out of her affairs. I told her she should be straight with you, not tell you all these lies. She's dealing with a lady, not some bit of a girl. See, she won't do no good on her own, she'll be back on the booze, and then this new job, they'll never let her get away with it. The drink's a real problem, I told Debs the same I'm telling you. We were both sorry you didn't come to the party. Her was it? Told you not to come? She's got a cheek. I nearly threw her out.'

I'm shaken. The last vestigial respect I have for Dannie is being ripped away. Can I have been so deceived? Was it all a lie, from beginning to end, all her sweetness, all her dedications, her kisses, her love making? Stripped bare of this pretence, her past, the rape, her treatment at the hands of her long term lover who she said had wasted all their money and made her sell her car and her motorbike, and all the rest of her ego boosting stories, what remains? Skeletal, shadow thin, swathed in swirling mists, barely visible, hardly human, I no longer know what she is, why she is, what I have been to her, and why this ghost has selected me to haunt.   Do I even care anymore?

As I drive Bridget she tells me more.

'Did she tell you she was mugged and got her briefcase damaged?'

'Yes.'

'All lies. A woman threw her down the stairs for flirting with her girlfriend. Dannie was drunk. Another time, a customer threw her out, she was drunk at ten in the morning. Honest Adrienne, you don't know her. She been so crafty with you. Her biggest conquest boosting her ego. Do you understand what I'm saying?'

I do. I do not want her to fail. I don't want to hear that she has a drink problem. I want to believe in her. Yet Bridget would not say these things were they not true. I am suddenly angry, but do not show it. I feel a great warmth for Bridget, doing her best for me, but I wish she weren't saying these things. I touch her knee, and say thank you. I can see she is troubled with split loyalties. But Dannie. I want you to be again, what you were five months ago, the golden being full of light, sweet sensuous, caring, full of respect for me. Sunlight slips silently, sinks, slinks away to be replaced by grey miserable mistiness, and settles clammy cold, envelops my body, and infiltrates my shocked seared soul.

By the time I reach Janet later, I am in good form, revived by Bridget and Debs, but strengthened by anger at this ghost which haunts and hounds, and I feel as happy as I have in a week. Instead of going to James's lonely flat, I stay overnight with Janet and Paul, but I do not sleep well. In the night my mind dwells on her and I am savage. For the first time it has sunk in how she has deceived me. She even had me thinking that I was insecure, obsessive, over possessive, when all I wanted was the normal response one would expect from a lover. Why has she treated me so? Just what does make her tick? I try to figure it all out, and come to some conclusions.

I doubt that she is capable of having a full time relationship as I think of it. As with Leslie, she would like to be able to go out flirting in the bars and clubs without me. 'What do you want to come for? We don't get up to anything, just see whether we can pull, does our egos good.' And what of my ego Dannie? What would it do for me? I would become as paranoid, jealous, suspicious, unhappy, maybe even violent, as Leslie has been according to Dannie. Is it surprising that one's live in partner should feel hurt when she is flirting? Did she not seduce me on her sofa in front of Leslie? I was ashamed of that at the time, but Leslie appeared to not even notice, but then she was senses dulled with three bottles of wine. Was that all a planned seduction? Had they arranged that I should be their victim? Is there an evangelic movement, an intent, to convert, subvert the hetero world? Or is it Dannie's sport, to conquer and seduce, just as in the hetero world? And Bridget admits to being promiscuous, and says that Dannie is as much so. What have I got into here?

My night is disturbed. The bed is uncomfortable, the covers on an unseasonably cold summer's night, keep coming adrift, and then a child keeps crying out. The sound is intensely disturbing. I imagine physical abuse, abandonment, severe sickness, and I picture this child imprisoned, even tortured. It is a horrible sound. I have horrible thoughts too, of Dannie and what she has done to me.

At half past five a dog is released into the yard, and keeps barking at an imaginary cat. Janet tells me later that this happens every morning, and that the child is mentally handicapped. That explanation at least relieves the distress of hearing the haunting human voice. I awake, dress and prepare to depart, knock on their door and say that I am going. They tell me to come in.

'How are you today?'

'OK,' I say.

'Really?'

'Yes. I've been thinking about her all night. I have to have this out with her, then that is it, finished.'

'Can you do it? Do you mean it?' Paul asks.

'I feel strong. I'm going to kick her arse. I've had enough.'

'Good for you,' Paul says.

Janet has leapt nude from the bed. She throws her light robe on, we have the same one, bought separately, without knowledge of each other. She follows me down the stairs to the door, giving me moral support, not against Dannie, but making me think about myself and giving me back some self-respect. We kiss then I walk to the car. I feel better than I have for weeks.

The dawn is full fledged, but the sun is hidden behind clouds. It is a light morning, bright with promise, but as yet a cold light, very white, the sky a peculiarly light creamy white. I look at my hands upon the wheel, and see knuckles which match the hue of these cold clouds, and my hands which are usually warm, are chilled. I switch on the heater, even though August is not yet done. At seven, the roads are uncrowded, and the six miles to the Isle of Dogs takes me just fifteen minutes. I love the architecture, but as yet this new town lacks a soul. I have the feeling that something has died here in this place, and although a body has been produced from the ashes, it lacks life. There is beauty without charm, line without object. And all the water gives a cold feel, acres of reflective surface, ground become sky, with upside down images, which in my low state confuse my mind still further. There is no softness to take away the stark, brave cold, no weeping willows as in Cambridge, no old architecture and buildings of warm brick leaning across the canals as with Venice, or a mixture of both as in Amsterdam. I cherish the memory of Dannie looking up at the magnificence of Canada house, her face full of a schoolboy's wonder. I loved her so much for that.

The house is quieter than a church. The water seen from the rear windows, which sometimes looks creepily calm and of a greenie hue, today is rippled by an early breeze, and reflects the sky of creamy cloud and palest blue. I heat the water for my bath, and breakfast and iron my blouse while waiting for it. By the time that is done the bath is ready. I soak lazily. There are no tears this morning. Am I at last escaping the spell she has put me under? I hope so.

No wonder Leslie is in such a state.

I make two calls, both on customers in Westminster. I try phoning her between visits, but her line is engaged. Is this another ruse? My third customer visit is cancelled, and I have time to sort this out.

Eventually as I walk up Victoria Street, she answers. The voice is guarded, apprehensive, as she says 'Hello'. I sense that she has dreaded my call.

'How are you today?'

'Pretty bad. Still a lot of pain.'

'So you'd rather I didn't come over?'

'Where are you?' Why does that matter, I wonder?

'London.'

'I don't feel well enough.' Because I am close?

Suddenly I am really angry. I'm convinced that she is not so ill that she cannot see me. I feel sure that she is using illness to avoid me, and I am now sure that she has used it in the past to cut our meetings short. The great lover. The up front tough guy.

'I'm fucked if I care what you feel. It's always you and what you want. What about me, how do I feel?'

There is total silence on the line. I wait for her to answer, but all I have heard is an intake of breath, sharply shocked. After what I reckon to be ten seconds, I speak again.

'I have been bloody good to you. If you can't spare me fifteen minutes, it's a very poor thing. How about it?'

'OK.' She breathes the word.

I press END, and the line goes dead. I wonder now whether to bother, whether to apply a little cruelty of my own and just let her wait, forever. But she has things of mine, discs of Mozart piano concertos, and a manuscript which she requested and hasn't had the good grace to read. She could have done, out of friendship, out of interest in me, in curiosity perhaps, but she is a lazy reader. She is no reader. Others have read it and enjoyed. I want these items back, particularly the manuscript, but why should I let her have the discs? I have given enough, but would have given the world.

The gate to the flats is unlocked, left open by the painter who seems to be doing this whole block alone, and the front door is propped open with a large tin of paint. I climb the stairs with a heavy heart, leaving the sunshine behind as I enter the dull staircase, when once I climbed them as if to heaven, hungrily hoping for the kiss, the fix, the orgasmic welcome. Somehow today the stains on the carpet seem even more obvious. When I come to her door, I stop in the dark hallway, not with fear exactly, but with emotion. Anger gives me the strength to go on. I knock.

She opens the door wide and stands back as I stalk past her. I have never seen her looking so sullen, like a naughty schoolboy caught wanking. Her face has a peculiar colour, a bluish white, almost purple. Is she really ill? I have never known anyone's complexion to change as much as hers. She can look country bumpkin fit one minute, and like a corpse the next. But then she is full of contradictions, in sex, her androgynous pose, her frailty and outward strength, her words and her actions. She was described as a compulsive liar, but that seems to even affect her complexion. I walk into the sitting room, suddenly ill at ease, then sit on the sofa, where she seduced me, four months ago. Two months of euphoria, and two months of cringing, spineless, fearful love have passed since then.

To my surprise, she presents me with a cup of coffee immediately.

My anger has died down. I look at her. Her face is flat, there is no expression except in the eyes, which are wide and fearful. I love her fine smooth skin.

'I've been really good to you. What can I have done for you to treat me like this?'

'Nothing. I just want to be on my own.'

'That's fine, but why say you loved me, why feed me a pack of lies? Why hurt me, when I showed you nothing but love?'

'I'm sorry. You're a lovely lady.'

'You changed. Even before I went on holiday, you changed, then blamed my insecurity on me. It was you. And the letter I left you, I was trying to be as open and honest as was possible, and you said you liked my letter then turned it as a weapon.'

'You said several things in that letter, now look at us.'

She is referring to my wish that if she ever wanted to leave me, she would tell me and we would remain friends always. It had been an unselfish, giving, considerate letter, a dedication of myself to her, without bonds and ties.

'What I said too was that you should always be honest with me. The basis of love and friendship has to be honesty. I've said that to you. You haven't been.'

'I'm sorry. I never meant to hurt you. I should have stopped it, after Janet spoke to me while you were asleep upstairs. You are a lovely lady.'

My anger evaporates in the face of her capitulation. Her face looks tortured. She looks so young, and compared to me, in years she is. Is not some of the fault mine, to believe that a thirty year old could love me at fifty three? And I knew from the start that I would be burned by this desire. Yet she had made the advances. True she thought me only in my forties, but surely it was me she said she loved, not my age? I think if she had been stronger, she would have been able to handle any jibes about falling for the older woman, but she hasn't that strength. We start to talk of other things, what is troubling us, work, our pressures. I tell her that we cannot discuss work any more. She seems surprised, then gives her sly smile. It is all about Dannie. Nothing matters, no subterfuge, no lie, no hurt, as long as she wins, and even my livelihood is as dust beneath her feet.

She says that Bridget has rowed with her, without knowing I know why. This affects her, there are tears in her eyes. I know that she values that friendship above anything she has felt for me, and once I told her so. I know that she wished Bridget and Debs would split, so that she could be with Bridget again. Lads together, out on the town, pulling and flirting.

I say I want to remain friends, and we begin to talk more amicably. She is on about Leslie, and her arrangements to collect her belongings, and how she is ringing up all the time, saying she wants another chance, and that she knows Dannie really loves her. Poor Leslie, she has suffered more than me. Dannie has done a proper job on her. I will not be like that, I will not beg her, I know that is a recipe for disaster, and I respect myself too much. She tells me a story about Leslie on holiday. It is disgusting. But I know that they had difficulties from the beginning of their relationship thirteen months ago. I fear that on Dannie's part, it was only a matter of monetary convenience.

'We're still going skiing.' Is it a question? 'Not Christmas, but later, I won't have the money at Christmas, I just want to forget that this year. But January.'

'I didn't think that would still be on the agenda.'

'Oh.'

'Perhaps.' I don't know how I feel about this. I am taken by surprise. It has been my dream to go with her, she said before her holiday, 'When I come back, we'll look at the brochures, and the second weekend we'll go windsurfing.' What happened? Why were these wonderful plans just dumped. That has been one of the hardest blows of all, my expectations of the shared future absolutely shattered.

'I suppose we don't have to be lovers to go.'

She seems surprised by this. Looking at me, she says almost silently, 'No, I suppose.' Is she disappointed by this? I wanted to hurt her when I came here today. She had said once, 'I don't think you will ever hurt me.' I replied that I never would, but hurt begets hurt, and I would punish her if I could.

'You'll get your two hundred pounds back, for the bike.'

I think she expects me to waive this debt. I do not. 'I better, or Ron and Roy will be round, they've got big dicks.'

'I don't like dicks.'

That's why I said it, darling.

I show her my description of her, and she reads it laughing at one or two things, and says, 'You remembered well.' I ask if she likes it? 'It's about me, and I like myself,' she says, and I cannot believe she has said that.

As I leave, I give her my cheek at the door. She kisses me on it, then on the lips, and I know I still love her, but the spell has gone. Her complexion is pale, still unhealthy, but the blue hue has gone, and her face has relaxed. She still has a sheepish look, but there is a touch of the cheeky chappie. The pallor was fear.

Later, on my way home, I call her. We are both glad to have met and sorted things out between us. Now perhaps we can get on with our lives.

I spend Saturday night with Bridget and Debs, and for the first time see the gay scene, see the flirting, the excitement of it all, the desperate need to prove one's attraction and worth. We go to a cafe bar in Covent Garden, fight with three hundred other gay women to get a drink at the bar. I stand in a basement club in Piccadilly, the music booming, watching, assimilating, the almost frenetic cruising, the undercurrents, the jealousy and promiscuousness. A visit to the loo can be embarrassing, questions from strangers, remarks, advances, 'who are you darling, you're sweet, where have you come from?' Dannie is in love with this. Before, I had compared it all with a hetero club, the young men there just to try to pull, but this is different, it all means so much more, yet is full of make-believe, girls being boys, girls pretending girls are boys, girls making an obvious show of lesbian love for effect, or just simply feeling free enough to let their inhibitions drop. I dance, after a time I stop feeling threatened.

I have been in a bar with three hundred other women, and then in a club with more of them till four a.m. Gay women are as diverse as the rest of the population, fat and incredibly thin, short and tall, beautiful and unattractive, with cropped or long hair, educated and ignorant. They are all here in this zoo I have come to see. I have cruised and been cruised, got a phone number and given one. I know who I am, and who they are. A girl called Carol shows interest. Suddenly I am as desperate as they all appear to be, but I remain passive. Carol kisses me goodbye.

Now I understand Dannie. The lepidopterist through some contagion has metamorphosed and become a butterfly. I know now what is in her head, and I am her. The butterfly has caught me in her net. I forgive her everything, true and imagined, and wish her happiness, and I would be her friend forever. Dannie my friend, I love you, not just want you, but I know that you will hurt me if I let you near, for you cannot play fair, you would have me dangle on my puppet strings, subject to your pulling and manipulation, and I am hurt enough.

I cry for a month, on and off, a miserable wreck in private, yet somehow manage to keep up appearances. Carol provides a brief diversion. Kath replaces Carol. Here is another drunk flirtatious lesbian, cheating on her partner. They are diversions, allowing my heart to mend enough for the crying to stop, yet you have me still, pinned in your collection Dannie.

CHAPTER 20.

It is seven years since that summer. Most of the forgoing was written then, in lonely hotel rooms up and down the country, sometimes in ecstasy, sometimes in despair and bitterness. It was a traumatic but cathartic task. I have written all night, with a heart singing of the joy of life, and, with tears running down my cheeks.

After that year, the newly established general sales force took over my sales duties, but did not necessarily reach the right parts of the organisations they were supposed to service. Change went on apace. Directors came and went. Heads rolled. Jobs changed. The whole organisation was shuffled, cut, shuffled again. They were preparing for privatisation.

I had a number of jobs. It was a time of score settling and if one's face didn't fit, there were suddenly a million ways to cast one out. I went into the office and found old friends gone. Eventually, having had enough of the management games, the merry-go-round of directorships, the realignments and job changes, I opted for redundancy. Nearly half the staff did likewise.

I came in from my travels one Friday afternoon, found a message to phone (in)Human Resources (my little joke), to be told that they had now got my release date, two weeks from that day, 29th April 1996. 'I'm owed two weeks holiday,' I said, 'so I'll go now.' I cleared my desk and walked out of the door. I left behind my office computer. The screen saver was a bouncing ball of the firms logo. To this I had added rats, chewing away at the edges and clambering across it. A parachutist descended, machine gun blazing, shooting lumps out of the bouncing ball.

I never regretted leaving. They had taken my best years and best efforts, and I had had enough of them. I keep in touch with a few women, Diana, Isobel, Hillary and Pam, and Maurice who was the best of men, but I do not need to belong to an old girls club.

There are one or two others that I hear from occasionally.

Derek G, one of the sales managers, with whom I worked only a short time, will phone me from Liverpool now and then. We worked together over three days up in Newcastle, doing an audit of DSS photocopiers, a mammoth task that occupied me for several months. I had written a report for management, from the pickings of our new sales force's brains. There was not a meeting that Derek would go to, but he would wave my report and suggest adopting my recommendations.

He was fun to be with, short and thickset, a northerner who had knocked about a bit, had seen success, lost it and found it again. A man with a commercial eye and acumen. A man's man and a gentleman. He was also a good husband when home and by all he said, a loving father. He was one of the few men, along with Maurice and Cass, who, confident of their own sexuality, were not afraid to associate with me.

We had one of his salesmen with us in Newcastle, Chris, a good looking fellow, but on the lazy side. We contacted a supplier up there who was having a team- building afternoon at a cart track and we were invited to take part. I was pitted for a penalty lap for shunting someone onto the top of the tyre wall, then did the second fastest lap time. We came away, our faces black from rubber thrown up from the tyres. In the hotel, we washed up before going out to dinner. Chris arrived down, dark lines still round his eyes, much to Derek's and my amusement. I told him he still had lines beneath his eyes, like carefully applied kohl. 'I know, thought it made me look interesting,' he said. Derek now has his own company and is making his fortune I am pleased to say.

I still speak to Cass, and saw him briefly a few months ago. He is still a lovely man, although with his own family troubles and ill treated by his company as so many are these days. He tells me of Dannie, with whom I have lost touch.

Dannie lost that first post that she had used her connection with me to get, because the promises she made to the new employer, were not fulfilled. I know for a fact, that instead of being out working, she was in her bedroom when I passed by that way. She lost the next job when that company was taken over. She then asked Cass to return to her old company, but the stories I had repeated to Cass, of her binge drinking, of her turning up drunk at the Ministry of Transport and the way she had let us down, spoke against that. She had soon found a new partner whom I met, Dannie made sure of that. She was a nice petite Irish girl, who with her two small children, had left an abusive husband. I had the feeling that she had met this young woman while I was in Portugal. That would explain Dannie's change towards me.

Carol picked me up in the Picadilly club I had gone to with Bridget. She was a yarn spinner, working for a video production company. Originally, I was being chatted up by her boss, a very masculine looking woman in a bright red blazer, not my sort at all, but a good conversationalist. Carol butted in, monopolised my attention and her boss left the club looking hurt. Carol had been a pupil at Summerhill, the controversial boarding school in Suffolk, and Daddy was supposed to be a millionaire with a Rolls . While waiting for her, in the Angel four weeks later, Kath introduced herself by chatting me up, then feeling my knee and discovering a stocking top. These two rebound liaisons eased me out of the trauma caused by Dannie. There is nothing like a rebound romance as a cure, as long as you recognise it for what it is.

In Norwich, I did some work for Lesbian Line, a help line for lesbians. There were some strange calls, some from men, looking for a bit of spice in their sad lives. There were several from women, mid-life crisis calls, children grown up and, tired of their husbands, had found out who 'they really were', looking for a lesbian fling or lifestyle. Some calls were from youngsters, girls pretending to be boys, white T shirts, jeans, close cropped hair. Many would probably later settle down and marry as I had in an attempt at normality.

Others were the genuine article, gay women wanting to come out but not knowing how, afraid of offending their families, isolated in their minds, just as I had been. There were some heart rending cases of bullying families, particularly Jehovah's Witnesses, who cast their children out or subjected them to a casting out of devils. The lesbian scene was a turbulent place, relationships breaking up, jealousy, girls out for kicks, just as Dannie had been. It was immature, funny, sad, incomplete, a place of delusions and illusions and many disappointments. There were many disturbed women with severe social and personality problems. Violence was threatened, but seldom carried out. It was difficult to know who were friends and who were enemies.

In this frenetic society was a young police officer, whom I met one night after a drive back from London. During that drive, my director phoned me. Amidst nose to tail traffic in heavy rain, on the appalling A12, he told me that I had failed a selection board. With this heavily on my mind I called in to the pub frequented by these girls, and was introduced to Sam. I could see at once that here was a young woman with a brain, a pleasant change from some I had met. She was in a relationship she said, *of sorts*. When I left, she came out *'to see you to your car'*. She asked for my phone number. When I opened my bag to find a card, she had immediately noted every item in it, Kim's game for real. The next evening, sitting writing, the phone rang but no one spoke. It rang again, the same result. On the third ring, I said, 'Yes Sam. Speak if you're going to.'

'I've been studying all day,' she said, 'and I need a break. I wondered if you wanted a drink?' It was her little girly voice, the one she used I would find out when wheedling her way in for a seduction.

I met her in the pub, close to her home. We then walked her girl friend's dog round the pitch dark streets of the Norfolk village. In the cosiness of her girl friend's sitting room, we talked for half the night.

Monday morning, as I worked at my desk, she called again, asking if we could meet for lunch?

I met her at police headquarters, a fleece jacket pulled over her uniform. We sat and talked down by the river under the gaze of a detective on 'obs', observation of these known areas where motorists take girls, or young boys.

There was an immediate physical attraction between us, but more, there was a meeting of minds, enquiring, lively, cynical, searchers for the truth. I decided to be honest with her about my origins, right from the start, and I have to say, she never let me down. As her girl friend said, 'You are soul mates.'

We were lovers. I stayed at Hendon police college and attended lectures with her there and at Portsmouth University. At Hendon, the man in front of me for self service breakfast, dropped the spoon into the baked beans. I fished it out, cleaned it off and gave it to him. He thanked me, started to chat to me, which force, why was I there, how much service. This tricky conversation was interrupted by another officer. 'Morning Commander,' he said. Apparently I had been fraternising with and telling porkies to the head of the training college! It was an exciting time and we both felt the thrill of our illicit liaison. Sam though, was even more complex than Dannie. The switch between ardent and jealous lover and uncaring, almost brutal user, started to tear me apart. I told her, latterly, that I felt no joy when coming to see her, only apprehension. It could not go on and in the end, after a year and goaded beyond forgiveness, I ended it. She sat on my doorstep, left flowers but I had had enough of her sweet torture. I love her still, but now it is the love one might have for a child that strays. At a distance I can forget the bad parts of our liaison.

After some years, we picked up our friendship again. As that happened, other things happened in her career. As a known lesbian in the police force, a sergeant with a doctorate, she was bound to be set apart from her fellow officers. They proved themselves every bit as bigoted, chauvinist, sexist and racist as the media has painted them. Norfolk Constabulary in particular, has come in for criticism. Eventually, Sam was prosecuted by her own police force on a trumped up charge over a misdemeanour. In the eventual trial at Crown Court, Sam's history came out, the persistent victimisation by other officers, remarks like 'lesbian whore' written across a local newspaper report of her visit to Disney World in Miami with disadvantaged children that had been stuck on the station notice board.

The Constabulary received a bad press. The judge berated them and Sam was found not guilty, thankfully, for guilty would almost certainly have meant a prison sentence. It had been touch and go. Now she has left the force.

There are other friends I value greatly, another Janet and her husband Alan, especially Sarah and her husband Neil with their daughter, my God daughter, Alexandra. My pal Brian and his forbearing wife Valerie. My brother, who I fought with as a child and fight with now. My cat, with whom conversation was sadly one-sided, but who absolutely adored me secretly, and whom I adored died one month after my mother who died after her 100th birthday.

I am estranged from my other friend Janet. She let me down in several ways, firstly by telling her son, daughter, her parents and her friends about me, against my expressed wishes, and then by breaking arrangements so often that it became a habit.

Recently, there have been a glut of cases of transsexualism in the news. A doctor, two C of E priests, a public school teacher, a policeman, a soldier. Mostly they are met with greater understanding than even five years ago. Often now, they just carry on the same job in their new role. The latest medical research, as explained earlier in chapter 10, has clearly shown a physical reason for the phenomenon. Yet, still there are doubters, like the Bishop of Lewes, who says there is no physical reason and he doesn't agree with 'sex changes'. He asserts that counselling is the correct treatment. Presumably, he has this information from God. It is just this sort of blind prejudice, that at the age of fourteen, helped me discover the church to be a sham staffed mostly by abject fools and charlatans. I therefore examined the whole faith question and rejected it wholesale over the next few years. I wrote to the 'good Bishop', but did not expect to convince him.

Meanwhile, the Governmentof the United Kingdom, has at last recognised the plight of transsexuals. A transsexual can at last change a birth certificate, so that they now are treated under the law as being their assigned sex. In 2005 the Gender Recognition Act came into force, twenty one years after EEC Directive 79/7 commanded all member nations to give equal opportunity regardless of sex or sexual orientation

Personal freedoms are hard won in this country, whether for gays in the forces or for freedom of expression, or for children to be prosecuted in a juvenile court. The people of the UK are constantly petitioning the European Court of Human Rights, to acquire the rights already acknowledged by most of our European partners. We live in a secretive and oppressive society, yet believe as we have been told, that we are superior to other nations. Unfortunately that is far from the truth.

We have some of the worst housing; the worst poverty; the greatest poverty gap; a failing Health Service even after a huge amount of cash because the format was made for the 1950s and not the 21st millennium; the most congested roads; execrable railways and other public transport; poor education with a large minority of under achievers; poor pensions and punitive care systems for the elderly. Our taxation system is dishonest, in that it portrays light taxation because income tax is low, but catches the poor in its net for a disproportionate amount because all their income is spent and subject to VAT and other taxes. We have the fewest acute care beds in hospital, the fewest doctors and nurses, for example, the European standard is five patients to one nurse, we say eight to one. No wonder Stafford Hospitable killed off patients.

The conclusion is that Thatcherism was a total success, in that the rich have gotten a whole lot richer at the price of essential services and the poor. It is not good to be a minority here. Blair's New Labour has completed Thatcher's work and has added other measures, gradually taking away rights of privacy, democracy and attempting the removal of habeas corpus. The Lords is now a shambles, a house of patronage and privilege, but in spite of Blair's best efforts still does its job of restricting his worst efforts. Faith schools have been encouraged at a time when it has been demonstrated that multi-culturalism does not work and integration under a common national identity is needed. Scotland and Wales, dependant on English money are better ruled than England.

It has therefore become a hobby of mine to write to the Times, one small way to fight back and hopefully, if not to convert, at least to make some think about their attitudes. Sometimes, these published letters result in threats or gobbledegook from cranks.

I paint lazily and there are my paintings in private collections in the UK, the United States and Holland.

My favourite occupation is skiing, but I enjoy watching many sports.

My mother died in December 2004 in a nursing home at the age of 100 and five months. I had supported her except for the last four months of her life. My daughter who had ignored her grandmother for years, had said the word grandma with a sneer and was estranged from us both, then decided she wanted to attend the funeral. I forbade it. Since, I have offered to meet, to try to settle things between us, but to no avail. I have given up seeing the children again.

My cat died the following month after a mystery illness that disabled her jaw. Early 2005 was a bleak time, but as usual, I bounce back. I have two rescue cats, Marble and Mudge a real delight.

In 2004, I returned to my old school on Old Boys Day. We separated into small groups to tour the school accompanied by a sixth former. One of the old boys wives walked with me, a lady of about seventy. 'Whose wife are you?' She asked.

'I was a pupil.' I replied.

'Oh, when did they start taking girls?'

'I was a boy.' I said, carefully avoiding the gaps in the paving slabs in my stilletto heels.

'How exciting!' She said, brilliantly.

They asked me to sit with them at lunch too, where I was joined with the director of development and the Headmaster.

I presented a copy of the book on art in Norfolk, 'Wide Skies', written by Brian and myself, and received a charming letter of thanks from the Headmaster with invitations to return for various other functions. The school has changed almost beyond belief. Now I would be counselled for my problem, but in my time they would probably have tried to beat it out of me. The facilities are wonderful. There are a number of young women teachers. If only they had been around in my time.

The oak tree I knocked a golf ball over still stands. The grass is intensely green. Sports are still important, but hockey and tennis are now played on astroturf. Uniform is still observed, but caps have gone. Shirts are tucked in, shoes shined, mainly.

My dear friend Brian died in September 2006 after a six month one-sided battle with cancer. He lusted for me, begged me for a kiss even in the London Eye, never reciprocated yet I loved him deeply as a friend. I miss him.

I am in touch with my daughter and I am going to her daughter's wedding. They have fallen out with their mother, who let them down badly after they had extended their home for her.

My daughter says that her mother gave them a miserable childhood by marrying an appalling individual after she was shot of me. My daughter also tells me that Margaret married me to escape her mother, not for love. That explains why, when I was in so much trouble, she tried to poison me rather than offer help, then managed to manipulate Social Services to ban me from seeing the children. My daughter says that she respects me for at least trying to be a man, husband and father and does not blame me. That means so much. As Dr Randall said, my leaving the family is no worse than any other marriage break-up, I am no more guilty. As my daughter says, 'You tried your best.'

In 2014 my daughter and I are again estranged and this time I see no way back. My life is too short to bother anymore.

I fought the Pensions Service for my state pension from age 60. Six months before my 60th birthday, I had in my absence, an unexpected visit from a young man from Inland Revenue (Pensions). He left a card asking that I contact him. It was extremely disturbing. I phoned and we made a further appointment. On the day, he phoned to say that he could not make it due to car trouble. He refused to say what the matter was about. I tried to contact him again but he did not respond. Eventually I tracked down his manager and wrote demanding an explanation. He responded by telephone, not a satisfactory way of doing business in my opinion. He told me that the young man was new, and didn't like to be the bearer of bad news. In other words he had funked the meeting. I was, he told me, still male in the eyes of the Pension Service so I would not receive pension until my 65th birthday. I said this was absurd. The NHS, a part of Government, had paid for my treatment. The Civil Service employed, paid and treated me as female. The Passport Office also recognised my new status as did Inland Revenue and DVLA. Under the 2002 ruling of the European Court, the Government was forced to fall in line with every other nation bar, Albania, Eire and two minute principalities to give transsexuals the rights of their assigned sex. They would have to pay Pension from the correct age.

This deplorable Government, led by the almost messianic Blair, then decided that to qualify they had to draw up a law, laying down certain conditions. This took two years to complete. They were using delaying tactics once more. The conditions were easy, that one lived in the assigned sex, permanently. That ones records, bank, passport, driving licence, medical records all agreed, precisely the argument I had made 4 years ago. I applied for pension and it was refused. I appealed and the Pension Service rejected the appeal. I applied to the Tribunal, I cited EU law, English law. I threatened that I would not go away even if it meant going to Strasbourg myself. The Tribunal commented that first the Pensions Service told us that we could not apply for Pension then later told us we could not qualify because we had not applied in the correct form and at the correct time, i.e., within 12 months of our 60th birthday. The Tribunal found in my favour and quoted a decision by the Pensions Commissioner under the 1977 Equal Opportunities Act which the Pensions Service had not divulged. This was Government at its worst, but there are many other injustices. The treatment of or lack of treatment for ex soldiers; Gulf War syndrome; diseased blood given to haemophiliacs; pitifully small recompense for all those injured by an arm of Government; minute Pensions; prisoners released after a successful appeal and having served many years jail and found innocent after all, made to pay for their living expenses while in prison. One suspects the prudent Mr Brown at work.

The Pensions Service received leave to appeal this decision. After a further barrage, they caved in and agreed to implement the Tribunal finding. They paid me and I also qualified for compensation for maladministration and loss of advantage.

However, later claimants were not so lucky. They were forced to go to Upper Tribunals and then awarded enhanced pensions rather than lump sums. Pensions take cases as far as the Supreme Court and lose. They have to pay transsexuals still married to their pre change spouses. Yet they will still only pay in increments to pensioners who are already over 70. At this rate it will take them twenty years to get the money back they should have been paid. With another trans woman, I visited the Minister with two of our MPs. They agreed at least to contact these people personally advising them of their rights, but will not give in on lump sums. It is a disgrace, yet I am not surprised by any of the under hand ploys of officialdom or the Government of the United Kingdom. Politicians, bankers and the media, are all corrupt to an extent and lacking moral fibre.

It is now 2014 and although victories have resulted against Department of Works and Pensions, we are still fighting battles. We have been greatly assisted by some MPs and especially large law firms working pro bono for us. Pensions service have consistently purposefully misread, misinterpreted the law. Their behaviour has been disgraceful. The same attitude exists throughout Government and our Government of both parties has a cynical attitude to its promises.

Paul left Janet in the end, soon after I'd had a parting row with Janet. He said he no longer loved her, but I guess it was her insecurity and constant need to have her ego bolstered that killed his love. I loved her as a sister. I have tried to get in touch but received no reply. I am sad.

I missed so much, missing my childhood and puberty as a girl and the romance of boys and all the other facets of growing up as a young woman. Probably I missed most, the difference in attitudes towards a young woman rather than those displayed to a young man and the company of girls of my own age. In a way, Dannie provided that.

My goddaughter is now 14 and having her first date. How I envy her. I know it may be as painful as my liaison with the dreadful Dannie, but it is an essential part of life that I missed.

I have just heard, My goddaughter kicked the first romance into touch. She was not ready nor has the time. She admits to her mother that she prefers her family life without the encumberment of some boy. She plays five instruments, is very clever, rides and although not a natural athlete, has no fear to have a go. I love her parents too.

It is difficult to explain to anyone who is not a transsexual, but before the change, every day is a day of regret, not just for dressing as a woman, but for having the wrong body with the wrong appendages and being unable to relate to the world at large as one would wish and in the way which is a natural instinctive reaction.

It is confining, imprisoning, a seeming life sentence to greyness. I escaped.

Many girls utter the words, 'if I were a boy', but it does not mean they aspire to masculinity, it means that in this male dominated world, they would have more opportunity and scope. In actual fact Transsexualism is an escalating phenomenon. The reason is not known. It could be the fact that it is a better known syndrome or there could be environmental reasons like the amount of oestrogen now present in the world. Certainly changes in species like fish have been noted. The median age for transition is 42. Four times as many boys want to be girls as girls to become boys, 80/20.

http://gires.org.uk/assets/Research-Assets/Prevalence2011.pdf

All has turned out reasonably in the end. But if only..............I so enjoy being a girl!

Thanks go to my doctor, Paul Everden

Thanks also to my MP, Norman Lamb.

Thanks especially to my friends and family.

CPSIA information can be obtained
at www.ICGtesting.com
Printed in the USA
LVIC04n1413140515
438520LV00001B/1